Praise for previous editions:

"*The State of the World Atlas* is something else – an occasion of wit and an act of subversion…These are the bad dreams of the modern world, given color and shape and submitted to a grid that can be grasped instantaneously."

New York Times

"Unique and uniquely beautiful...a discerning eye for data and a flair for the most sophisticated techniques of stylized graphic design; the atlas succeeds in displaying the geopolitical subtleties of global affairs in a series of dazzling color plates…tells us more about the world today than a dozen statistical abstracts or scholarly tomes."

Los Angeles Times

"Coupled with an unusual non-distorting map projection and a series of brilliant cartographic devices, this gives a positively dazzling set of maps. It deserves to be widely used."

New Society

"A super book that will not only sit on your shelf begging to be used, but will also be a good read. To call this book an atlas is like calling Calvados, applejack – it may be roughly accurate but it conveys nothing of the richness and flavour of the thing. Its inventive brilliance deserves enormous rewards."

New Scientist

"A striking new approach to cartography...no-one wishing to keep a grip on the reality of the world should be without these books."

International Herald Tribune

"Outspoken cataloguing of global oppressions and inequities, painstakingly sourced."

Independent on Sunday

"Packed with fascinating facts and figures on everything from the international drugs industry to climate change."

Evening Standard

"A political reference book which manages to translate hard, boring statistics into often shocking visual statements... required reading."

NME

"No-one wishing to keep a grip on the reality of the world should be without these books." *International Herald Tribune*

Available now:

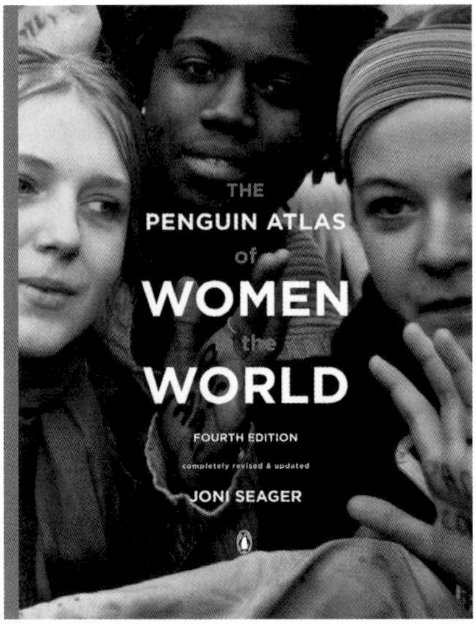

Available March 2015:

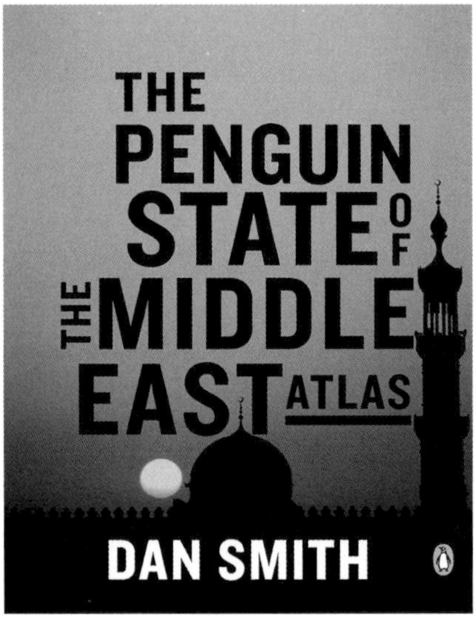

"Invaluable...I would not be without the complete set on my own shelves."
Times Educational Supplement

"Fascinating and invaluable." *The Independent*

"A new kind of visual journalism." *New Scientist*

THE PENGUIN STATE of the WORLD ATLAS

Completely Revised and Updated
Ninth Edition

Dan Smith

PENGUIN BOOKS

PENGUIN BOOKS

Published by the Penguin Group
Penguin Group (USA) LLC
375 Hudson Street
New York, New York 10014

USA | Canada | UK | Ireland | Australia
New Zealand | India | South Africa | China
penguin.com
A Penguin Random House Company

This ninth edition first published in Penguin Books 2012

ISBN 978-0-14-312265-4 (Penguin paperback)

Produced for the Penguin Group by
Myriad Editions
59 Lansdowne Place
Brighton, BN3 1FL, UK
www.MyriadEditions.com

Edited and coordinated by Jannet King and Candida Lacey
Designed by Isabelle Lewis and Corinne Pearlman
Maps and graphics by Isabelle Lewis

3 5 7 9 10 8 6 4

Contents

8 About the author

9 INTRODUCTION

16 The problem with maps

17 Acknowledgements

18 PART ONE
Who We Are

20 **THE STATES OF THE WORLD**
Most states are relatively recent creations.

22 **POPULATION**
Global population continues to grow but the rate of increase is slowing.

24 **LIFE EXPECTANCY**
Average life expectancy is higher than ever before and rising.

26 **ETHNICITY AND DIVERSITY**
People divided by ethnic difference live side by side in peace more often than they fight.

28 **RELIGIOUS BELIEFS**
Differences within religions are often as intense as differences between them.

30 **LITERACY & EDUCATION**
More teachers are needed if the trend towards greater school enrolment is to continue.

32 **URBANIZATION**
For the first time in history, most people live in cities.

34 **DIVERSITY OF CITIES**
Cities reflect the diversity of the world.

36 PART TWO
Wealth & Poverty

38 **INCOME**
Economic growth continues to outpace the growth in world population.

40 **INEQUALITY**
While 2.6 billion people live in poverty, there are more billionaires than ever.

42 **QUALITY OF LIFE**
Rich countries inevitably offer a high quality of life.

44 **TRANSNATIONALS**
The revenues of the largest corporations outstrip those of many countries.

46 **BANKS**
Despite everything, bankers continue to reap huge financial rewards.

48 **CORRUPTION**
Corruption is pervasive, some countries run on it.

50 **DEBT**
Debt has soared but not everybody, everywhere is equally in debt.

52 **TOURISM**
Tourism is predicted to rise, bringing much-needed income to many smaller economies.

54 **GOALS FOR DEVELOPMENT**
Development progress is real but patchy.

56 PART THREE
War & Peace

58 **WARS IN THE 21ST CENTURY**
This is an era of growing peace, despite the wars that persist.

60 **WARLORDS , GANGLORDS, & MILITIAS**
Armed conflicts fought between non-state armed forces are proliferating.

62 **MILITARY MUSCLE**
Despite the global economic crisis, military spending remains buoyant.

64 **THE NEW FRONT LINE**
Warfare has evolved and is now entering cyber space.

66 **CASUALTIES OF WAR**
Data on war deaths are incomplete and contentious.

68 **REFUGEES**
30 million people are refugees from war and repression.

70 **PEACEKEEPING**
After a period of rapid increase, the number of peacekeeping missions has started to decline.

72 **GLOBAL PEACEFULNESS**
Understanding what makes societies peaceful is a significant step towards the world becoming more peaceful.

74 PART FOUR
Rights & Respect

76 **POLITICAL SYSTEMS**
The global trend is for more countries to become democratic.

78 **RELIGIOUS RIGHTS**
Almost a quarter of the world's states have formal links to a religion.

80 **HUMAN RIGHTS**
In some countries the greatest menace citizens face comes from the state.

82 **CHILDREN'S RIGHTS**
Although respect for children's rights is increasing, millions still stuffer terrible abuse.

84 **WOMEN'S RIGHTS**
Though gender equality is advancing, women worldwide remain financially and politically disadvantaged.

86 **GAY RIGHTS**
Gay people experience varying degrees of acceptance from fellow citizens and authorities.

88 PART FIVE
Health of the People

90 **MALNUTRITION**
Many of the world's poor suffer from diets deficient in calories and/or vital nutrients.

92 **OBESITY**
Many of the world's rich suffer from diets deficient in nutrients, but over-packed with unnecessary calories.

94 **SMOKING**
Between a third and a half of smokers die from tobacco-related diseases.

96 **CANCER**
As countries become more prosperous, and their lifestyles and diets are changing, their cancer rate is rising.

98 **HIV/AIDS**
Education and treatment are beginning to slow the rate of new HIV/AIDS infections and deaths.

100 **MENTAL HEALTH**
Poor countries lack the resources needed to treat mental and behavioural disorders.

102 **LIVING WITH DISEASE**
Years of healthy life are lost to disease and disability.

104 PART SIX
Health of the Planet

106 **WARNING SIGNS**
Things are changing in the natural world – and not many of the changes are to the good.

108 **BIODIVERSITY**
Efforts to slow the loss of species of animals and plants have not been successful so far.

110 **WATER RESOURCES**
By 2025, two-thirds of the world population will have an inadequate supply of water.

112 **WASTE**
Waste, especially plastic waste, is a serious global problem on both land and sea.

114 **ENERGY USE**
World energy use is increasing, especially in the most rapidly developing economies.

116 **CLIMATE CHANGE**
The build-up of carbon emissions has reached a critical point.

118 **PLANETARY BOUNDARIES**
There are limits beyond which human impact on the Earth's balanced ecosystems will have as yet unknown consequences.

120 PART SEVEN
Vital Statistics

122 **WORLD TABLES**

138 Notes & Sources
143 Index

ABOUT THE AUTHOR

Dan Smith is Secretary General of the London-based international peacebuilding organization International Alert, and former Director of the International Peace Research Institute in Oslo. He has also held fellowships at the Norwegian Nobel Institute and Hellenic Foundation for Foreign and European Policy and was, for over a decade, the Chair of the Institute for War and Peace Reporting.

He is the author of *The State of the Middle East,* as well as successive editions of *The State of the World Atlas* and *The Atlas of War and Peace.* At International Alert he produced the path-breaking *A Climate of Conflict* (2007) report on the links between climate change, peace, and war. He is regularly invited to advise governments and international organizations on policies and structures for peacebuilding, including through his membership of the Advisory Group for the UN Peacebuilding Fund, of which he was Chair until 2011.

He was awarded the OBE in 2002, and blogs on international politics at www.dansmithsblog.com

Introduction

Ours is a period of change – continual, multi-form, and multi-level – technical, scientific, economic, and political.

Scientific discovery feeds into technical innovation at dizzying speed, changing how we communicate with each other, what we can know about far-flung parts of the world and how quickly we can know it, how we do business, what we understand about the natural world and how the human brain works, how many diseases we can cure, and the kinds of energy supply we can utilise. In every corner of our lives as individuals and as communities and societies, there is change.

THE THREE GREAT CHANGES

The theme is repeated in the big global picture. Five major issues and how the world – its leaders, governments, companies, international organizations, individuals, everybody – responds to them will define our future. To take them on, change is needed. And three great changes at approximately ten-year intervals over the past two decades will set the terms and the tone of how that response shapes up.

In the 1980s, the Cold War seemed stuck fast, likely to be a long-enduring feature of world politics. Yet in half a year in 1989 its basic components unravelled, and in a second series of events the Soviet Union came to an end in five swift months of 1991.

For the 1990s, then, the USA seemed set to enjoy a golden age as the sole superpower while its allies basked in the security it generated. Those comfortable assumptions were detonated in 2001, not only by the force of the 9/11 terror attacks on New York and the Pentagon, but by the wide-reaching, aggressive, and ultimately self-defeating, US "war on terror". The golden age was gone and there was a widespread sense of insecurity as the 9/11 attacks were followed by others in Bali, Madrid, London, and elsewhere, as well as by the wars in Afghanistan and Iraq.

Underneath that, however, was a different kind of security. Economic growth and prosperity seemed broadly dependable. There were winners and losers as always, but for most people in the rich world times were pretty good, and for many people in poorer countries conditions were also improving a little.

Much of that was destabilized by the third great change of the recent era, as unsustainable patterns of lending and borrowing fed a shattering credit crunch in 2007 and 2008, triggering recession and a financial catastrophe whose full effects had not played out some four or five years later.

If we look back over those 20 years, we can see how quickly confidence about the future can be generated and then lost. We need something rather better than that moodiness, something more stable and persistent, if we are going to be successful in facing up to the five big challenges we face as a global community: wealth and poverty, war and peace, rights and respect, and the health both of the people and of the planet.

WEALTH & POVERTY

The world is marked by large inequalities of wealth. Multiple further inequalities flow from that starting point – dramatically different degrees of access to education, health care, good food, clean water, sanitation, reasonable housing. Though the proportion of the world's population that lives in the extreme poverty of less than $1 a day is declining, progress is slow and more than one-third of all people live on less than $2 a day. The benefits of economic growth are not being distributed evenly or anything like it, and at the same time the model of economic development is environmentally unsustainable.

At the start of the century, world leaders undertook to make a major new effort to help developing countries move forward. In the confident spirit of that time, more money was committed and targets were set with a fixed date of 2015. These Millennium Development Goals have guided Western countries' official development assistance ever since. In the much less confident spirit in which these donor governments are working a decade on, still reeling from the economic aftershocks of 2008, it is clear that there has been progress but the targets will not be met. And some of the most significant economic development and alleviation of poverty in the last decade seems to have owed very little, if anything, to the Millennium Development Goals.

Above all, on the economic front, the events of 2008 and since have generated a growing realization of another axis of change. For a long time it has been recognized that the economic output of China and India was growing much more quickly than that of Europe and the USA. China's eventual assumption of the position as the world's largest economy – and India's as the third largest, with the USA staying second – has been long anticipated. Whether that makes them in a meaningful sense two of the three wealthiest countries is another matter, because their output per person remains much lower than in the USA and Europe. There is, nonetheless, a distinct political weight that comes with economic size. And the effect has been emphasized because, while the USA's recovery from 2008 has been halting and uncertain, Europe has faced a serial crisis and renewed recessions. The contrast with China has only served to emphasize its rise. The European Union's combined economic scale remains huge; it is the largest single market in the world. But the combined political weight of its member states, which has always seemed less than the sum of its parts, has diminished because of the political leaders' seeming inability to find a solution to Europe's problems that retains credibility for more than a few months.

WAR & PEACE

This is not a peaceful world, and yet it is more peaceful today than at any time since before the First World War and, some argue, ever. Military spending remains high, and armed conflict remains a major cause of death, yet by comparison with earlier times, there are markedly fewer wars and they are less lethal. There has been an avalanche of peace agreements in the two decades since the end of the Cold War, and a major, sustained if quiet effort not only to make peace, but then to lay the foundations for long-term peace in conflict-affected countries.

Two decades of growing peace
Number of wars

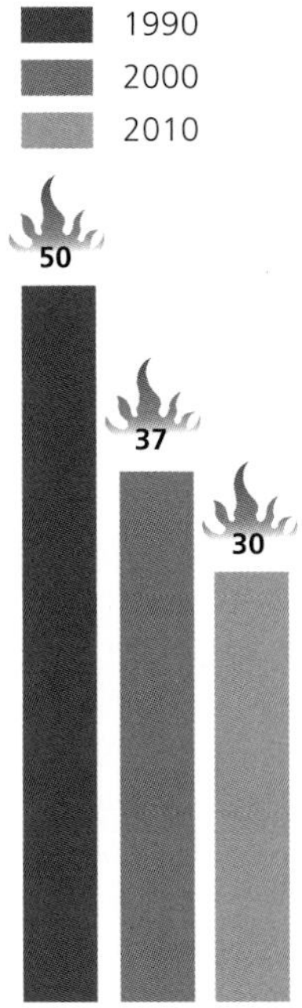

It would be wrong to look at the issues of war and peace and declare job done. In many countries, it is not so much a case of having achieved peace as, rather, of bottling up conflict. Indeed, declaring job done prematurely is a repeated failing of the Western governments who often offer themselves as custodians of peace processes in war-torn countries. In many countries, there are patterns of violent conflict that are from a different mould than civil wars. They are generated by, and reinforce, a dangerous intersection between crime and politics, and in several cases they revolve around the trade in illegal narcotics or other illegal and massively profitable enterprises. The main international institutions on which we rely for responding to armed conflicts are strikingly ill-prepared for this kind of violent conflict. A high United Nations representative can be sent to negotiate with even the most despicable of dictators, but the same space and the same role does not exist between a government and a drug lord.

There is, further, a risk that the number of civil wars could increase. The environmental, demographic, and economic pressures are there. The United Nations has become quite adept at generating norms that manage violent conflict, but a new round of conflict pressures might encounter a deficient response because the governments that have tended to fund peace efforts include several that have been hard hit by economic crisis. With repetitive demands for bailing out countries and banks, these governments may simply conclude they have too many competing calls on economic resources for it to be politically feasible to support long-term peacebuilding. If no new actors appear to take their place, the peacebuilding enterprise could collapse.

These are all risks – the potential is there. Even so, if the United Nations as an organization and those governments that have been particularly committed to the work of ending armed conflicts can stay focused and keep their efforts properly resourced, there is every reason to expect a reasonably successful record of building peace to continue.

RIGHTS & RESPECT

This is the ninth edition of this atlas. The last one before this came out in 2008. At that time, 43 per cent of the world's population lived in established democracies. In this atlas, it is recorded that in 2012 48 per cent live in established democracies.

For all its flaws, viewed from the perspective of ordinary citizens and their shared interests, democracy is by far the best, most stable, and freest political system. It is based on a bargain that concedes power to the state as long as it is accountable to the people. It is a system in which the social and economic elite has to accept constraints on its power. When it works properly, it protects us from the negative consequences of our own short-sightedness and tunnel vision. And it does so on the basis of our consent. It is the system that has, on average, been associated with the most successful economies.

It is, however, like peace, a trend and benefit that needs safeguarding; it cannot be taken for granted. Achieving democracy is perilous, and is closely associated with violent conflict. And when it is well established and the struggle to achieve it has been forgotten, it often seems barely to be taken seriously by those who could most benefit from it. In countries that have recently entered a democratic transition, there will always be false friends of democracy, ready to try for power that way if that's all that's possible, but to grab and hold it against the democratic will if that becomes possible. Similarly, in the established democracies there are always economic and social elites who are content with democracy as long as they can rig its rules in their favour, but are ready to cry foul if it ever threatens to rule against them.

These fake and shallow supporters of democracy reveal themselves by trying to call the language of rights into service for one segment of society and not for others, or by claiming exemptions from national and international legal responsibilities whenever it suits them.

HEALTH OF THE PEOPLE

Without our good health, what can we do? Providing for our own and each other's health is fundamental to us, both as individuals and as social beings.

Living and dying with HIV/AIDS
Adults and children
1990–2010

---- new HIV Infections

—— AIDS-related deaths

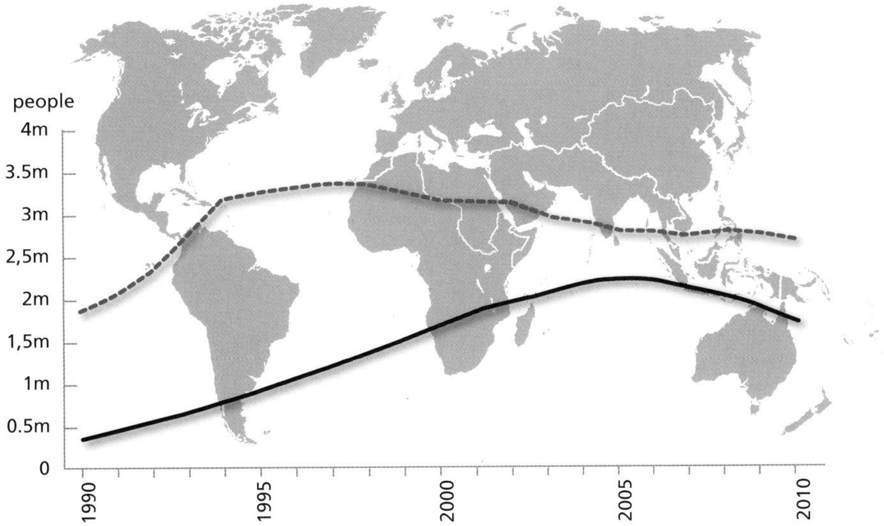

Many societies do not generate the wealth required to be able to look after the health of the people on a more or less fair basis. Others have the resources but the political and social will to do so is lacking. Challengingly, even where and when the resources are available and are deployed to provide health care for all, that is no guarantee that our patterns of behaviour will be healthy. For that is a matter of personal responsibility and individual action; government can make it easier or harder, can educate the citizens or neglect the issues, but in the end it is impossible to enforce healthy behaviours.

Even so, people's health is improving. There is still too much suffering from curable and preventable conditions and, in many countries, the way that mental and psychological disorders are handled primarily by silence and taboo is as big a health scandal as any. But medical science is advancing, the sequencing of the human genome has been worked out, the genetics of cancers are being unlocked, and new treatments are being and will be developed. The progress is encouraging but there is further to go because many of these conditions have social causes – lifestyle diseases whether of poverty or spreading prosperity. What is required now is to increase the capacity to address those causes.

HEALTH OF THE PLANET

On top of all this, there is growing awareness about the unfolding crisis in the natural environment. Compared to the other events that have shaped the spirit of our time, changes in the natural environment are slow moving. By the standards of 21st-century political culture, they do not deserve the name of crisis at all – but the timescale in which they should be understood is much longer than a four- or five-year political cycle, which is the maximum we are used to thinking in.

Of the five key issues that we must as a world community resolve in order to prosper, our relationship to the natural environment is the most tangled, the one in which knowledge is most essential to understanding, and the one that has the highest stakes – yet the one on which we seem unable to act on the scale that is needed. Though we cannot yet make out all the details of the interaction between different components of this crisis – between the different ways in which we are damaging the environment – we can clearly see the critical moment bearing down on us. Yet generating a united and viable response is currently beyond us. Calm reflection reveals that, on the basis of what we currently know, there is time to act effectively as long as we act now. But each day that passes increases the depth and scale of change that is required.

PROBLEMS & SOLUTIONS

These five key challenges are in principle all amenable to solution. In one sense, that is illustrated simply by there being successful approaches to significant aspects of three of the five. Problems remain in the realms of war and peace, rights and respect, and people's health, but progress is visible. There is less war, though violent conflict persists. There is more democracy and more respect for human rights, though abuses persist and the transition is often dangerous. Improvements in treatment for many of the major ailments are available, though lifestyle diseases are on the increase. Undernourishment is slowly reducing as a problem, but obesity – perhaps a different kind of malnutrition – is now a global epidemic.

What holds us back from pressing through to greater improvements on these three fronts and to sorting out at least some of the big issues of wealth, poverty, and the natural environment is the condition of our politics and our international political institutions. In Europe in the years since 2008 we have seen signs of a breakdown in the fundamental relationship between citizens and state – the implicit bargain that power is both real and accountable. There is now such a deep resentment about taxpayers being forced to pay the cost of the failings, incompetence and, in some cases, apparent crimes in the major banks that it is building towards refusing consent to be governed. The social and economic elite has shown a combination of incompetence and the arrogance of impunity, and would-be political leaders continue to cosy up to that elite so shamelessly that they are threatening the continued viability of the contract of government.

It is, in the end, unlikely that this will erupt into any kind of revolution and, if it does, the odds are that it will be profoundly unpleasant for ordinary people. But it is the kind of deep-seated problem that may make it next to impossible to generate new policies and approaches to prevent environmental degradation and successfully address the other major issues.

Our enemies in trying to generate new and better approaches are inequality, unfairness and social exclusion, short termism, and blinkered allegiance to norms and policies that used to be functional. Anything and everything that limits the amount of knowledge that can be brought to bear on a problem, and the number of knowledge-holders that can get engaged, is an obstacle. Part of this problem resides in the limitations of the institutions we have developed to regulate our affairs. We need new ones. There is energy available that has not yet been harnessed and connected to engines of change. The old power formats are creaking but the new ones have not yet emerged.

KNOWING THE WORLD

Getting things more or less right on these five issues will be done by international agreement or not at all, for no single government can handle – or should even dream of handling – the whole set of issues alone, and much of it will in turn be based on shared knowledge and understanding.

Of course, knowledge is not the same as wisdom. You can know all the facts and still not be able to act wisely. But without knowledge, it is harder to be wise – even if what wisdom tells us is that knowledge is very often provisional and that we cannot wait to have certainty about every fact before we act.

DAN SMITH
LONDON, JULY 2012

THE PROBLEM WITH MAPS

The aim of this atlas is to look at the world through the lens of world problems. That means mapping those issues onto the world – and there we encounter the standard problem of atlases. Because the world is virtually a sphere, it cannot be accurately depicted on a flat, rectangular piece of paper. Peel an orange and flatten out the skin and the problem is immediately understandable. Choices and compromises must accordingly be made – choices, essentially, about how to be inaccurate. These choices are packaged into the projection of the world that is utilised in drawing the map.

The most widely seen world maps use projections that retain the shapes of the continents and islands, and therefore wildly distort their size. The first and most famous of these projections is the one developed by the 16th-century Flemish cartographer, Gerardus Mercator. Using that projection, the sizes of regions far from the equator are exaggerated. Thus Europe looks bigger than it is, while China and India look smaller. The most notorious distortion of area in Mercator is that Greenland looks similar in size to Africa, which is actually 14 times bigger than Greenland. Mercator's choice of projection was determined in part by his wish, as the sub-title of the original atlas put it, to produce an aid for navigators. Navigation was at the forefront of Europe's advance into the world from the 15th through the 18th centuries. It was the scientific precondition for sailing to far-flung destinations for trade and conquest.

There have been numerous attempts over succeeding centuries to correct the illustrative weakness in the Mercator projection. The best known today is the one proposed in 1973 by Arno Peters, drawing on work in the 19th century by a Scottish clergyman, James Gall. The Peters or Gall-Peters projection is more accurate on the size of different regions but distorts the world's appearance in other ways. There are geographers who believe the depiction of the world on rectangular pieces of paper should be stopped.

The projection employed in this atlas makes a different set of choices and compromises. It is the Winkel's Tripel, first used in 1913, compromising between the three elements of area, direction, and distance. Distortion is not completely eliminated but is minimized. The curved lines of latitude and longitude make the projection useless for navigators, but the result is fairer and reasonably familiar, especially since it was adopted by the US National Geographic Society in 1998.

Below: Myriad's world map based on the Winkel Tripel projection, and a cartogram based on population size.

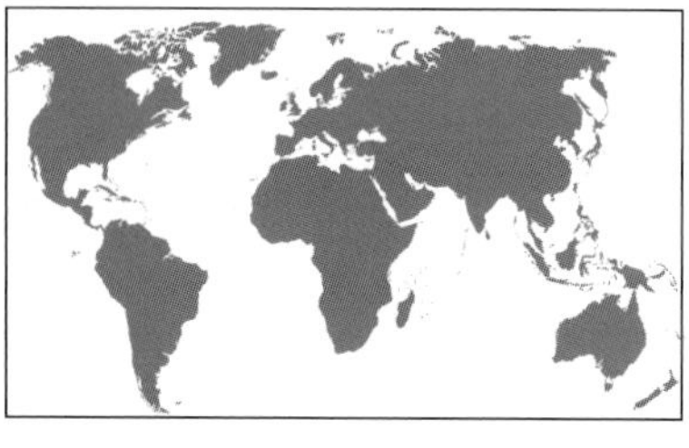

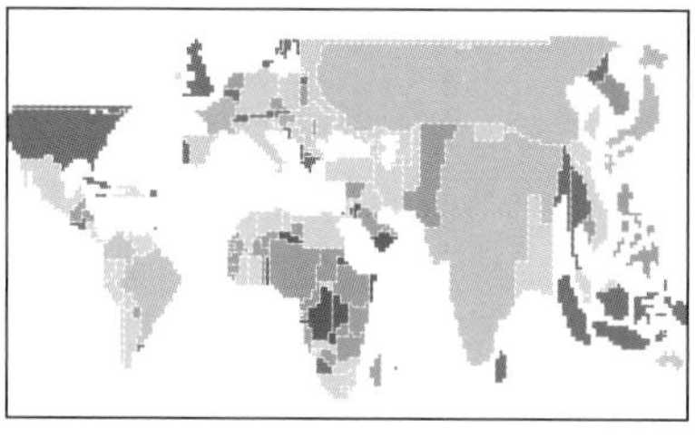

ACKNOWLEDGEMENTS

The atlas is the work of a team. Jannet King has been the editor, assiduous and detailed in her work, and respectful of a wayward author's prerogatives. Isabelle Lewis provides the basic cartographic design work without which the whole atlas approach would be impossible, and throughout showed her talent for coming up with innovative ways of displaying the information. The overall look and feel of the atlas is down to the design coordination of Corinne Pearlman. Candida Lacey ran and coordinated the Myriad team and was always a joy to work with. Elizabeth Sarney was an extremely diligent research assistant without whom the basic research for the atlas could not have been done; she also offered insightful comment on the draft layouts for displaying the data. Nicolle Nguyen made sure I stayed up to par on my day job and was another source of comment and feedback on draft designs. Ilaria Bianchi and Selena Mirams were a responsive focus group at a critical stage. Åsa Frankenberg provided thoughtful reflections on the look and functioning of the spreads, and was a source of strength throughout. Felix Smith-Frankenberg reminded me of what life is about at moments when I thought it only consisted of missed deadlines. I thank all of you unreservedly.

PHOTOGRAPHS

The publishers are grateful to the following for permission to reproduce their photographs on the following pages: 18 © Mark Henley / Panos Pictures; 30 Mexico City: Milan Klusacek / iStockphoto; New York: Candida Lacey; London: Ivan Mateev / iStockphoto; Paris: JB Russell / Panos Pictures; Lagos: George Osodi / Panos Pictures; Sao Paulo: AM29 / iStockphoto; 31 Istanbul: George Georgiou / Panos Pictures; Karachi: Giacomo Pirozzi / Panos Pictures; Shanghai: Manfred Leiter; Tokyo: Wikimedia Commons / Chris 73; Jakarta: Martin Adler / Panos Pictures; Cairo: ictor/ iStockphoto; Mumbai: Candida Lacey; Tehran: Frank van den Bergh / iStockphoto; 36 Ian Teh / Panos Pictures; 56 Iva Zimova / Panos Pictures; 74 Philippe Lissac / Panos Pictures; 88 Teun Voeten / Panos Pictures; 104 Alvaro Leiva / Panos Pictures; 120 Dieter Telemans / Panos Pictures.

Below: The world map based on the Mercator, Gall and Peters projections.

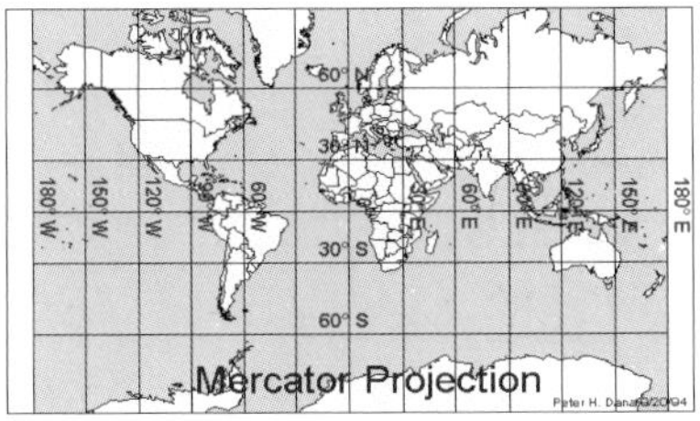

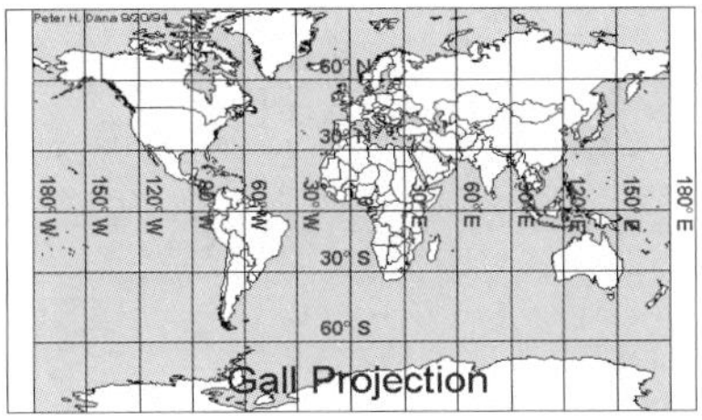

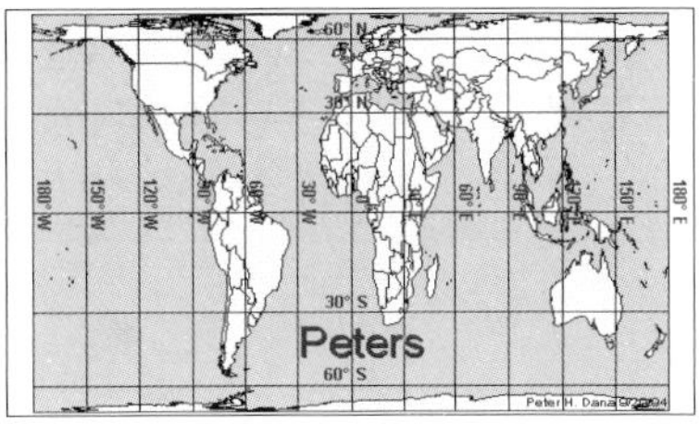

PART ONE
WHO WE ARE

This is the age of more, most, and never before. There are more people, living in more countries, and more of us living in cities, than at any time in the past.

It is only 200 years ago – less than a blink of an eye in the timescale of the planet, and not much more than a blink in the timescale of human beings walking the planet – that the world's human population passed the 1 billion mark. Today there are just over 7 billion of us. At that time, some 3 per cent – just 30 million people – lived in cities. Today, the corresponding figure is about 50 per cent, or some 3.5 billion people.

Current projections are that these figures and percentages will all increase. World population is expected to grow, as will the proportion of us who live in cities. The total expected population increase by 2030 – about another 2 billion people – is about the same as the expected rise in the urban population, as increasing numbers are born in cities or move there.

Humanity has never before experienced demographic change on such a huge scale. The movement from the countryside to the cities in the industrial revolution two centuries ago has nothing on this. The migration from Europe to the New World of the Americas from the mid-19th century to the early 20th numbered some 30 million. In the first ten years of this century, global population grew by some 100 million a year and urban population even faster.

But the issue is not just population increase. There is the matter of resources. According to one estimate, our seven-times-larger population compared to 1810 produces 50 times as much in economic output, and uses 60 times as much water and 75 times as much energy. Seen in a longer timescale going back to the beginning of recorded history some 5,000 years ago, that astonishing increase in the production of wealth is as wholly unprecedented and wildly abnormal as the increase in population itself.

The figures testify to the creativity unleashed through the industrial revolution. They are the evidence against fears, widely expressed over the past two centuries, that population increase must end in starvation and mass misery.

It is no new thought, however, to wonder how long this growth of output and consumption can be sustained, to question what may happen as the emerging economies of China, India, Brazil, and other countries, with increasing economic growth in Africa and many parts of Asia, successfully produce and consume ever-increasing amounts of everything, just as we have done in Europe, North America, and Japan.

This growth in production both owes much to, and has fed, the extraordinary growth in human knowledge over the past 200 years – as, indeed, does the underlying population growth because of the improvements in public health that have made it possible. Whether knowledge generates wisdom is, as we all know, questionable. But if we are seeking to compare ourselves to the past in the effort to understand who we are today, one thing is that we are better educated. We know more and, despite the way it may seem, we understand more.

Among other knowledge, we know more about each other than ever before. There is more travel and more communication, leading to more encounters and more information. As we encounter each other, we see our diversity – of background, race, ethnicity, belief – and how we handle that diversity will have much to say about whether we will in the end be able to rise successfully to the great challenges we face today. It is possible to see every day how the encounter between people and groups of diverse backgrounds can be on the one hand a benefit – a source of interest, pleasure, or mutual gain – or on the other hand a source of danger and potential loss – of jobs, fellow-feeling in the community, or security.

It is paradoxical how we are divided and united by our needs. Because so many of our needs are the same, there is a risk of clashing over our attempts to meet them. And when there is a possibility of clashing and sides get chosen, we are more likely to choose the side that looks, sounds, feels, and thinks like us. Perhaps if our needs were as diverse as we are, they would mesh and be complementary.

Especially when communities are under pressure, the need to band together against the outsider gets stronger. The multiple sources of change in today's world are a constant source of pressure and thus of danger. Those who once sought world government based on the recognition of all that we have in common are destined for disappointment. We have chosen instead to be divided, creating more and more independent countries and following different faiths.

Yet there is also plenty of evidence that different ethnicity and faith do not prevent people living together peacefully. As more of us cram into cities, bringing our different traditions and social norms into close proximity, being able to draw on that part of humanity's experience will become more and more important.

The States of the World

Some of our sense of who we are comes from where we were born and grew up – our countries, most of which are quite recent creations. In 1945 the United Nations was founded by just 51 states, some of which were not fully independent at the time (and the defeated states in World War II were initially excluded). Today, the UN has 193 members.

Over the past century, states have won, lost, and regained independence, often against a background of war and bloodshed. Some have become formally independent before achieving real independence; with others, it has been the other way round. This atlas shows many ways – economic, environmental, political – in which independent states do not have full sovereignty in the modern world – yet the evidence is clear that sovereignty is a highly desirable political commodity. The age of forming new states is not yet over.

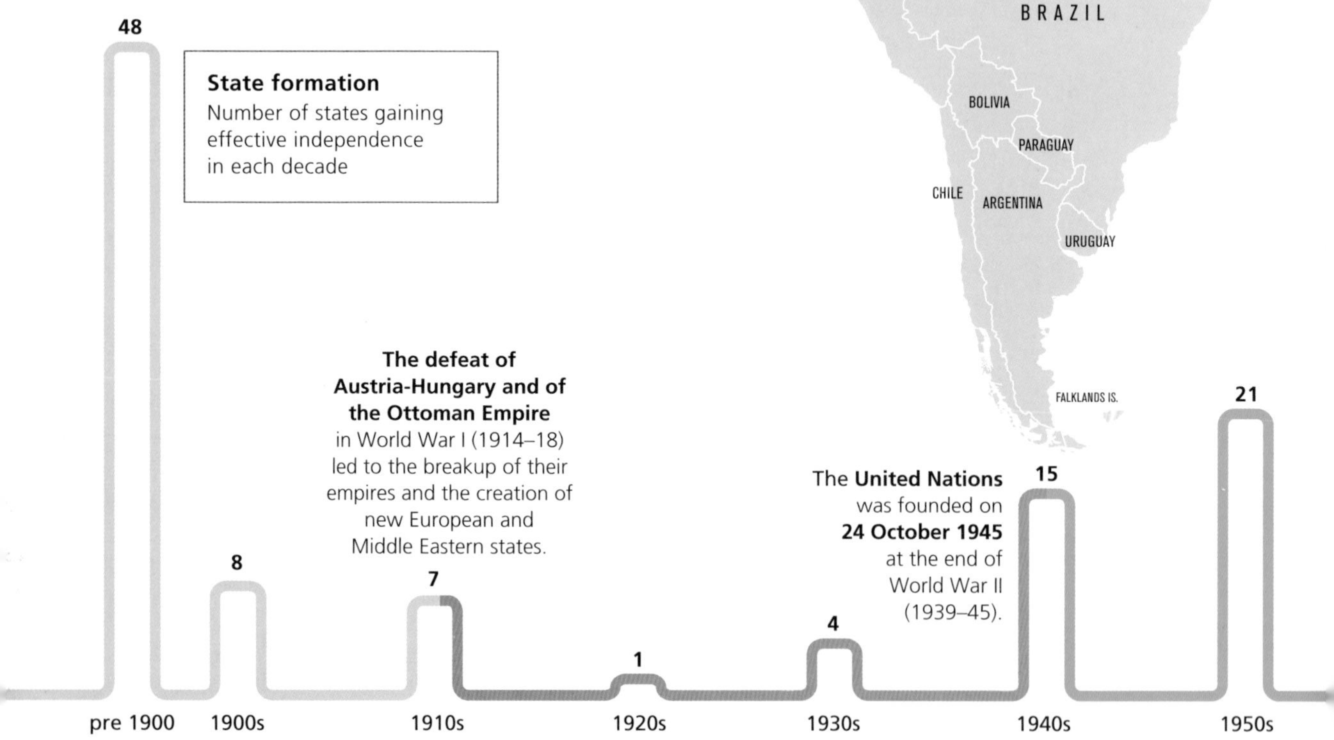

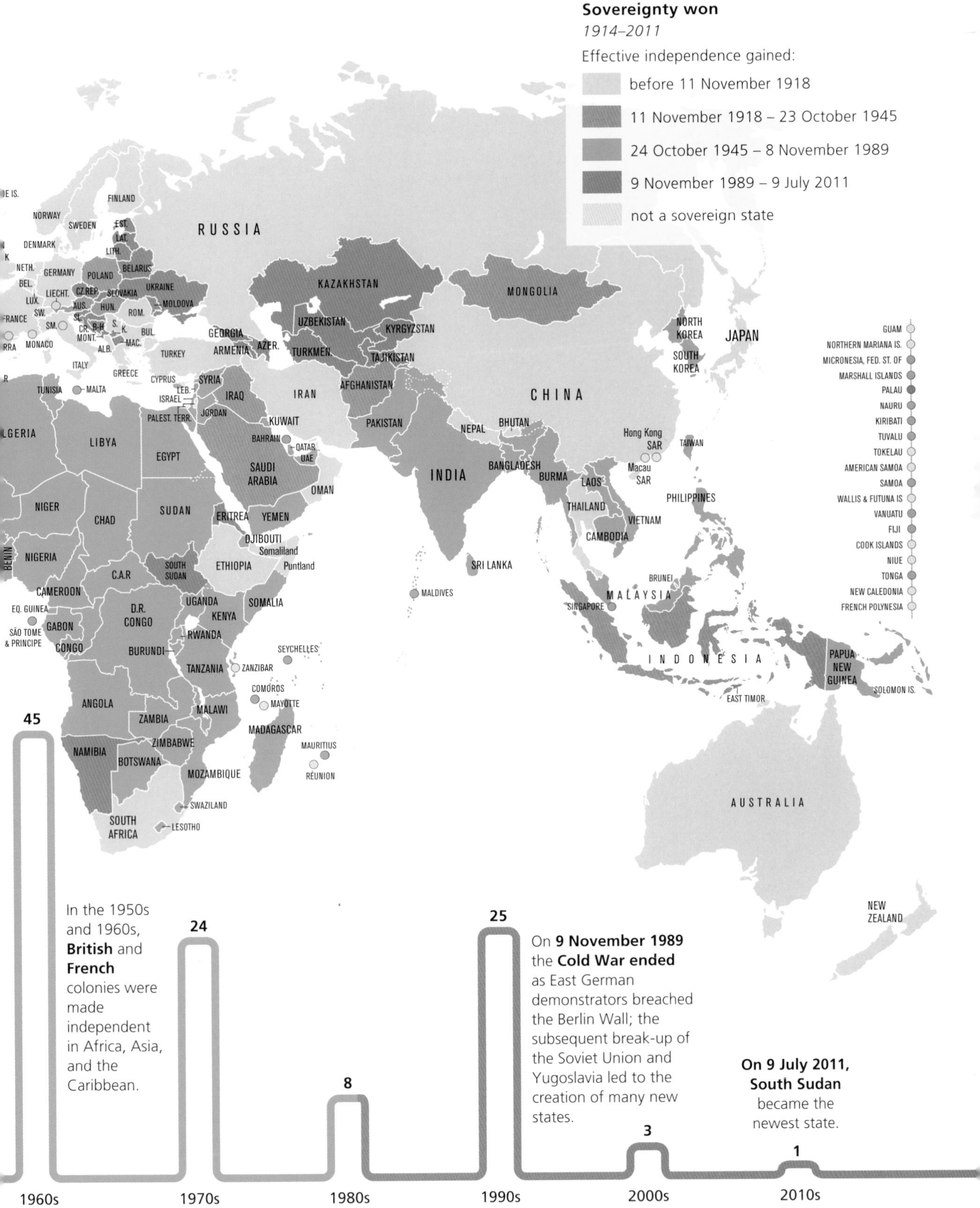
Sovereignty won
1914–2011
Effective independence gained:
before 11 November 1918
11 November 1918 – 23 October 1945
24 October 1945 – 8 November 1989
9 November 1989 – 9 July 2011
not a sovereign state
FINLAND
NORWAY
SWEDEN
EST.
LAT.
LITH.
DENMARK
RUSSIA
NETH.
GERMANY
POLAND
BELARUS
BEL.
LIECHT.
CZ.REP.
SLOVAKIA
UKRAINE
LUX.
AUS.
HUN.
MOLDOVA
FRANCE
SW.
SL.
ROM.
SM.
CR.
B-H
S.
K.
BUL.
MONT.
MAC.
MONACO
ALB.
ITALY
GREECE
TURKEY
GEORGIA
ARMENIA
AZER.
KAZAKHSTAN
UZBEKISTAN
KYRGYZSTAN
TURKMEN.
TAJIKISTAN
MONGOLIA
NORTH KOREA
SOUTH KOREA
JAPAN
CHINA
TUNISIA
MALTA
CYPRUS
LEB.
ISRAEL
SYRIA
IRAQ
IRAN
AFGHANISTAN
PALEST. TERR.
JORDAN
KUWAIT
PAKISTAN
NEPAL
BHUTAN
BAHRAIN
QATAR
UAE
Hong Kong SAR
Macau SAR
TAIWAN
LGERIA
LIBYA
EGYPT
SAUDI ARABIA
OMAN
INDIA
BANGLADESH
BURMA
LAOS
PHILIPPINES
NIGER
CHAD
SUDAN
ERITREA
YEMEN
THAILAND
VIETNAM
CAMBODIA
DJIBOUTI
Somaliland
Puntland
BENIN
NIGERIA
C.A.R.
SOUTH SUDAN
ETHIOPIA
SRI LANKA
CAMEROON
MALDIVES
BRUNEI
MALAYSIA
SINGAPORE
EQ. GUINEA
D.R. CONGO
UGANDA
SOMALIA
KENYA
GABON
SÃO TOME & PRINCIPE
RWANDA
CONGO
BURUNDI
SEYCHELLES
TANZANIA
ZANZIBAR
INDONESIA
PAPUA NEW GUINEA
COMOROS
MAYOTTE
EAST TIMOR
SOLOMON IS.
ANGOLA
MALAWI
ZAMBIA
MADAGASCAR
NAMIBIA
ZIMBABWE
MAURITIUS
BOTSWANA
MOZAMBIQUE
RÉUNION
AUSTRALIA
SWAZILAND
SOUTH AFRICA
LESOTHO
NEW ZEALAND
GUAM
NORTHERN MARIANA IS.
MICRONESIA, FED. ST. OF
MARSHALL ISLANDS
PALAU
NAURU
KIRIBATI
TUVALU
TOKELAU
AMERICAN SAMOA
SAMOA
WALLIS & FUTUNA IS
VANUATU
FIJI
COOK ISLANDS
NIUE
TONGA
NEW CALEDONIA
FRENCH POLYNESIA
45
24
8
25
3
1
In the 1950s and 1960s, British and French colonies were made independent in Africa, Asia, and the Caribbean.
On 9 November 1989 the Cold War ended as East German demonstrators breached the Berlin Wall; the subsequent break-up of the Soviet Union and Yugoslavia led to the creation of many new states.
On 9 July 2011, South Sudan became the newest state.
1960s
1970s
1980s
1990s
2000s
2010s

76 Political Systems ►

Population

The global population is still growing, although the rate of increase is beginning to slow compared with that of the last 50 years. In 2010 the average number of babies born to each woman was 2.5; in 1990 it was 3.2.

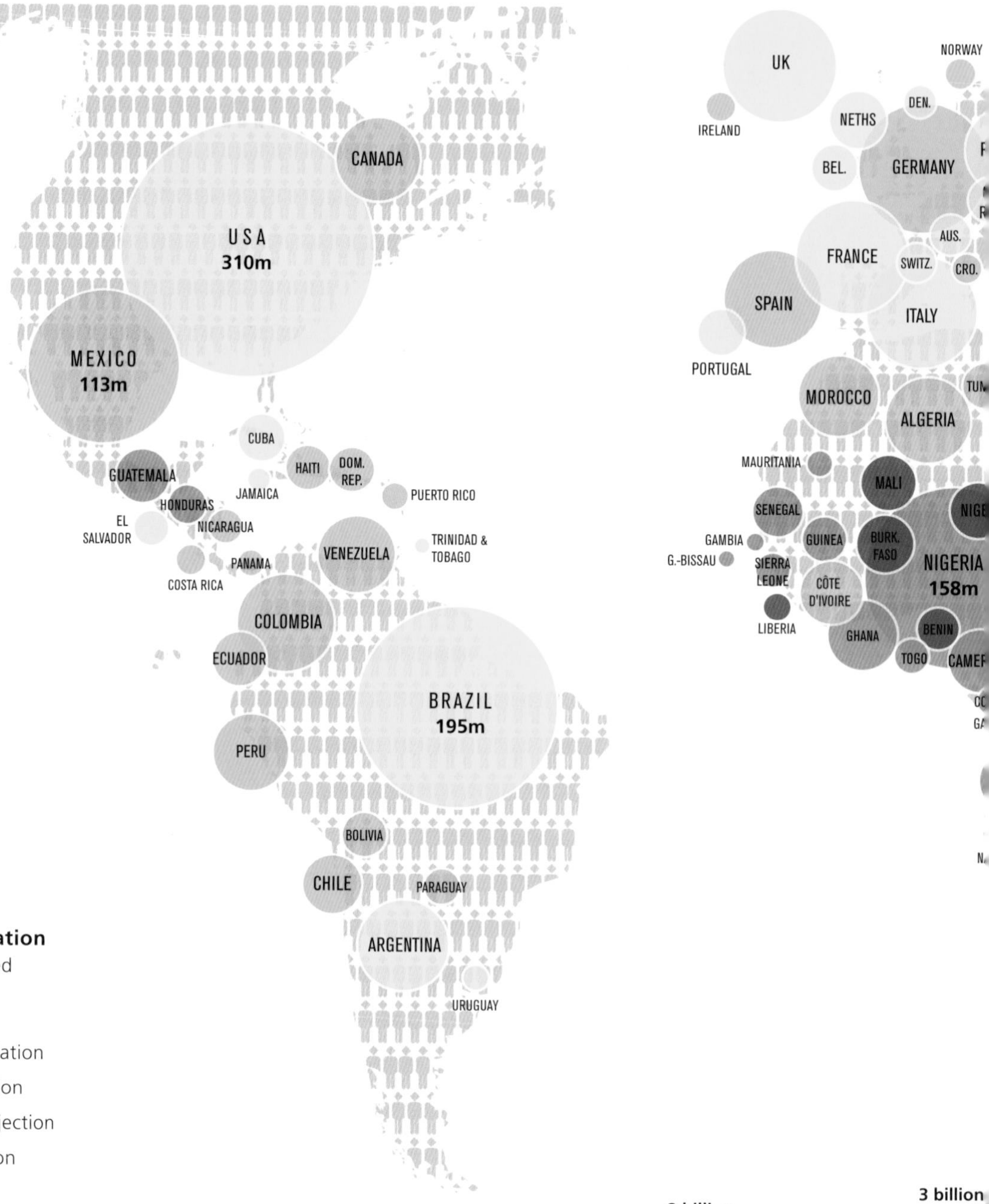

Changing population
Actual and projected world population
1810–2100

actual population
high projection
medium projection
low projection

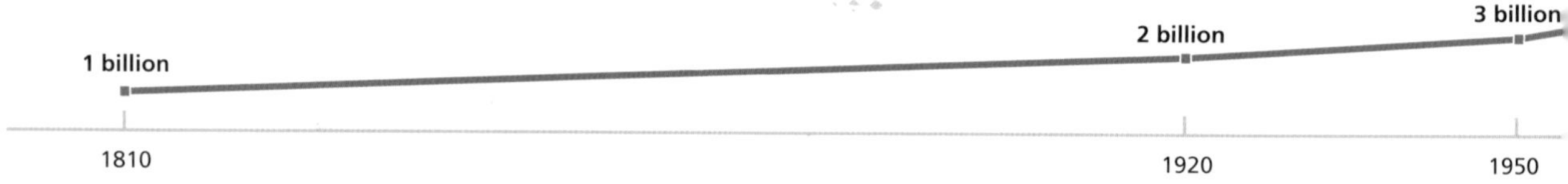

People in the world
2010

○ = 1 million people

Annual percentage change
3.0% or more
2.0% – 2.9%
1.0% – 1.9%
0.0% – 0.9%
-0.1%– -2.8%

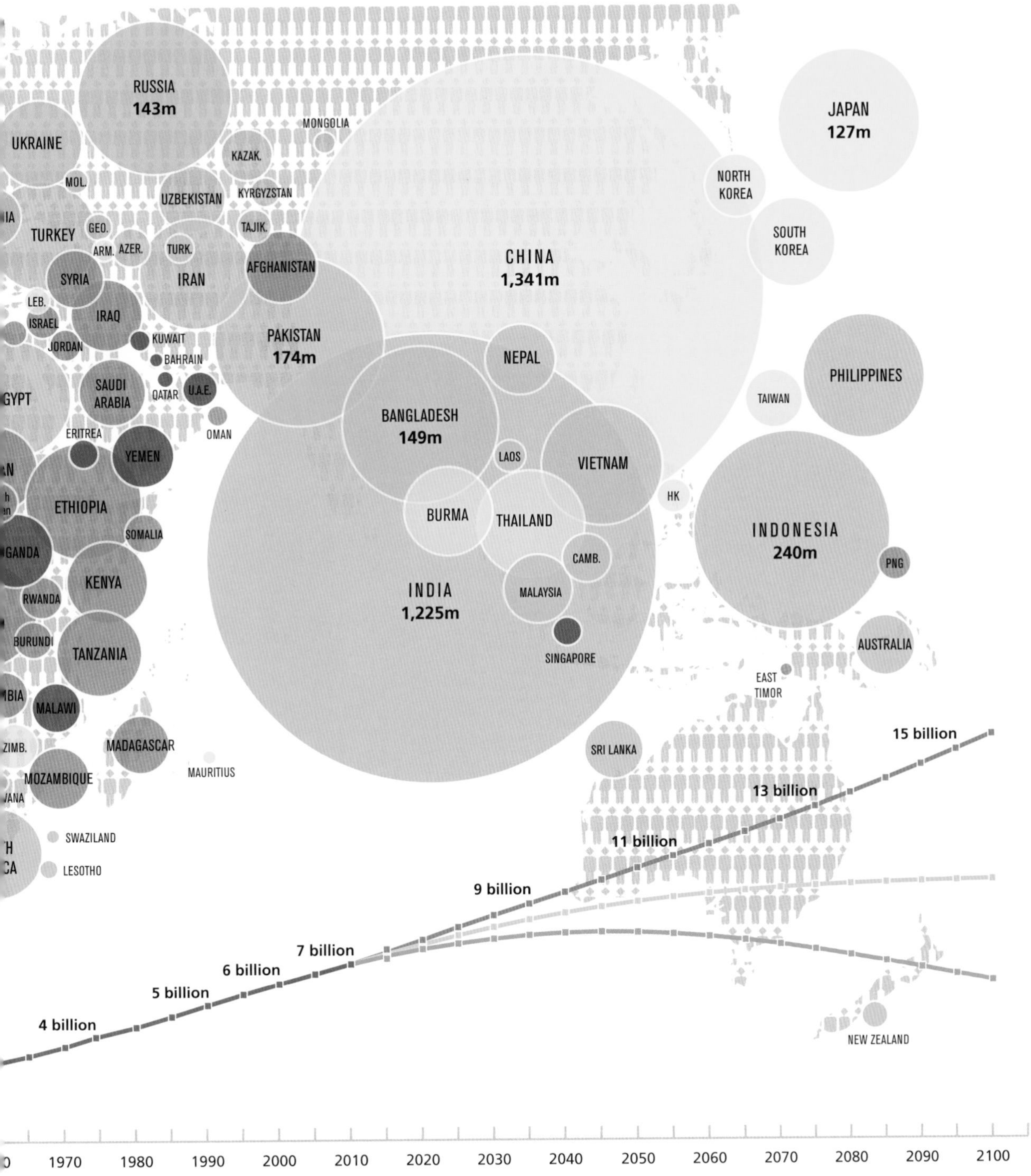

32 Urbanization ▶

Life Expectancy

Average life expectancy has never been higher, and continues to grow as general levels of health and public sanitation continue to improve.

In southern Africa, the proportion of the population infected by HIV/AIDS was 12 to 30 times the world average during the 2000s. This has combined with other diseases to reduce average life expectancy in the region.

Being homeless in England cuts life expectancy by 30 years to just 47, one year less than in Afghanistan and Central African Republic.

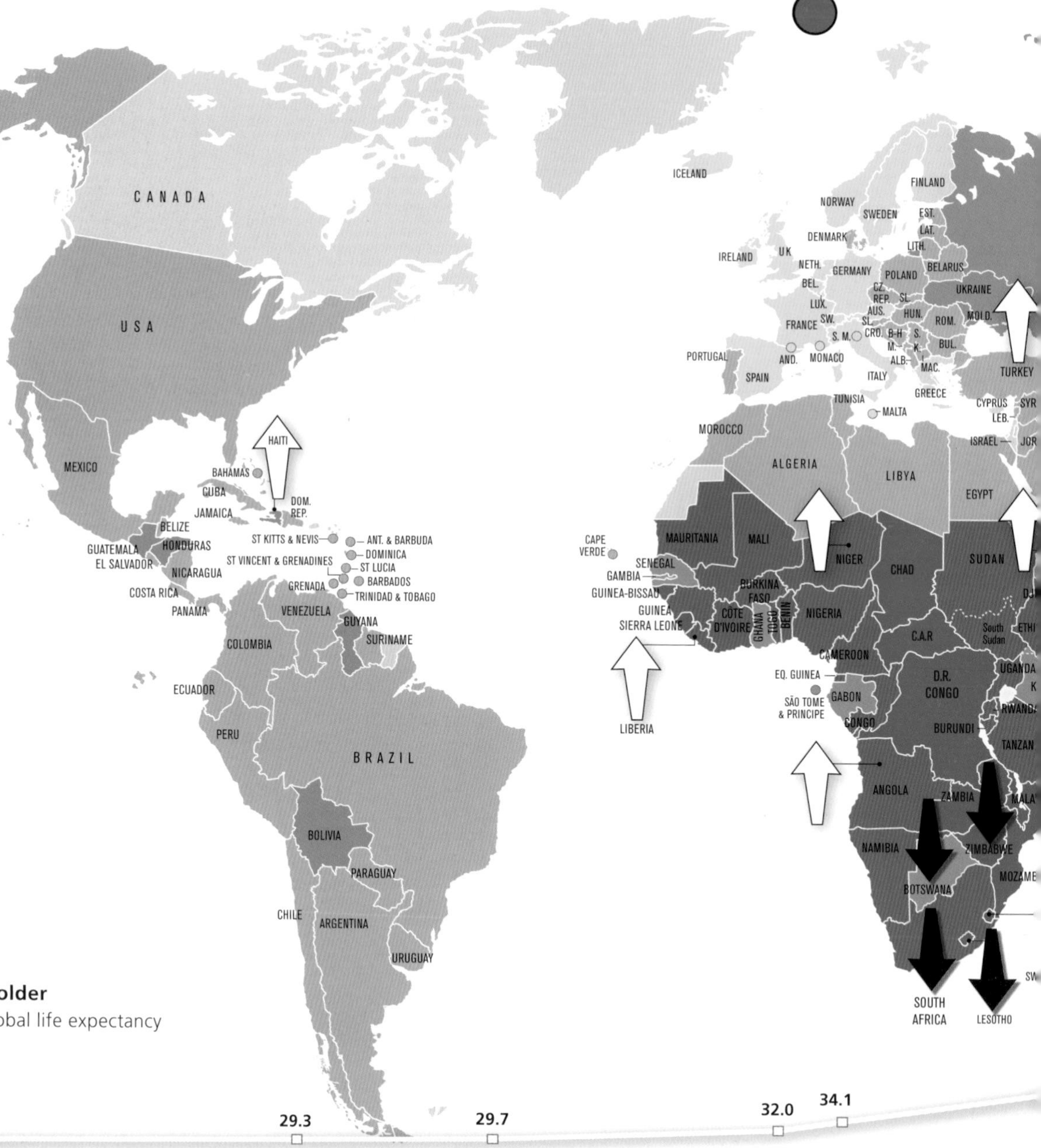

Growing older

Average global life expectancy at birth

1800–2009

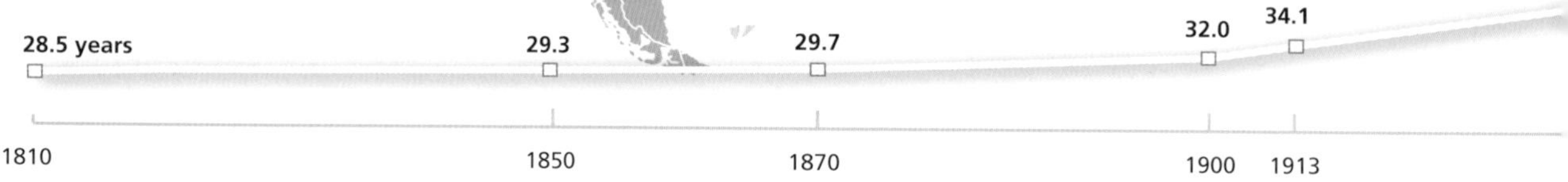

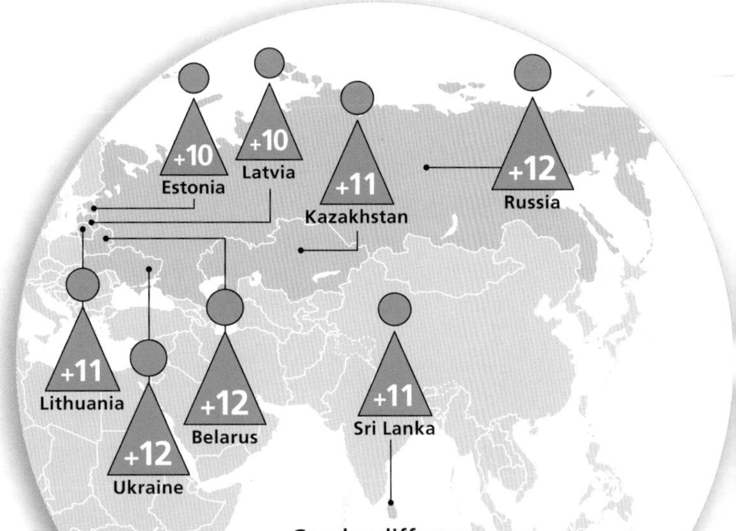

Gender difference

On average women live five years longer than men. In eight countries, women live at least ten years longer; seven of these are in the former Soviet Union.

2009

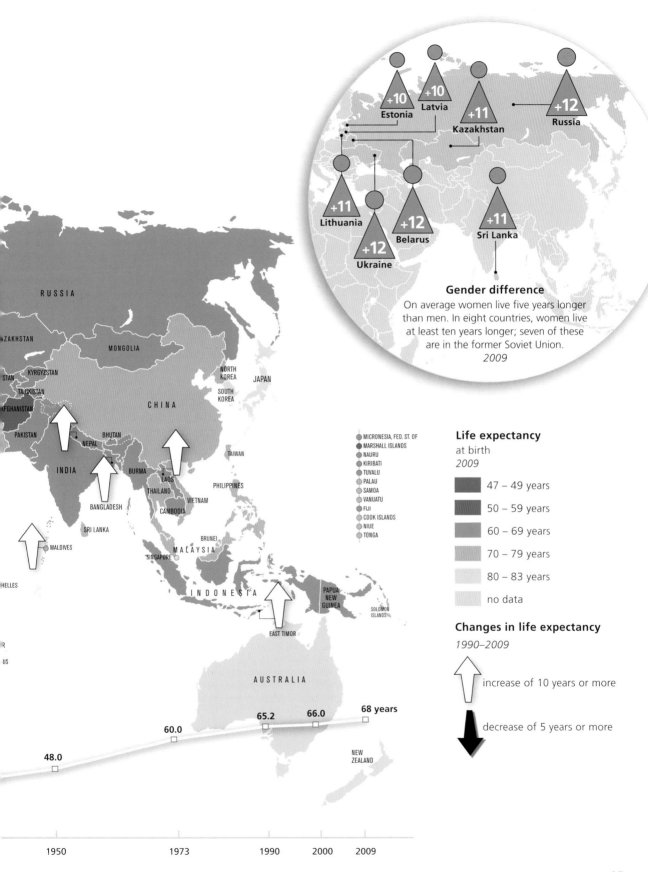

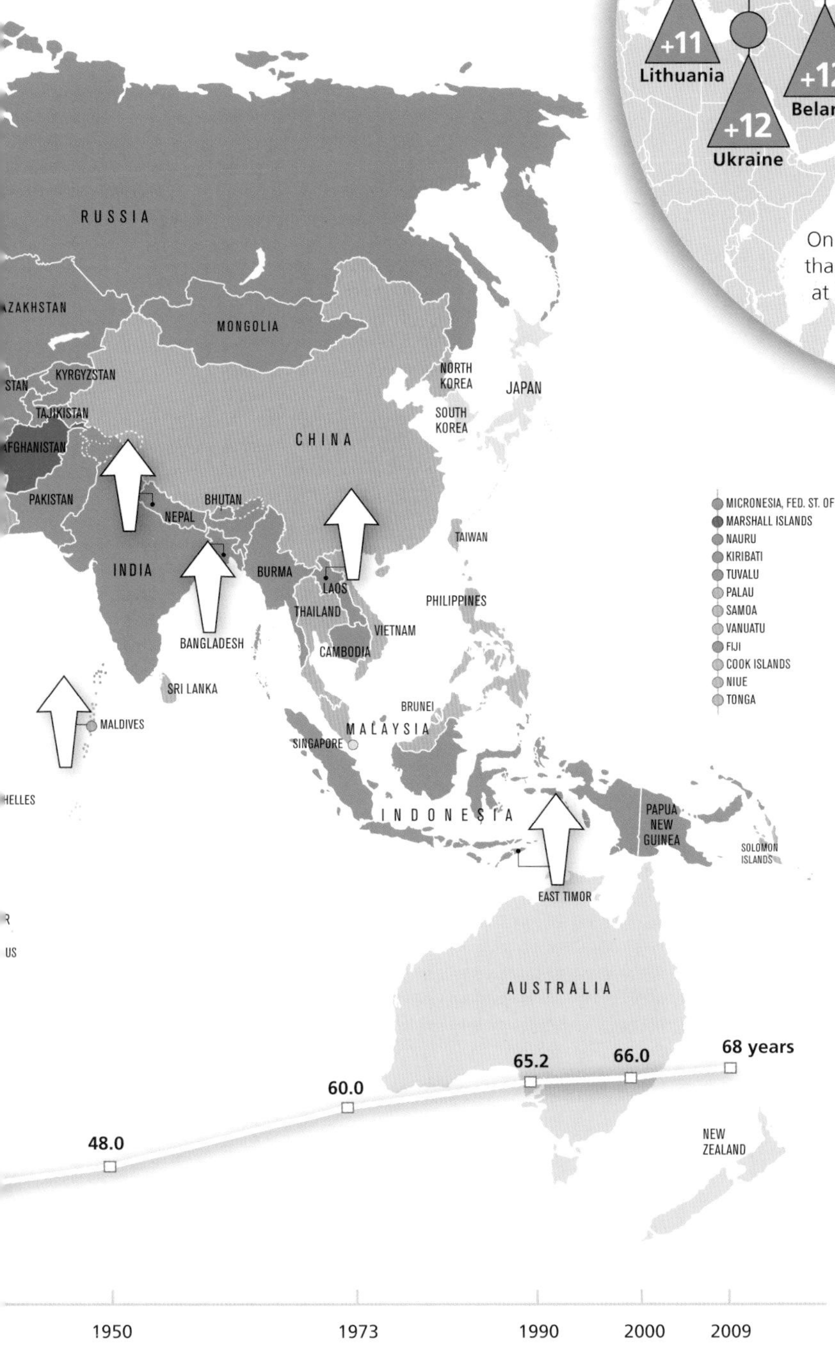

Life expectancy

at birth

2009

- 47 – 49 years
- 50 – 59 years
- 60 – 69 years
- 70 – 79 years
- 80 – 83 years
- no data

Changes in life expectancy

1990–2009

- increase of 10 years or more
- decrease of 5 years or more

40 Inequality; 98 HIV/AIDS ▶

Ethnicity & Diversity

Part of human diversity lies in our membership of large groups – nations, ethnic groups, races, tribes, clans. How these are defined varies from one culture to another. How important they are varies both from one person to the next and from time to time. Groups take on the most explicit importance for their members when they are or feel threatened – whether by day-to-day discrimination and ill treatment or by traumatic events as in war.

National ceremonies such as independence days, martial anniversaries and royal weddings offer rituals for coming together in spirit to renew identity bonds. For the rest of the time, ethno-national and racial identities tend to be little considered even though a lot of life is quietly shaped by them. Ethnic and national differences are often part of war but there are far more instances of diverse groups living peacefully together.

Ethnic and national identity is at stake in **50%** of 21st-century wars

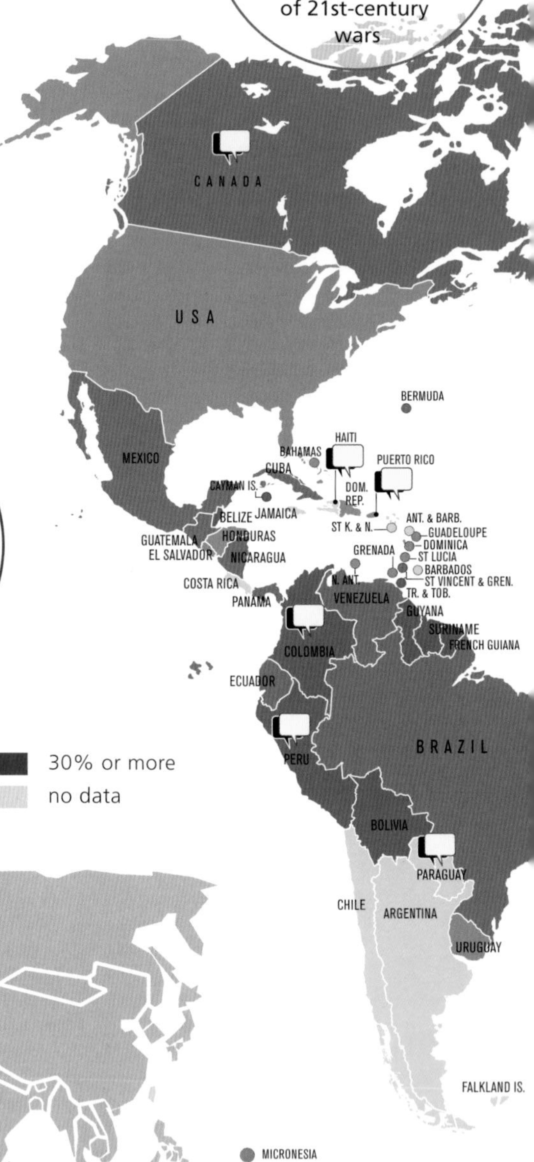

215 million people live outside their country of birth

Migrants

People living in country other than that in which they were born as a percentage of total population
2010

- less than 10%
- 10% – 29%
- 30% or more
- no data

Ethnic, national, and racial minorities
Minority groups as percentage of population*
2012 or latest data

*definitions differ among countries

- less than10%
- 10% – 29%
- 30% – 49%
- 50% or more *there is no majority group*
- data lacking or inadequate

The language of government
2012 or latest data

- more than one official language in use nationally and/or locally

Cyprus: Greek Cypriots make up about 80% of the total population, Turkish Cypriots about 20%. The island has been divided since 1974. Viewed as a whole, the island is nationally diverse; viewed separately, each entity is homogenous.

Researchers have identified 719 languages in **Indonesia**...

...and over 850 languages in **Papua New Guinea**.

58 War in the 21st Century ▶

Religious Beliefs

The vast majority of people profess a religious faith. Although professing a faith on a population census form and actually practising it are two very different things, their faith is, for many, a basic marker of identity. Shared religious conviction can unite people where other things divide them, and even between different faiths there is significant ethical common ground and a shared openness to the spiritual and immaterial.

But religious identity coincides with other markers of identity – regional, national, ethnic, and cultural. When and where religious leaders cannot or will not restrain the way in which adherents to different faiths express their differences, conflicts can overheat and explode. Some of the world's most brutal violence is – and has been throughout history – inflicted in the name of religion. And some of the worst violence is over differences within the same religion: between Protestants and Catholic Christians, or between Sunni and Shi'a Muslims. Yet common to all major religions is the over-riding value of peace.

Faithful countries

Countries with largest populations of Christians and Muslims

Christians   Muslims

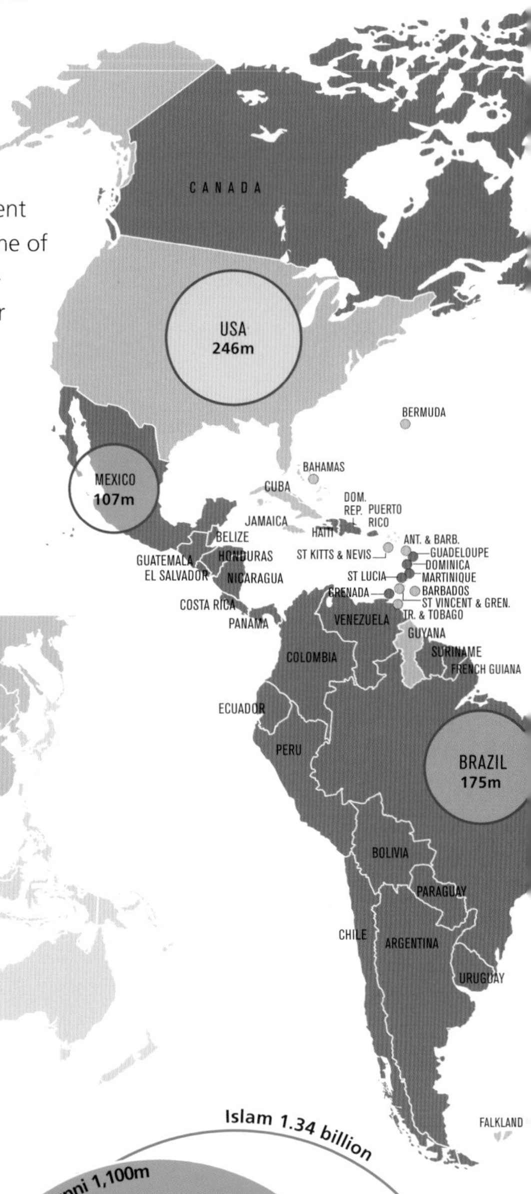

Non-believers

People who profess no religion as a percentage of population

2005

20% or more

10% – 19.9%

fewer than 10%

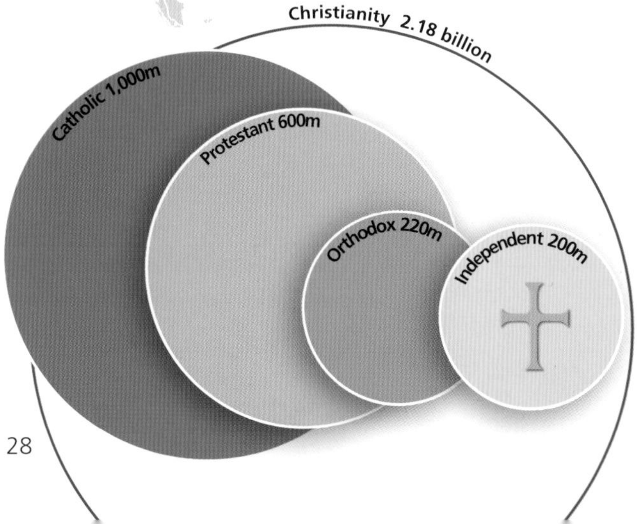

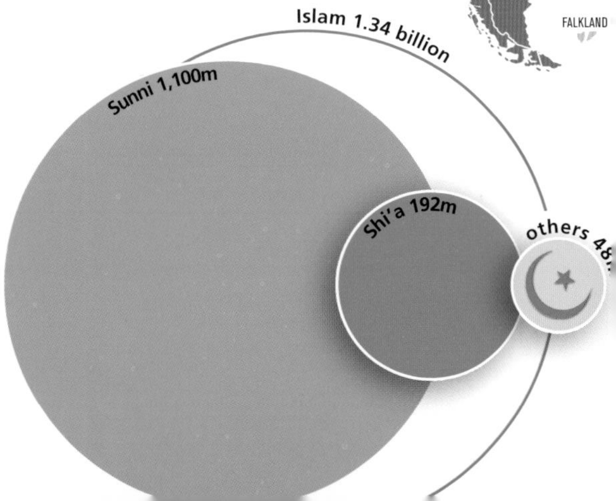

Believers
Most popular faiths
circa 2006–10

Buddhism
- Mahayana
- Theravada

Christianity
- Catholicism
- Protestantism
- Orthodox
- Independent

Islam
- Sunni
- Shi'a
- Ibadiyyah

Other religions
- Hinduism
- Judaism
- Indigenous
- officially irreligious

World faiths
Estimated number of followers
latest available data

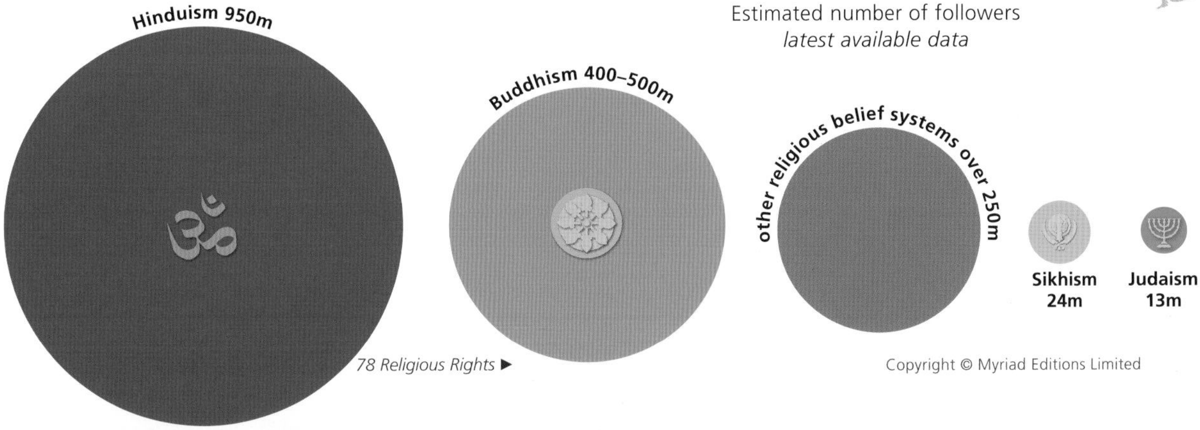

78 Religious Rights ►

Literacy & Education

Literacy is simultaneously a functional need for modern societies, a basic tool for individual advancement, and a personal source of knowledge, access to the world and satisfaction. Thanks to a major international effort, trends in the last decade have been positive. Although there remain places where adult illiteracy rates are still over 50 per cent of the population, and in Africa and some other areas, progress in secondary and tertiary education remains slow, primary education, where the foundations are laid, has registered real forward movement.

Nonetheless, the challenge remains steep. The UN estimates that the world needs 8 million more primary school teachers by 2015 in order to achieve its Millennium Development Goal for education. Of these, 6 million are required simply to replace others who will leave the teaching profession, while 2 million are necessary extra teachers. And of those 2 million, more than half are needed in Sub-Saharan Africa.

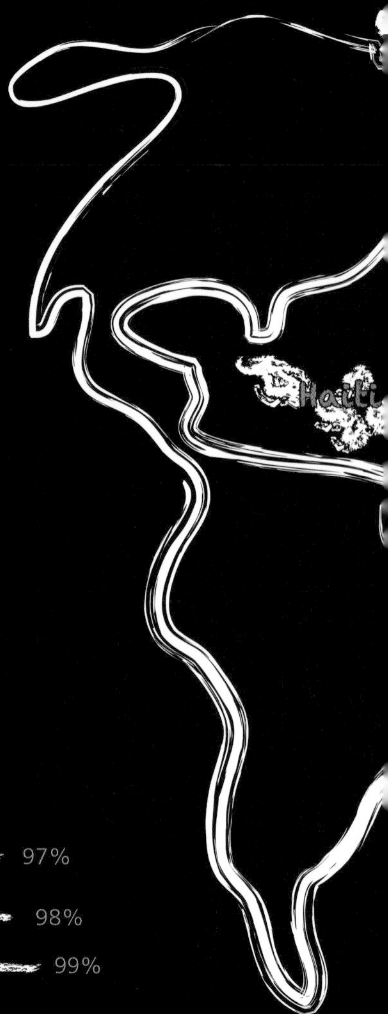

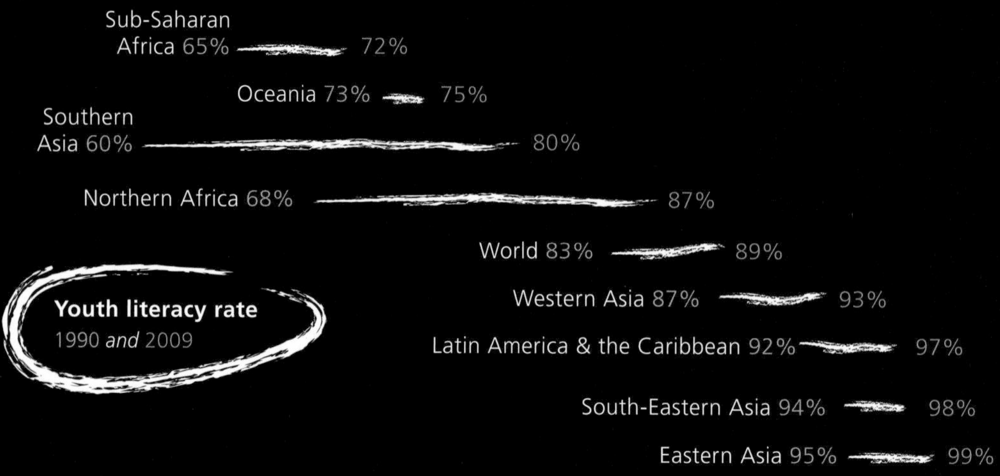

Enrolment in education
2010 or latest available data

- 90% or more
- 70% – 89%
- 50% – 69%
- 30% – 49%
- 10% – 29%
- fewer than 10%
- no data

Primary education

Percentage of children of the correct age enrolled in primary school

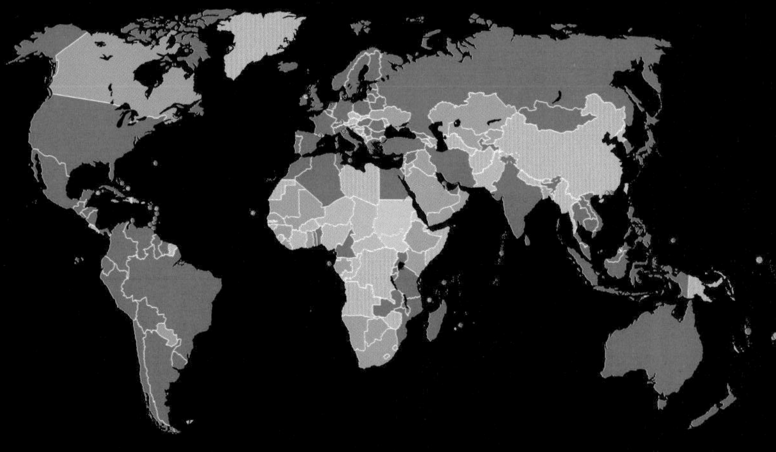

Secondary education

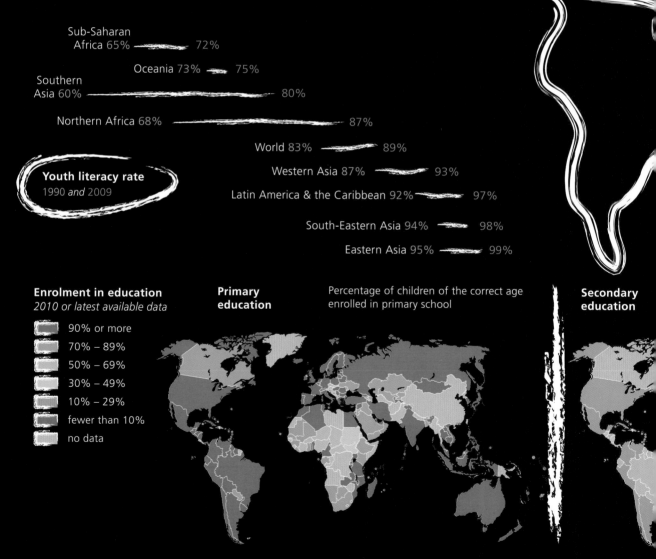

Adult illiteracy
As percentage of adult population
2010 or latest available data

Percentage of children of the correct age enrolled in secondary school

Tertiary education

Percentage of young people enrolled in tertiary college

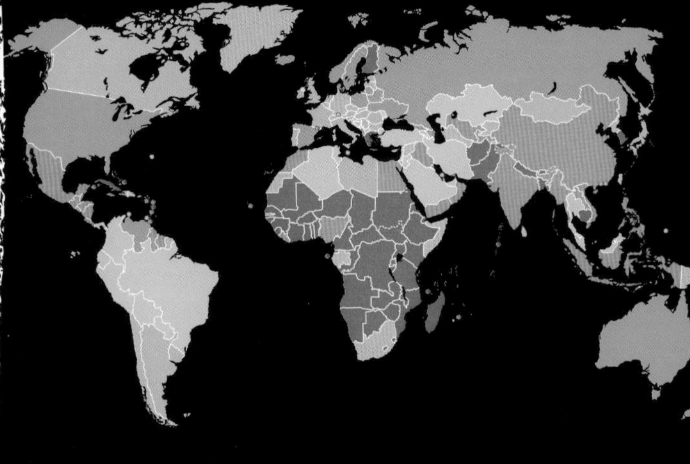

54 Goals for Development; 82 Children's Rights ►

Urbanization

Today 51 per cent of the world's people live in cities. In 1800 just 3 per cent were urban dwellers. Projections suggest between 60 and 70 per cent of the world's population will live in cities by 2030. New urbanization is largely concentrated in the developing countries. Most major cities in Europe are static or declining in size, partly because improved transport and communications are reducing the economic benefits of concentrating large numbers of people in a few places. In developing countries, however, big cities remain magnets for people seeking livelihoods when they can no longer sustain themselves in the countryside.

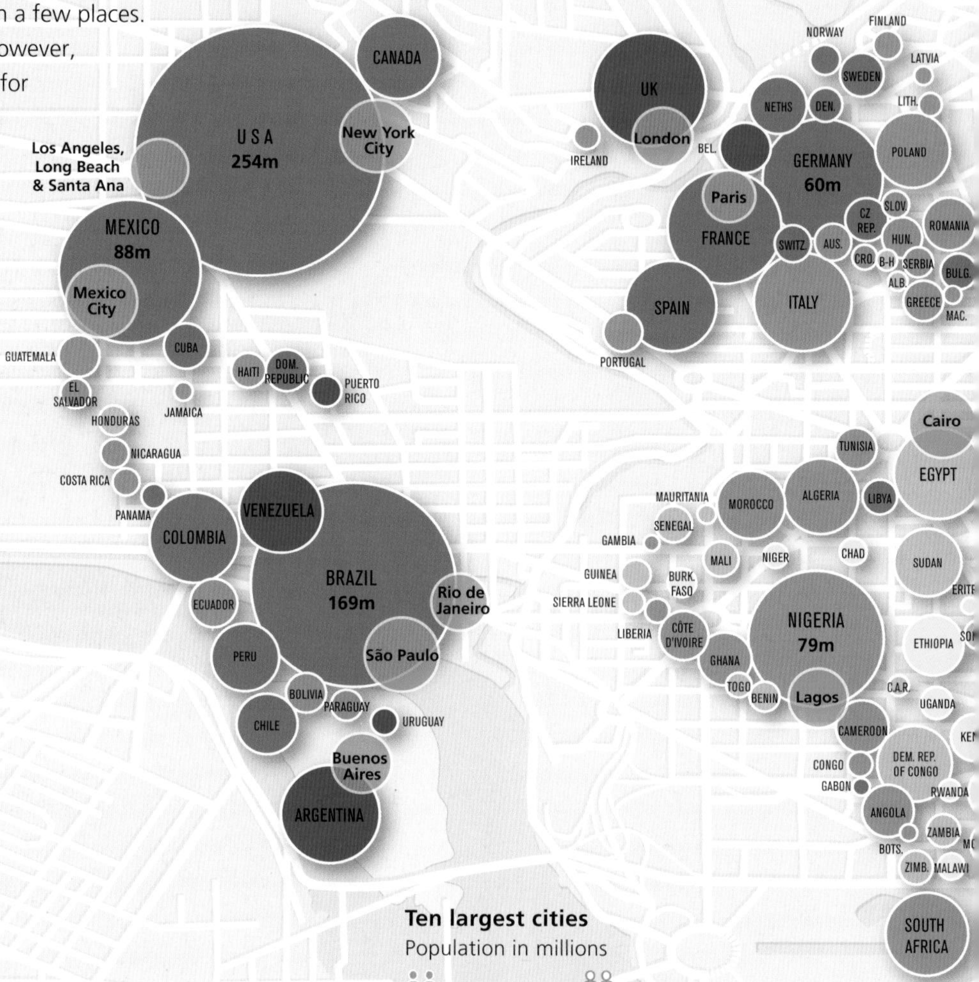

City scale

Number of people living in different sizes of urban conglomeration

2010

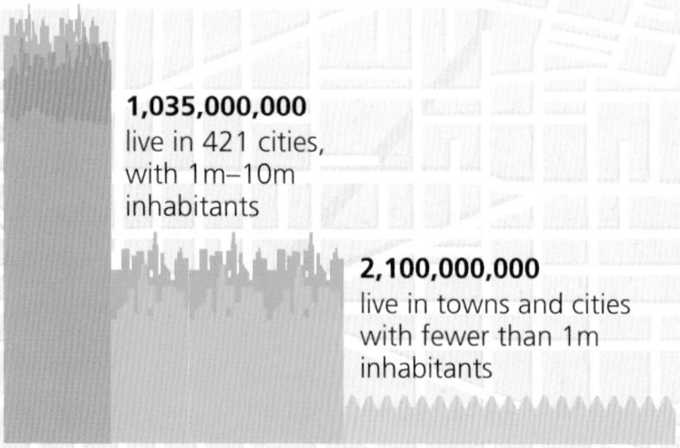

Ten largest cities

Population in millions

1950 2010

Arranged from west to east

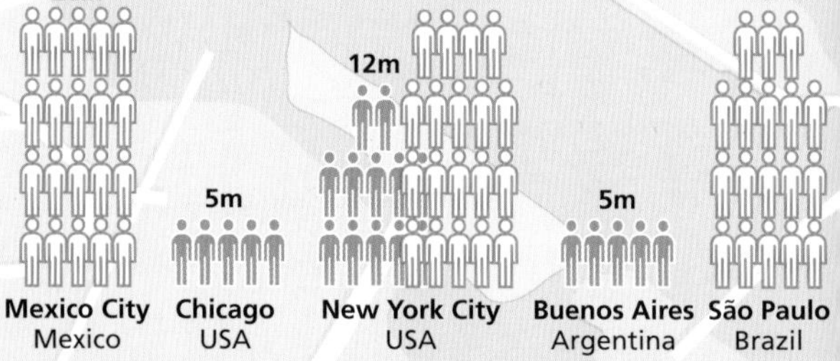

◄ 22 Population

Urban population
2010

= 10 million people

= 1 million people

Urban dwellers as percentage of total population

- 90% or more
- 70% – 89%
- 50% – 69%
- 30% – 49%
- 10% – 29%

city with over 10 million inhabitants *2010*

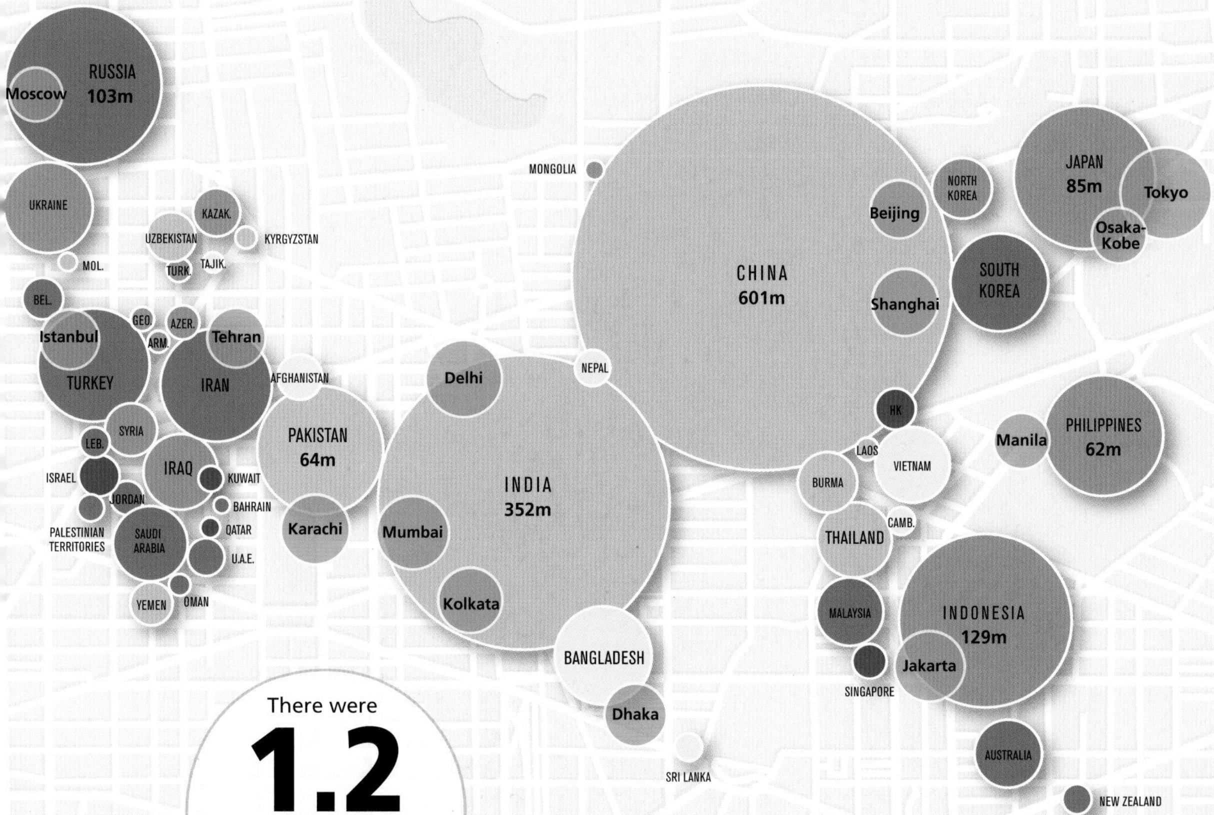

There were
1.2
billion
more urban dwellers in 2010 than in 1990

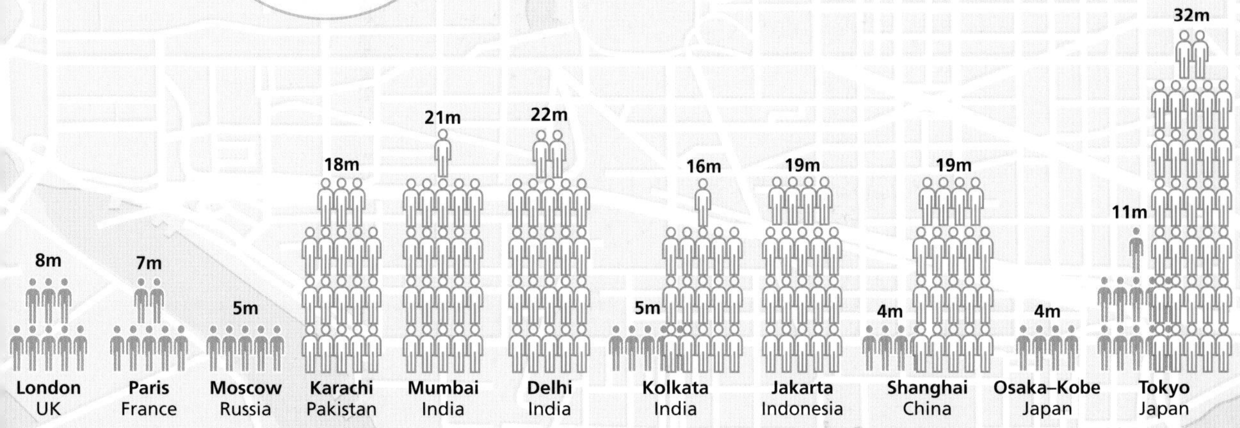

78 Religious Rights ▶

Diversity of Cities

The diversity of cities is as great as the diversity of the world. They hold, display, and generate great wealth – and equally great poverty. They are places of danger, and equally of opportunity, as continued urban migration shows. Worldwide, just under a billion people are believed to live in slums, almost one-third of the urban population.

- More than 300 languages are spoken in London.
- It has the world's oldest and second most extensive underground railway network.

- 20% of Parisians were born outside France.
- The city receives 28 million tourists a year, 17 million from outside France.

London

Paris

- About 45% of New Yorkers speak a language other than English at home.
- The urban legend of alligators in Manhattan sewers grew in the 1960s based on a colourful account by a retired city official.

New York

- Mexico City sits on a drained lake-bed of saturated clay that is subsiding as it continues to dry: in 100 years, parts of the city have sunk about 9 metres.
- Its metro system is the world's fourth largest and cheapest to use.

Mexico City

- Lagos has no overall city administration.
- The city population is growing at the rate of 1 new person every 2 minutes.

Lag

São Paulo

- "Sampa" is the world's largest Japanese city outside Japan, the largest Spanish city outside Spain, the largest Lebanese city outside Lebanon.

Comparative wealth of city dwellers

Number of hours someone needed to work for the average city wage in order to buy an iPod Nano (8GB version) in 2009

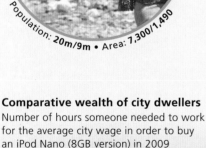

◄ 32 Urbanizatio

Cities around the world

2011 or most recent data

Size of metropolitan area:

metro area =1,000 km² (outer ring)

city area =100 km² (inner ring)

Population density: people per square kilometre:

- 20,000 or more
- 10,000 – 19,999
- 6,000 – 9,999
- 3,000 – 5,999
- fewer than 3,000

Istanbul, Turkey

Population: 13m • Area: 5,300

- Istanbul has 18% of Turkey's population and produces over 25% of national GDP.
- Its population grew tenfold in the second half of the 20th century.

Karachi, Pakistan

Population: 18m • Area: 3,500

- As Pakistan's financial and commercial capital, Karachi contributes 25% of national tax revenue.
- The city's population grows at the rate of 1 person a minute.

Shanghai, China

- Shanghai has the world's most extensive underground railway network.
- It has the world's busiest container port.
- The Shanghai Stock exchange ranks third in the world by trading volume.
- 99% of residents are Han Chinese.

Population: 19m • Area: 6,300

Tokyo, Japan

- 99% of Tokyo's population is Japanese by birth.
- 40% of the city is built on landfill.

Population: 32m/13m • Area: 8,000/2,100

anbul

Tehran

Cairo

Karachi

Mumbai

Tokyo

Shanghai

Jakarta

Tehran, Iran

Population: 13m/9m • Area: 1,300/730

- Tehran's population has grown fivefold in 50 years.
- Air pollution (80% cars, 20% industrial) kills about 10,000 people a year; in 2006, 3,600 died in the month of October alone.

Mumbai, India

Population: 21m/14m • Area: 2,350/660

- 16 major languages are widely spoken in Mumbai.
- With less than 2% of India's population, Mumbai pays over 33% of its taxes.
- About half of residents live in unregistered accommodation and lack sanitation.

Cairo, Egypt

- Almost 20% of Cairo's buildings date from 1997 or later.
- 60% of the population is aged under 30.
- Up to 25,000 people a year die from air pollution.

Population: 17m/6.7m • Area: 6,600/453

Jakarta, Indonesia

- 40% of Jakarta is below sea level.
- At least 35% and perhaps as many as 80% of residents lack a clean water supply.
- All Jakarta's rivers are polluted – 71% heavily.

Population: 19m/10m • Area: 5,100/740

a rs | Mexico City 95 hours | Cairo 105 hours | Mumbai 177 hours

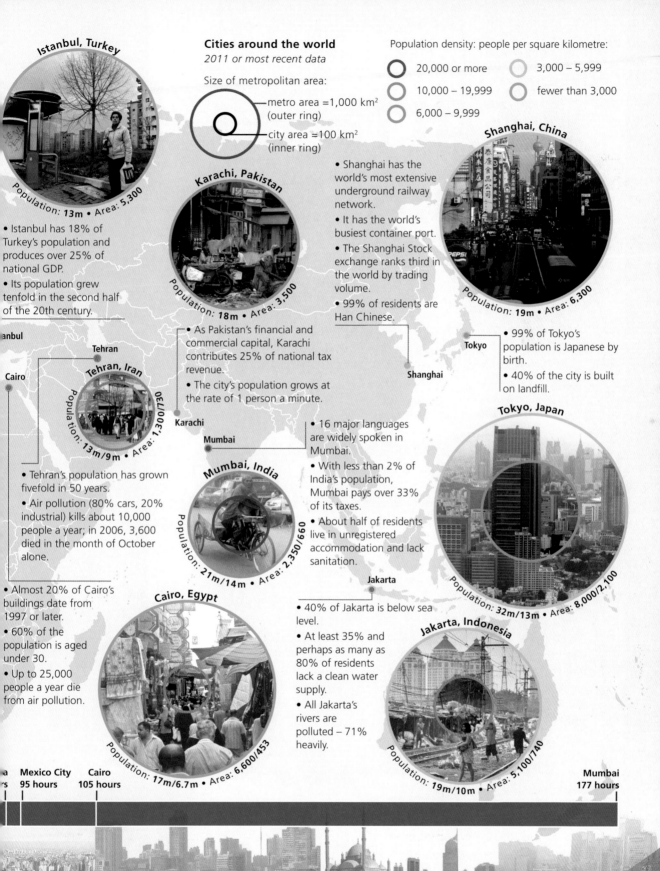

2 Tourism ►

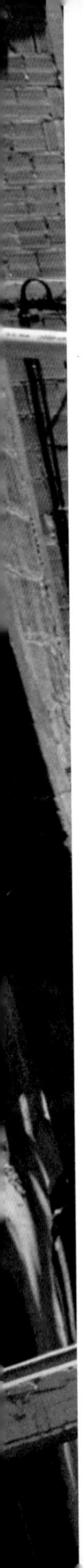

PART TWO

WEALTH & POVERTY

The two decades up to 2008 were hardly still waters in the global economy, and the sense of safety and certainty about the economy that opinion-leaders and policy-makers in the rich countries often expressed was always somewhat shallow and misleading. There was a severe downturn at the turn of the 1980s into the 1990s, followed by Japan's lost decade, and the costs and upheavals in eastern Europe and the former Soviet Union as they went through a massive economic transformation, then an Asian economic crisis in the late 1990s and the collapse of many new technology companies in the early years of this century. And in the countries where there was more or less steady economic growth, there were plenty of losers as well as winners, while global poverty persisted. But there was also an unmistakable – and now absent – sensation of forward movement, a confidence that economic problems were open to relatively straightforward solutions, and trust in many countries that the hands on the economic tiller were competent and dependable.

Today it feels so very different. And in the change of conditions brought about by economic events since 2008, it is sometimes hard to disentangle what has really changed and what not. As always, not everybody gains and loses equally. One line of inequality has been narrowing and there is every reason to expect it to continue to do so: the old idea of a sharp division in the world between rich countries and poor countries no longer holds in the same form. The contrasts are now more subtle, as other lines of inequality are getting broader. Some countries are richer than others, but in the rich countries there remains much poverty. India is no longer one of the poorest countries, not even when wealth is measured per head of the population. But there are more people living in poverty in India than in any other country. Worldwide, the number of people living below $1 a day is declining, but the number on less than $2 a day is over 2.5 billion – more than one person in three in the global population.

World leaders committed themselves at the start of the century to a major effort at international social and economic development, with the richer countries pledging to spend more on aiding development. Promises were

made and targets set for achievement by 2015. The record is mixed: development spending has increased, though that has been slowed by the economic downturn, and there has been considerable progress on some indicators in some countries. By and large the targets will not be met; they now seem to have been not only too ambitious but also flawed by being generic. Countries are different from each other; the policies that work in one place fail elsewhere. It is in particular countries that are affected by violent conflict and political instability where the millennium development effort is failing most comprehensively.

Among the factors that hold back some countries is their pervasive corruption. But it should not be thought that this is only a problem of poor, developing countries. A significant contribution to corruption in those countries is made by businesses headquartered in the financial capitals of the northern world.

And when looking at how the banks have performed – borrowing and lending up to 2008 in amounts and ways they could not keep track of, running a cosy system of mis-selling poorly understood financial products and fixing interest rates to their own benefit, their top managers paying themselves vast bonuses then seeking government hand-outs when their incompetence caught up with them, and then carrying on with the big bonuses – the concept of legalized corruption comes to mind.

The economic crash highlighted a global imbalance, in which the USA borrowed and spent while China saved and lent. On a smaller scale the same imbalance existed between Germany and much of the rest of Europe. But the USA had more collateral. This crisis has been a knock, a profound one, for the USA – but not the shattering disaster it is turning out to be in some parts of Europe.

Out of the crash of 2008, while Europe has stumbled into one hole after another, the USA has limped, several times seeming to pull itself clear of the wreckage only to fall back, while China has walked tall and the Indian economy has performed only a little less impressively. Yet, like the USA, the rising economic powers may be slowed and hindered by Eurozone stagnation. Globalization has harnessed everybody's economic fates together.

An economic system that has previously been marked not only by perpetual forward motion but by astonishing resilience has taken a terrible buffeting. So far the politicians have no solution. Each crisis summit is the solution, so it is declared, until the next one. In all probability, the resilience of the system will reassert itself over time – but most likely at high cost for ordinary people in many countries. There seems little doubt that less painful recovery requires new institutions to protect us all from the malign influence of short-term greed and the tunnel vision it generates.

Income

Despite the economic crash of 2008 and the recessions, depressions, and crises that have happened since, growth in the world's annual economic output continues to outpace by far the growth in world population. Yet extreme poverty persists.

Gross National Income
Per capita
2010 or latest available data
PPP$

- $25,000 or more
- $10,000 – $24,999
- $5,000 – $9,999
- $1,000 – $4,999
- less than $1,000

Economic output increased by over **200%** 1990–2010

Growth spurt
Percentage increase in GNI
1990–2010

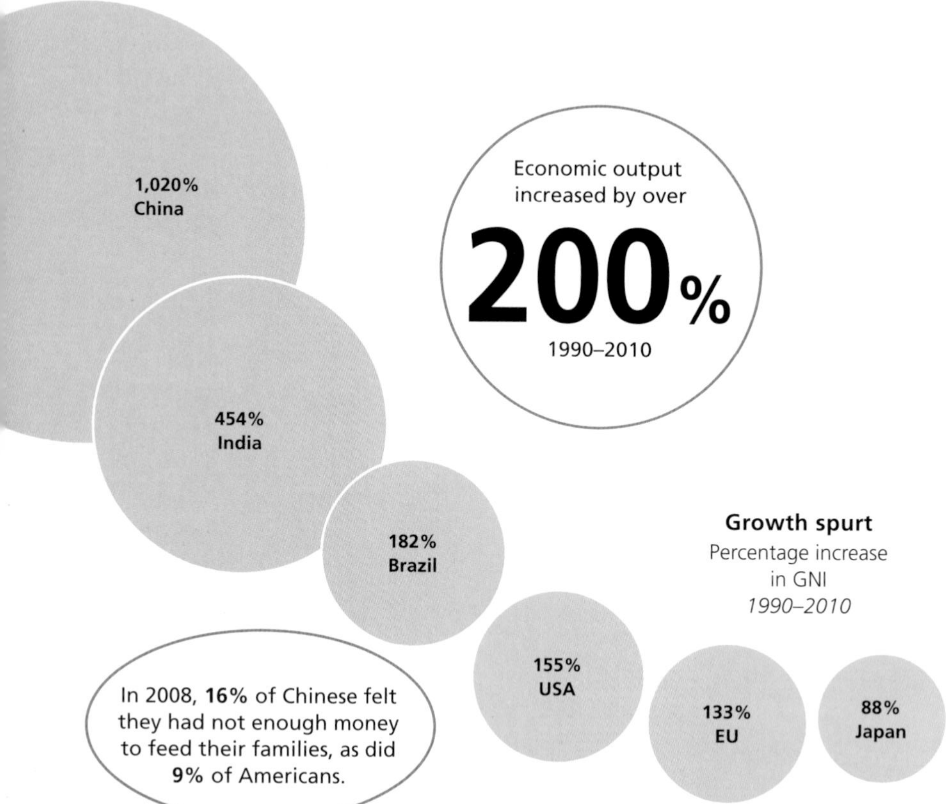

In 2008, **16%** of Chinese felt they had not enough money to feed their families, as did **9%** of Americans.

In 2011, **6%** of Chinese said they could not feed their families, as did **19%** of Americans.

Who crashed in the 2008 crash?
Change in GNI
2008–09

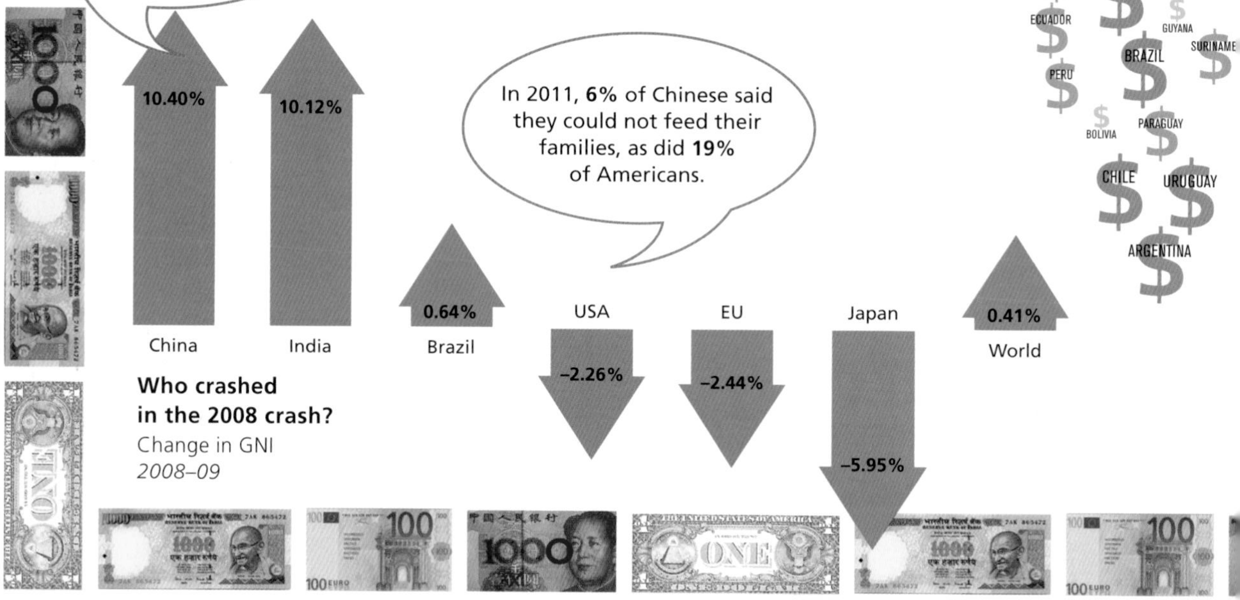

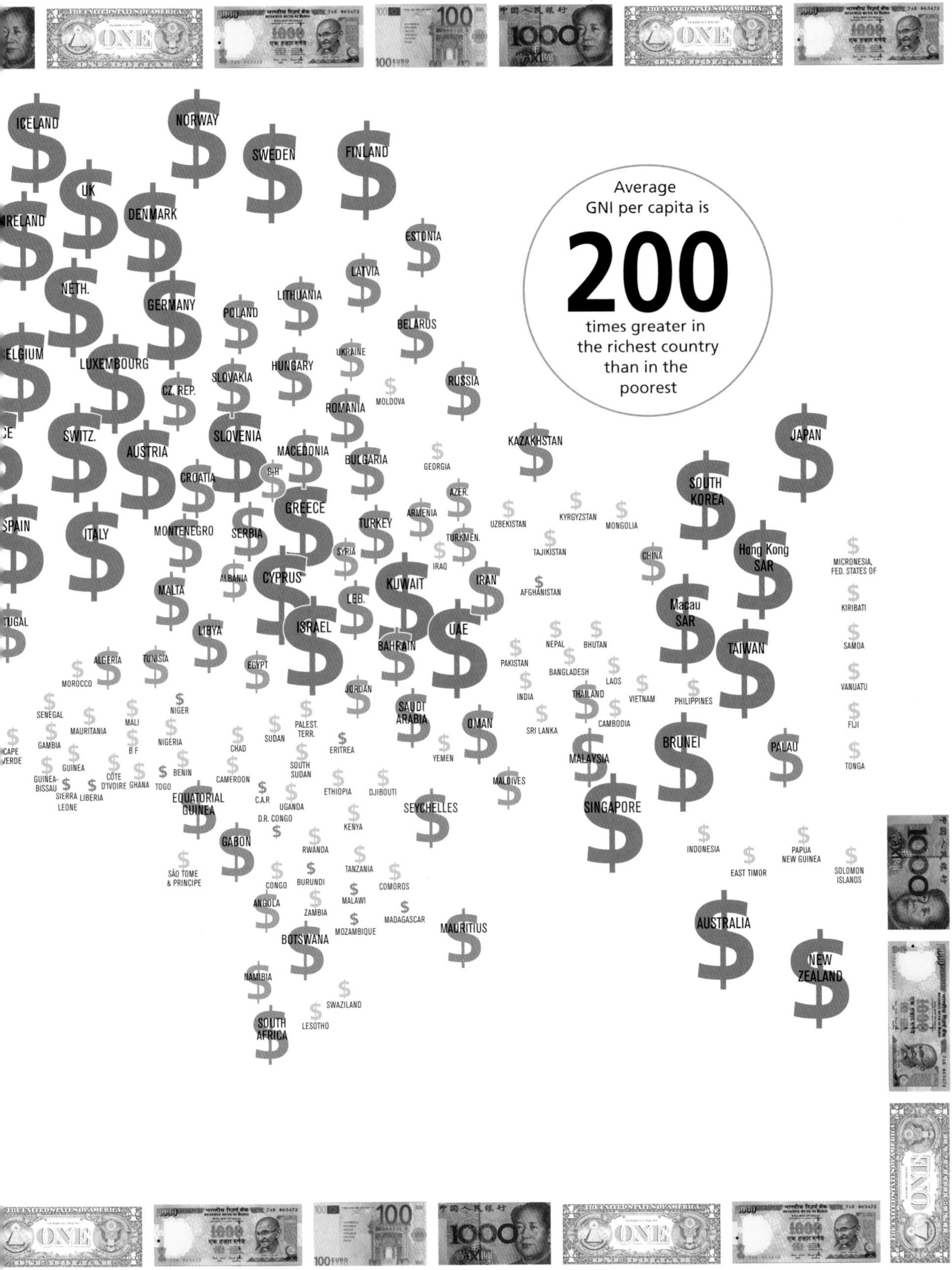

40 Inequality; 44 Transnationals; 50 Debt; 112 Waste ►

Inequality

The Gini index measures the degree to which the distribution of wealth within a country is different from a perfectly equal distribution. The higher the index, the greater the inequality.

Billionaires were hit hard by the global crash in 2008. They have recovered quickly.

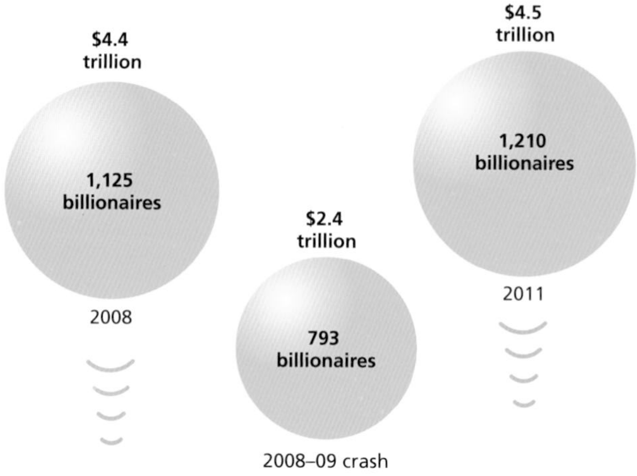

Bouncing back
Number of billionaires and their total wealth
2008–11

16%
of global economic output is owned by
0.000016%
of the global population

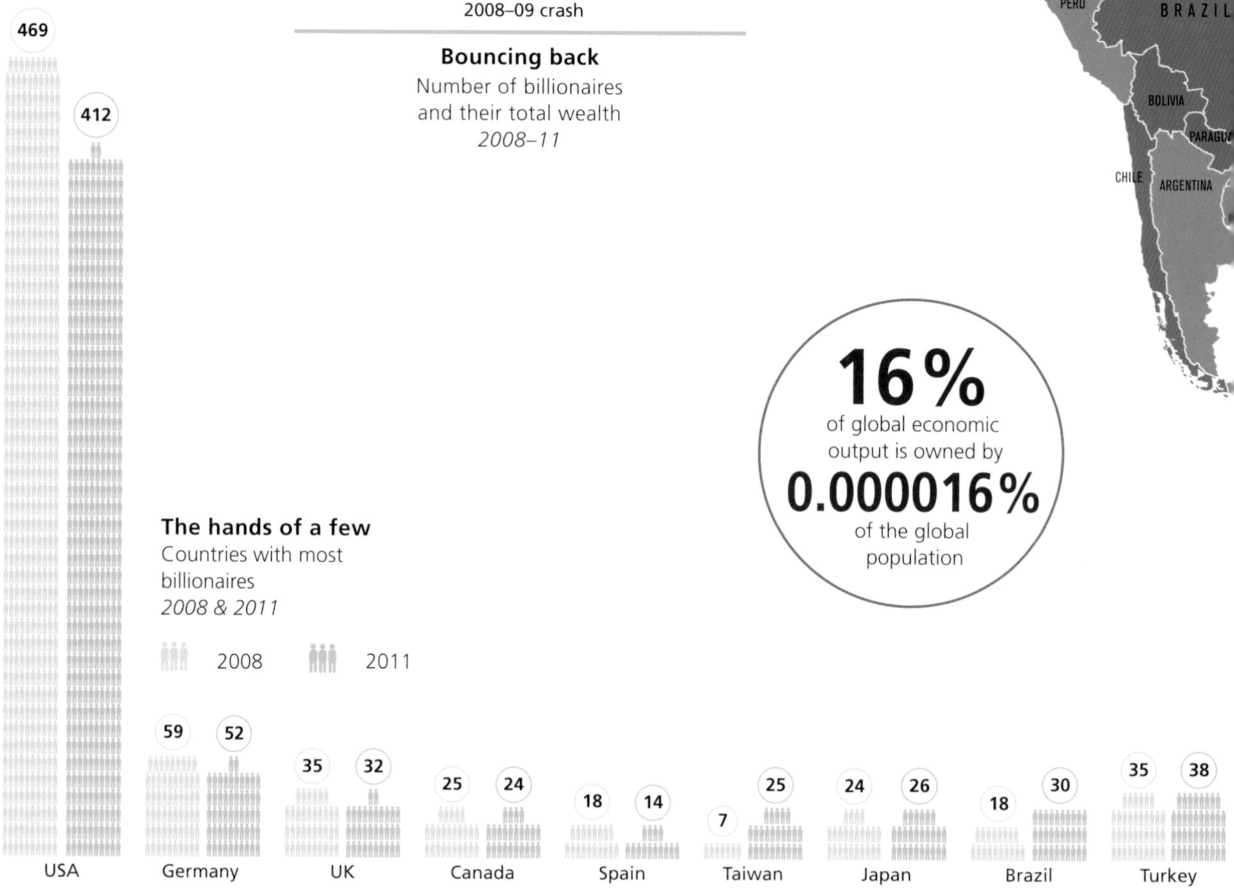

The hands of a few
Countries with most billionaires
2008 & 2011

◀ *24 Life Expectancy; 38 Income*

Distribution of wealth

Within a country
latest available data 2000–09
Gini index

- 50 – 68 *most unequal*
- 40 – 49
- 30 – 39
- 20 – 29 *most equal*

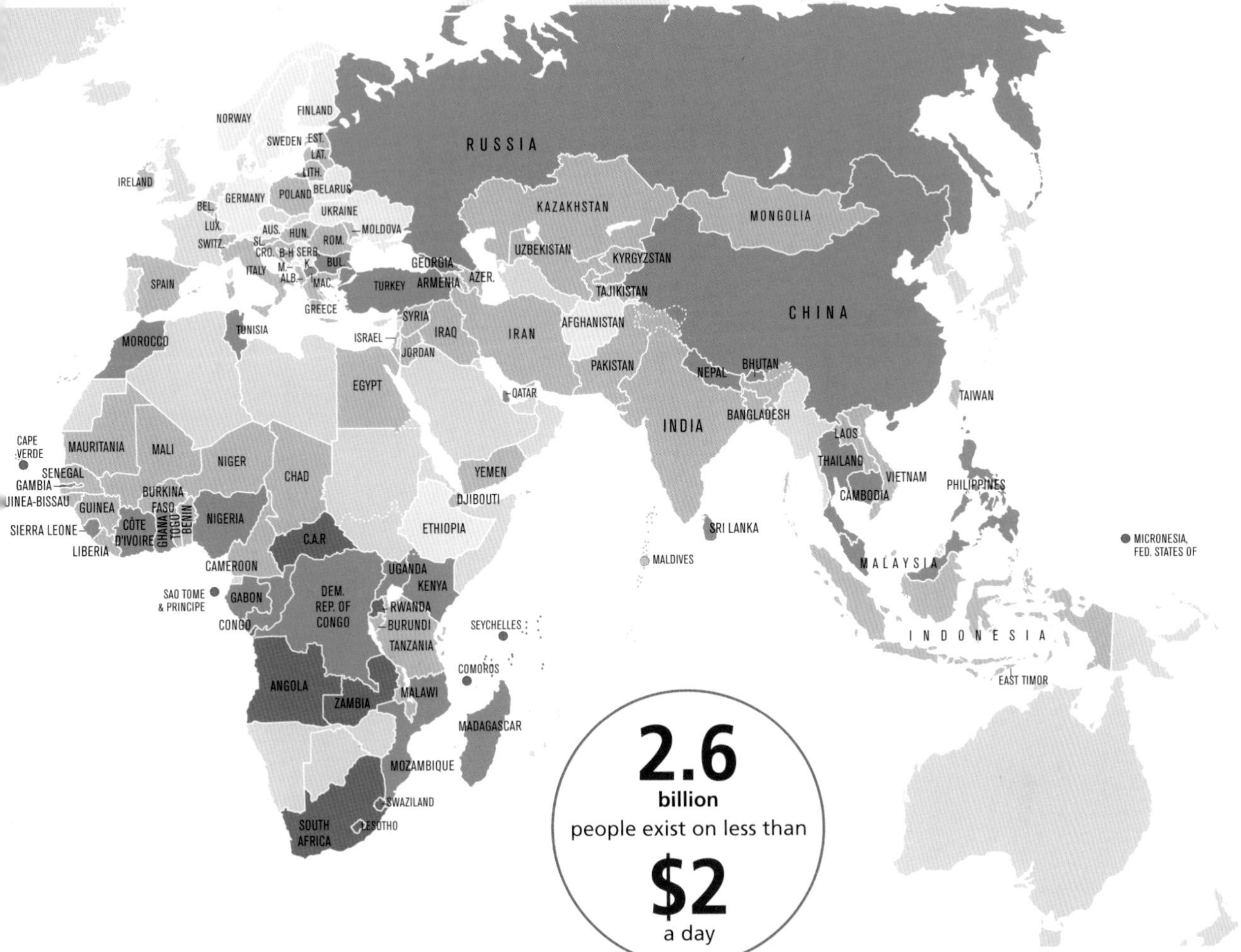

2.6
billion
people exist on less than
$2
a day

World poverty

Percentage of population living on less than $2 a day
latest available data 2000–09
PPP$

- more than 75%
- 51% – 75%
- 26% – 50%
- 25% or fewer
- no data

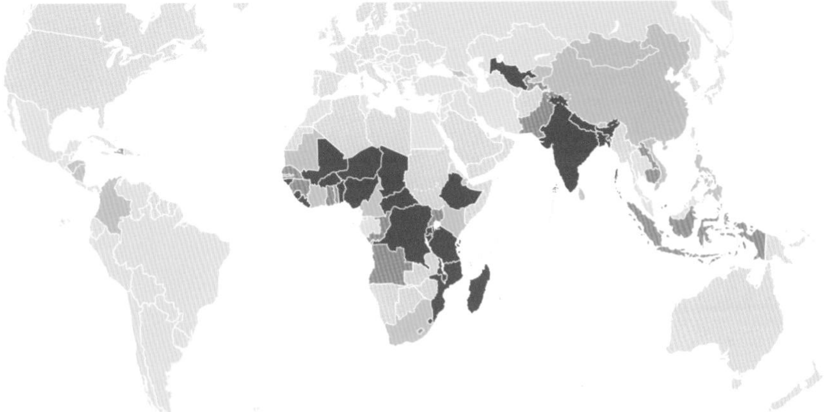

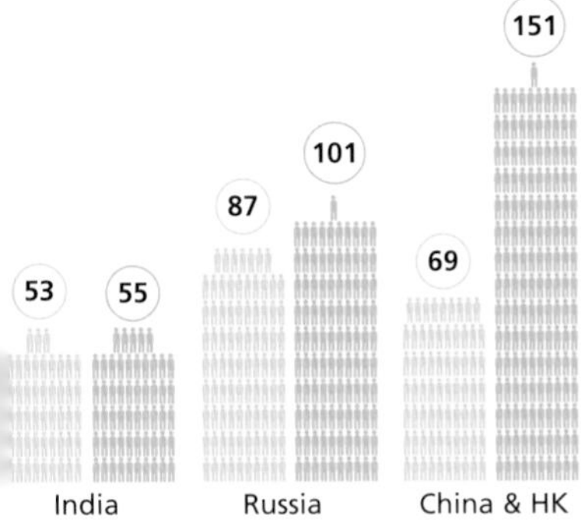

46 Banks; 54 Goals for Development; 100 Mental Health ►

Quality of Life

There is more to happiness than wealth alone – yet rich countries inevitably offer a higher quality of life.

The happiness league
Percentage of people who gave their current and future life high scores
2005–09

more than 50%
26% – 50%
25% or fewer
no data

How do I feel about my current life, and how do I envisage my life in five years' time?

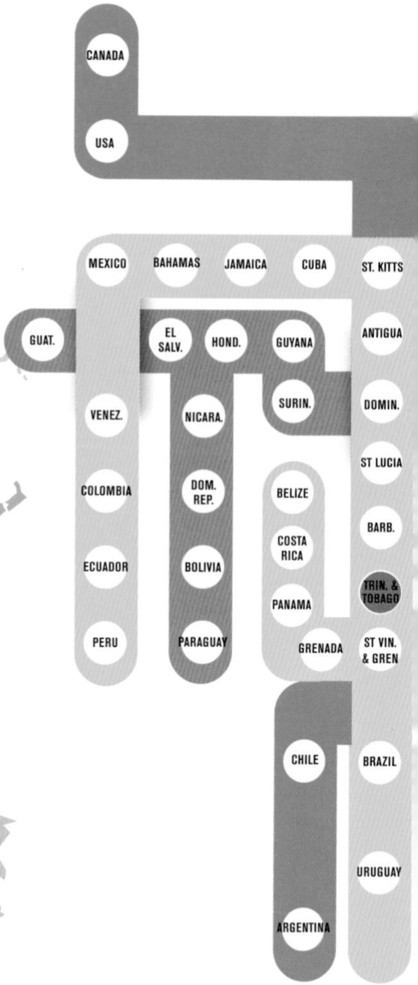

Daily experience of life
Average score out of 10 for evaluation of previous day
2005–09

7.5 – 8.4
6.5 – 7.4
5.0 – 6.4
no data

How do I rate my daily experience? Do I feel well-rested, respected, free of pain and intellectually engaged?

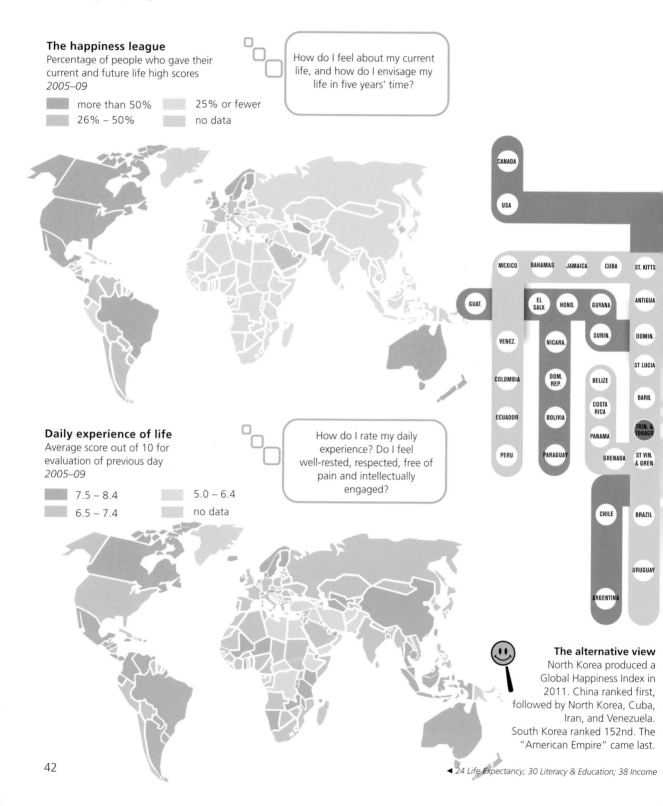

The alternative view
North Korea produced a Global Happiness Index in 2011. China ranked first, followed by North Korea, Cuba, Iran, and Venezuela. South Korea ranked 152nd. The "American Empire" came last.

◄ *24 Life Expectancy; 30 Literacy & Education; 38 Income*

Relative human development

Score on the Human Development Index (HDI)

2011

The Human Development Index (HDI) scores countries according to the life expectancy and educational level of their populations, and the national income per capita.

very high
high
medium
low

HDI ranking much lower than Gross National Income ranking. This suggests a country uses less than the average proportion of national wealth to improve quality of life

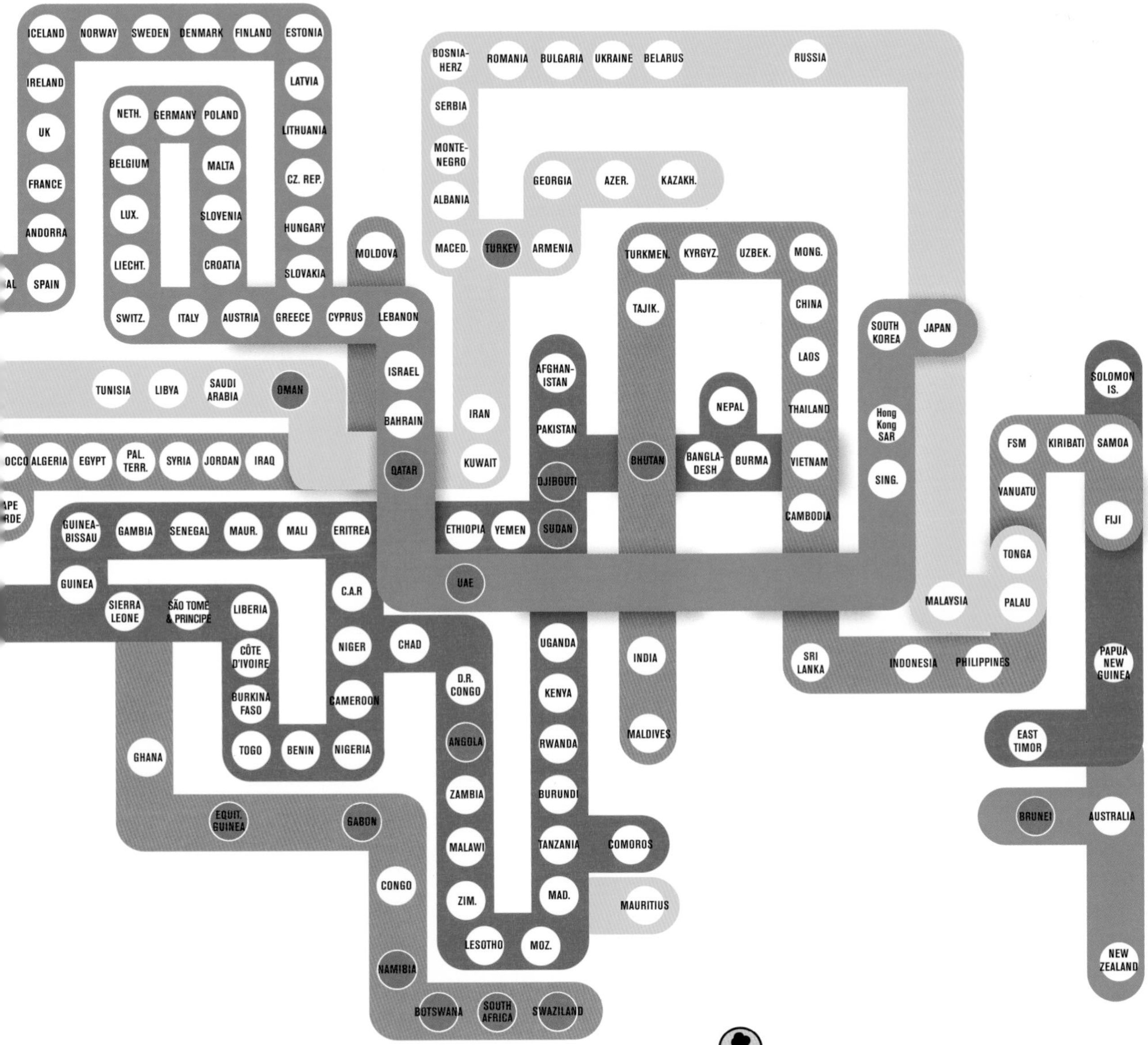

Quality carbon

Five of the 20 countries with the highest quality of life are also among the top ten carbon emitters, jointly responsible for about two-thirds of the world's CO_2 emissions.

72 Global Peacefulness; 102 Living with Disease; 110 Water Resources ▶

Transnationals

Transnational corporations represent enormous wealth and therefore power. Comparing countries' Gross National Income (GNI) with the revenue of some of the giants of the corporate world is salutary.

The largest corporation is Walmart. Only 27 countries have a GNI larger than its revenue, and some 50 countries have populations smaller than Walmart's global workforce. Operating in scores of countries, the biggest companies have interests that reach far beyond any single national loyalty.

Corporate wealth

Gross National Income (GNI) compared with the annual revenue of selected transnationals
2010 or latest available data

country's GNI larger than revenue of any transnational	
country's GNI smaller than: **Walmart** ($421.8 billion) but bigger than: Nestlé	Walmart employs 2.1 million people and sells to 100 million customers a week. Its 2010 sales revenue exceeded the combined GNI of the world's 62 smallest economies. 80% of its suppliers are in China. A legal case, started in 2000, sued Walmart for discrimination against 1.5 million current and former women employees. In 2011, the US Supreme Court dismissed the case on the grounds that the women could not pursue it as a single group.
country's GNI smaller than: **Nestlé** ($105.3 billion) but bigger than: Kraft Foods	Nestlé operates in 86 countries and has 30% of the global market for baby food. The way it sells substitutes for breast milk remains controversial. An international boycott started by consumer activists in 1977 is still active in over 100 countries.
country's GNI smaller than: **Kraft Foods** but bigger than: McDonald's	Kraft sells in 170 countries. 40 of its brands are more than a century old. It started in 1903. Its first-year losses amounted to $3,000 and one horse. In 1915 the company invented pasteurized processed cheese.
country's GNI smaller than: **McDonald's** ($24.1 billion)	McDonald's employs 1.7 million people and operates in 119 countries. It serves 68 million customers a day – more than the population of France or the UK.
no data	

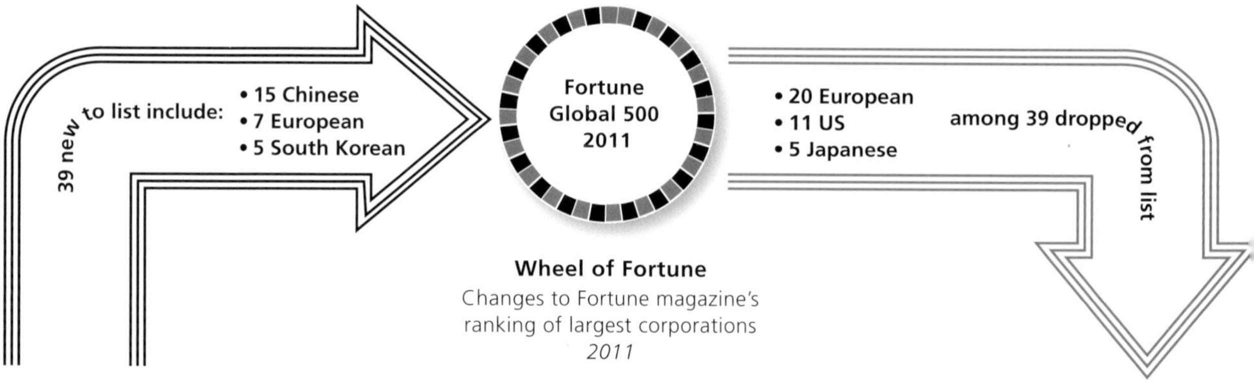

Wheel of Fortune
Changes to Fortune magazine's ranking of largest corporations
2011

◀ 38 Income

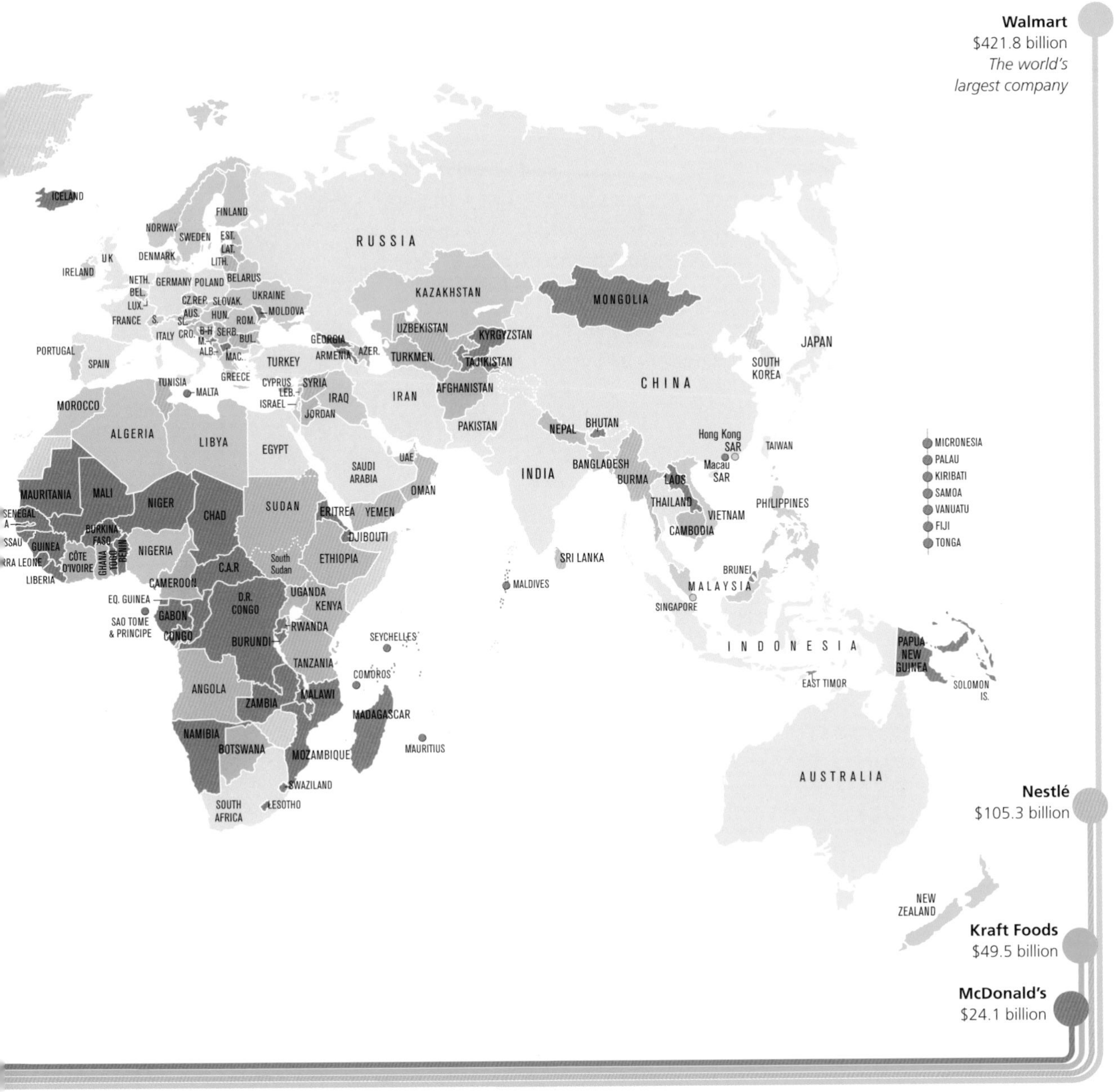

Profitability
The profits of these selected major companies are larger than the GNI of each of these countries
2010

Nestlé:
$32.84bn
≥ GNI of 82 countries

Paraguay • Trinidad & Tobago • Luxembourg • Cambodia • Honduras • Albania • Botswana • Estonia • Cyprus • Macau SAR • Senegal Macedonia • Georgia • Mozambique • Democratic Republic of Congo • Burkina Faso • Madagascar • Jamaica • Brunei • Gabon

Microsoft:
$18.76bn
≥ GNI of 62 countries

Mauritius • Zambia • Armenia • Equatorial Guinea • Papua New Guinea • Nicaragua • Mali • Laos Tajikistan • Namibia • Benin • Chad

Apple:
$14.01bn
≥ GNI of 50 countries

Congo • Malawi • Rwanda • Moldova • Haiti • Kyrgyzstan • Niger • Malta Guinea • Mongolia • Iceland • Bahamas • Montenegro • Mauritania • Swaziland Togo • Barbados • Sierra Leone • Lesotho • East Timor • Suriname • Fiji • Bhutan Central African Republic • Burundi • Eritrea • Guyana • Maldives • Gambia Djibouti • Belize • Cape Verde • Seychelles • St Lucia • Antigua & Barbuda Guinea-Bissau • Liberia • Solomon Is • St Vincent & The Grenadines • Vanuatu Grenada • St Kitts & Nevis • Dominica • Comoros • Samoa • Tonga • Micronesia Kiribati • São Tome & Principe • Palau

Banks

Bank failures lay behind the financial crash of 2008 that has fed the recessions and depression since then. There were failures in two senses: in the technical sense that some banks did not have enough assets to meet their liabilities; and in the ordinary sense that they and the people who ran them, as well as those who regulated them, failed. They didn't do their jobs properly. The top bankers, however, with only a few exceptions, have weathered the storm and continue to receive vast salaries and bonuses.

The consequences of that dual failure are so far-reaching because the banks are so big and because money and credit are fundamental to the functioning of a modern economy. When the credit system goes bust, it threatens to take the money system down with it. The peak (so far) of the fear this creates has been found in the Eurozone – 17 disparate members of the European Union who chose to enter a monetary union. Because of this fear, the current history of the Eurozone is a series of crisis meetings – another summit, another national bail-out.

From excessive levels of compensation, to shoddy treatment of customers, to a deceitful manipulation of one of the most important interest rates and now news of yet another mis-selling scandal we can see we need a real change in the culture of the industry.

Mervyn King, June 2012
Governor of the Bank of England

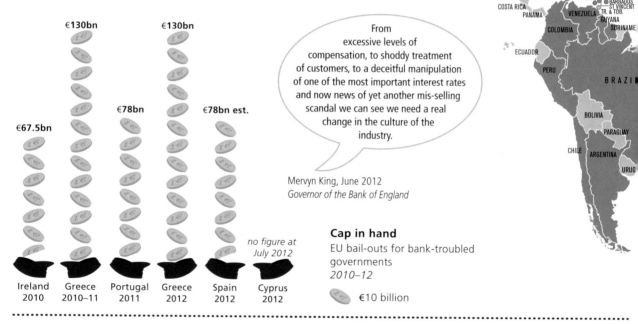

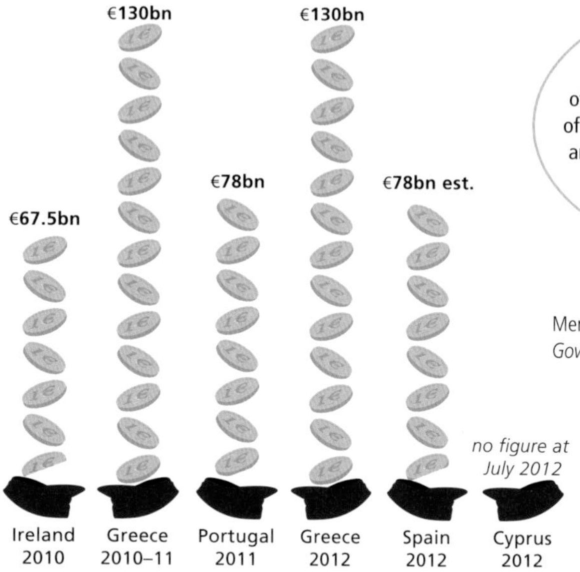

Cap in hand
EU bail-outs for bank-troubled governments
2010–12

€10 billion

Peaks and troughs of the banking crisis

2008 **Iceland**: Following the collapse of all three major commercial banks, Iceland effectively went bankrupt. The prime minister of the time has been convicted for negligence.

2008 **UK:** Economic bail-out commitment peaked at **£4.5 trillion** in loans, spending & guarantees.

2009 **USA:** Commitment to economic rescue peaked at **$12.8 trillion** in loans, spending & guarantees.

2011 **Bank boss bonuses:** Banks' average share price and revenues dropped in all financial centres AND top banks awarded their chiefs **$12.8m** on average – **11.9% more** than in 2010.

2012 **Spain:** As the banking crisis accelerated to bail-out, Spanish escorts **banned sex** with bankers until they started lending to small business and families.

2008 2009 2011 2012

◄ *40 Inequality*

Bank wealth
Gross National Income (GNI) compared with Bank of America annual revenue of $134 billion
2010 or latest available
GNI greater
GNI smaller
combined GNI of 41 smallest countries is less than the revenue of the Bank of America
no data
ICELAND
NORWAY
FINLAND
SWEDEN
EST.
LAT.
LITH.
DENMARK
IRELAND
UK
NETH.
GERMANY
POLAND
BELARUS
BEL.
LUX.
CZ. REP.
SL.
UKRAINE
FRANCE
SW.
AUS.
HUN.
ROM.
MOLD.
SL.
CRO.
B-H
S.
M.
K.
BUL.
ALB.
MAC.
PORTUGAL
SPAIN
ITALY
GREECE
TURKEY
GEORGIA
ARMENIA
AZER.
RUSSIA
KAZAKHSTAN
MONGOLIA
UZBEKISTAN
KYRGYZSTAN
TURKMEN.
TAJIKISTAN
JAPAN
SOUTH KOREA
TUNISIA
MALTA
CYPRUS
SYRIA
LEB.
IRAQ
IRAN
AFGHANISTAN
CHINA
MOROCCO
ISRAEL
JORDAN
ALGERIA
LIBYA
EGYPT
PAKISTAN
NEPAL
BHUTAN
Hong Kong SAR
TAIWAN
SAUDI ARABIA
UAE
INDIA
BANGLADESH
BURMA
Macau SAR
LAOS
OMAN
MAURITANIA
MALI
NIGER
SUDAN
CHAD
THAILAND
PHILIPPINES
SENEGAL
ERITREA
YEMEN
VIETNAM
BURKINA FASO
DJIBOUTI
CAMBODIA
GUINEA
NIGERIA
SIERRA LEONE
CÔTE D'IVOIRE
GHANA
TOGO
BENIN
C.A.R.
South Sudan
ETHIOPIA
SRI LANKA
LIBERIA
CAMEROON
MALDIVES
BRUNEI
EQ. GUINEA
UGANDA
MALAYSIA
SINGAPORE
D.R. CONGO
KENYA
SÃO TOME & PRINCIPE
GABON
RWANDA
CONGO
BURUNDI
SEYCHELLES
TANZANIA
INDONESIA
PAPUA NEW GUINEA
COMOROS
ANGOLA
MALAWI
ZAMBIA
EAST TIMOR
MADAGASCAR
MAURITIUS
NAMIBIA
BOTSWANA
MOZAMBIQUE
SWAZILAND
LESOTHO
SOUTH AFRICA
AUSTRALIA
NEW ZEALAND
MICRONESIA, FED. ST. OF
PALAU
KIRIBATI
SAMOA
VANUATU
FIJI
TONGA
Weighed in the balance...
2010
$134bn
Bank of America revenue
$128bn
Combined GNI of 41 smallest countries
World annual output 2010
$76 trillion
Assets of world's top 50 banks:
$62 trillion
Comparative wealth
2010
country GNI
assets of top banks
$14.6tn
$8.5tn
USA
$10.2tn
$8.2tn
China
$3.1tn
$4.6tn
Germany
$2.3tn
$8.2tn
France
$2.2tn
$9.1tn
UK
$1.5tn
$2.7tn
Spain

50 Debt ▶

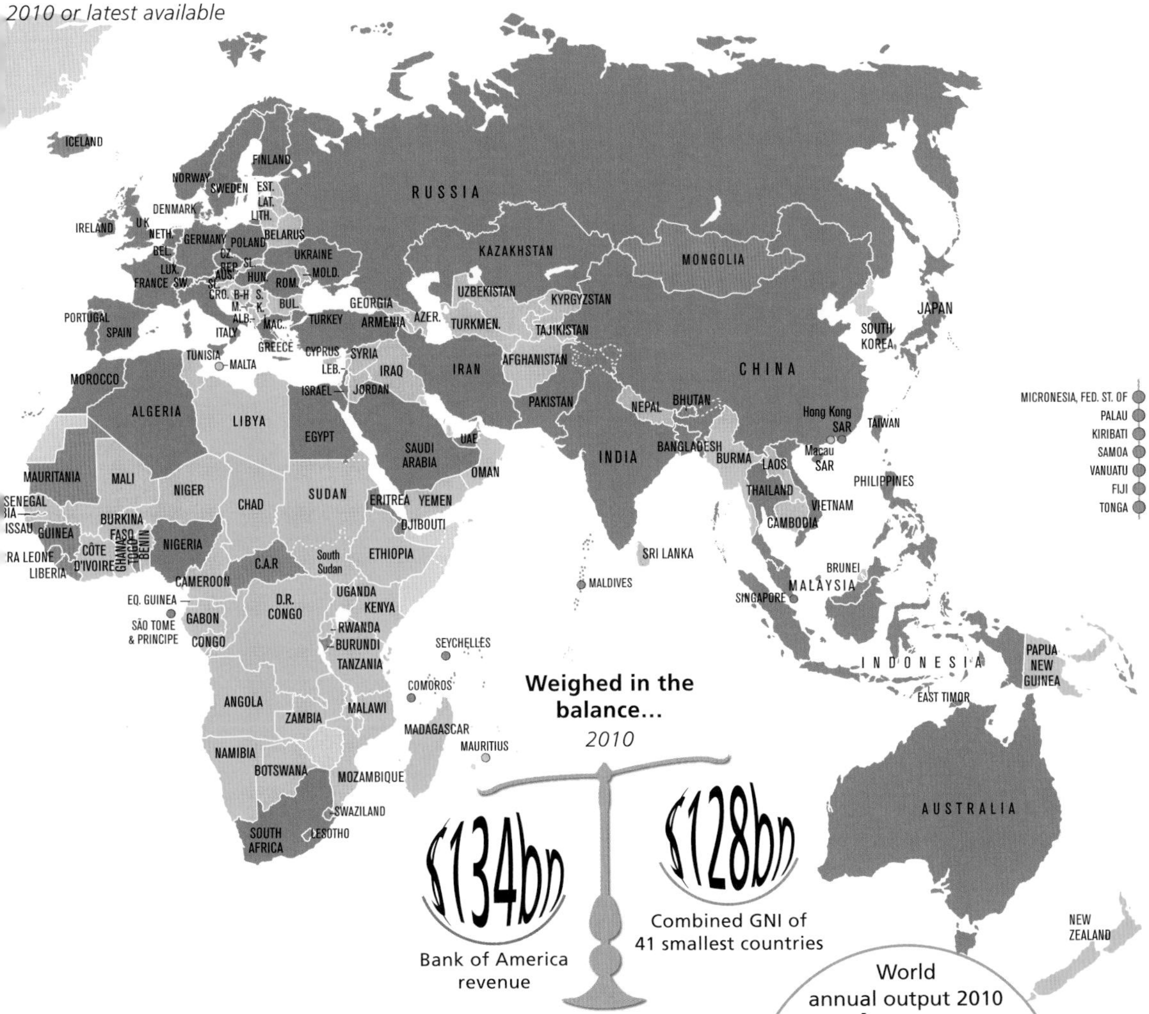

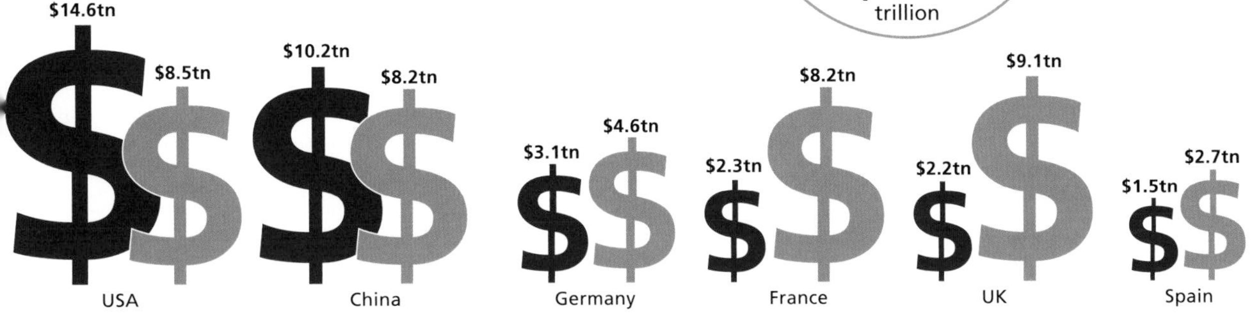

Corruption

Corruption is everywhere – officials taking bribes, companies and individuals evading taxes. It weakens governments and weakens public trust in them. Transparency International provides an index of corruption that is highly regarded, if often controversial, based on the perceptions of the citizens of the countries concerned.

The strength of the shadow economy is one indicator of a corrupt society. Although it may involve activities that are themselves legal, the failure to report the financial gains from those activities to the country's tax authorities – tax *evasion* – is illegal. It steals about 25 per cent of potential global tax revenue. Tax *avoidance*, on the other hand, is legal. It exploits loopholes in the law, differences between national laws, and the existence of tax havens. It probably costs as much if not more.

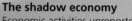

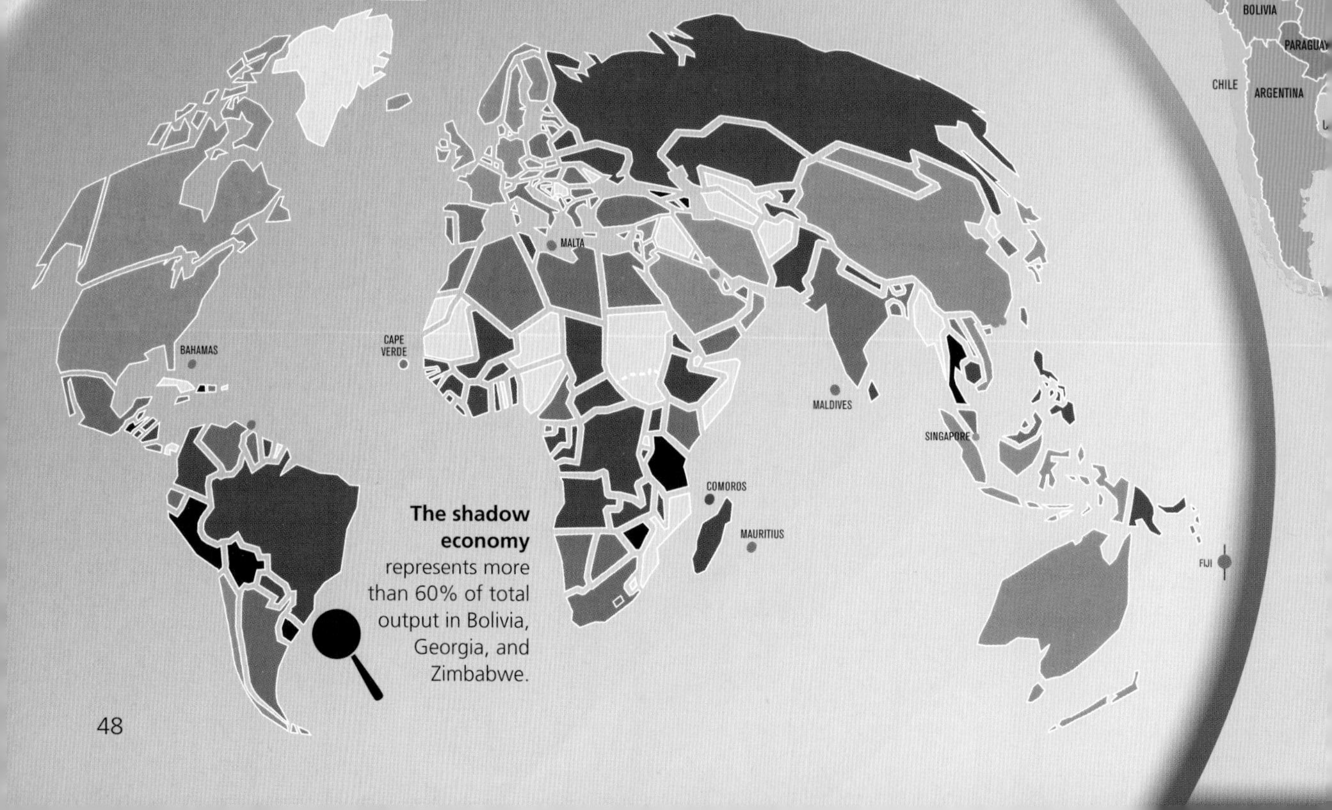

The shadow economy represents more than 60% of total output in Bolivia, Georgia, and Zimbabwe.

Level of corruption
Score according to Corruption Perceptions Index 2010
1.0 – 2.5 highly corrupt
2.6 – 5.0 significantly corrupt
5.1 – 7.5 reasonably clean
7.6 – 10.0 very clean
no data
ICELAND
FINLAND
NORWAY
SWEDEN
ESTONIA
LATVIA
RUSSIA
DENMARK
LITHUANIA
IRELAND
UK
NETH.
BELARUS
GERMANY
POLAND
BEL.
CHANNEL IS
LUX.
CZ. REP.
SL.
UKRAINE
KAZAKHSTAN
MONGOLIA
FRANCE
SWITZ.
AUS.
HUN.
MOLDOVA
ROM.
SL.
CRO.
B-H
SERB.
BUL.
UZBEKISTAN
KYRGYZSTAN
NORTH KOREA
JAPAN
PORTUGAL
SPAIN
ALB.
MAC.
GEORGIA
ARMENIA
AZER.
TURKMEN.
TAJIKISTAN
ITALY
TURKEY
SOUTH KOREA
GREECE
TUNISIA
MALTA
CYPRUS
LEB.
SYRIA
IRAQ
IRAN
AFGHANISTAN
CHINA
MOROCCO
ISRAEL
JORDAN
KUWAIT
PAKISTAN
NEPAL
BHUTAN
ALGERIA
LIBYA
BAHRAIN
QATAR
UAE
Hong Kong SAR
TAIWAN
EGYPT
SAUDI ARABIA
INDIA
BANGLADESH
Macau SAR
OMAN
BURMA
LAOS
MAURITANIA
MALI
NIGER
SUDAN
PHILIPPINES
CHAD
ERITREA
YEMEN
THAILAND
VIETNAM
SENEGAL
BURKINA FASO
DJIBOUTI
CAMBODIA
GUINEA
KIRIBATI
NIGERIA
SOLOMON IS.
SIERRA LEONE
CÔTE D'IVOIRE
GHANA
TOGO
BENIN
South Sudan
ETHIOPIA
SRI LANKA
SAMOA
LIBERIA
C.A.R
BRUNEI
VANUATU
CAMEROON
MALDIVES
MALAYSIA
EQUATORIAL GUINEA
UGANDA
SOMALIA
SINGAPORE
TONGA
KENYA
SÃO TOME & PRINCIPE
GABON
DEM. REP. OF CONGO
RWANDA
CONGO
BURUNDI
SEYCHELLES
TANZANIA
INDONESIA
PAPUA NEW GUINEA
COMOROS
EAST TIMOR
ANGOLA
MALAWI
ZAMBIA
MADAGASCAR
ZIMBABWE
MAURITIUS
NAMIBIA
BOTSWANA
MOZAMBIQUE
AUSTRALIA
SWAZILAND
SOUTH AFRICA
LESOTHO
NEW ZEALAND
Estimate of assets held legally in tax havens:
$21 trillion
Estimate of revenue lost to illegal tax evasion:
$3 trillion
5.9 billion people live in countries considered significantly corrupt
Copyright © Myriad Editions Limited

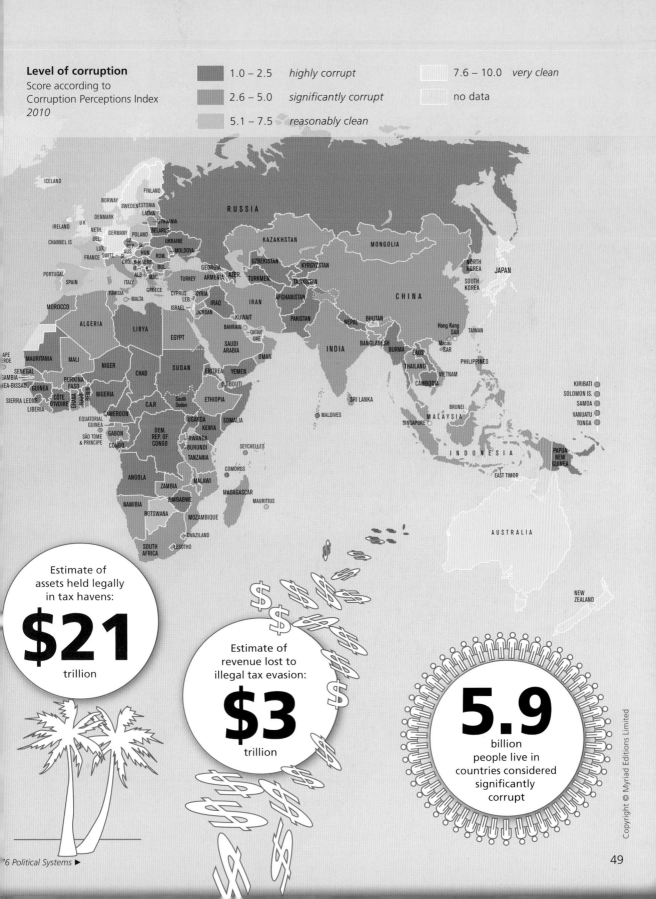

Debt

The credit crunch of 2007 to 2008 that turned into the economic crash of 2008 to 2009 that became the fiscal catastrophe of 2010 and beyond has been fuelled by the unsustainable and unrepayable debt of governments, private companies, and individuals. But not everywhere and everyone is equally indebted. American borrowing had largely been thanks to China's willingness to lend, leading to a major imbalance between the mountain of savings in China and the pits of debt in the USA.

In Europe, governments responded to the magnitude of debt with austerity policies. Banks, having lent too much, cut back sharply on loans. The combined result of the original ills and this remedy was economic slowdown and unemployment, financial crises and new bail-outs every few months, and growing political uncertainty.

In the USA, the treatment applied to the economic problem was less harsh, but recovery was slow, and confidence about the future was low.

Current account balance
2010 or latest available data
US$

Deficit of:

- $470 billion
- $11 billion – $68 billion
- $1 billion – $10 billion
- $999 million deficit – $999 million surplus

Surplus of:

- $1 billion – $100 billion
- $166 billion – $305 billion
- no data

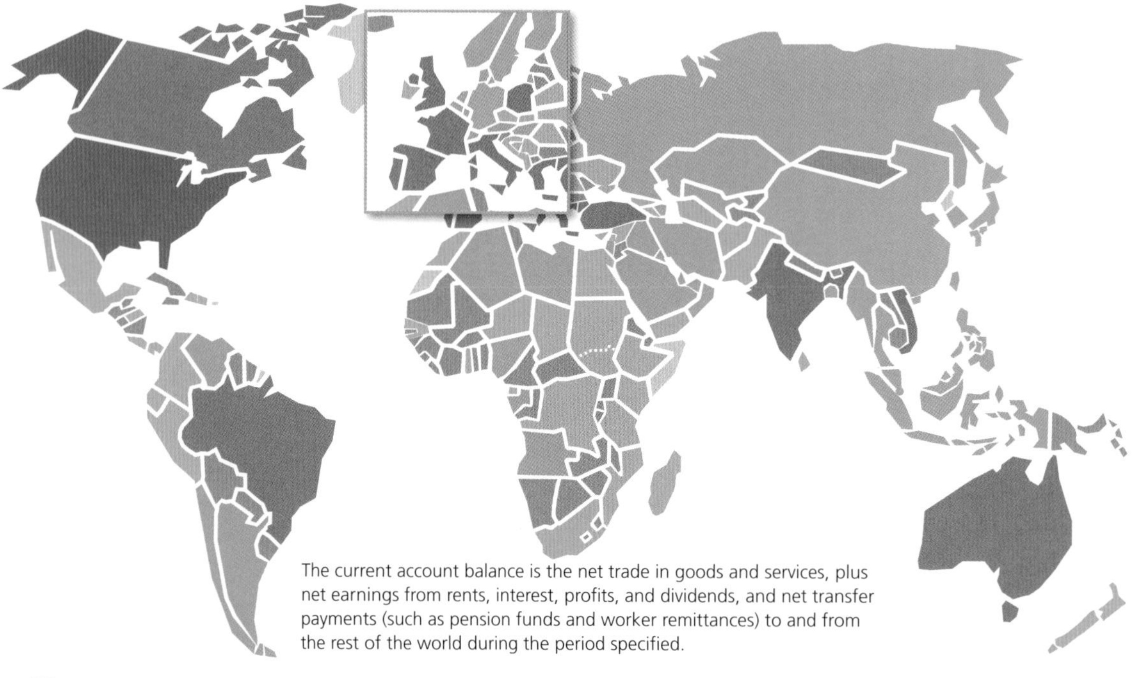

The current account balance is the net trade in goods and services, plus net earnings from rents, interest, profits, and dividends, and net transfer payments (such as pension funds and worker remittances) to and from the rest of the world during the period specified.

◀ 38 Income; 46 Bank

Government gross debt
As a percentage of GDP
2010
200% – 220%
101% – 145%
61% – 100%
41% – 60%
11% – 40%
10% or less
no data
Gross government debt is everything the government owes to any creditor at home or abroad.
NORWAY
SWEDEN
FINLAND
ESTONIA
RUSSIA
LATVIA
LITHUANIA
RUS.
DENMARK
UK
NETH.
GERMANY
POLAND
BELARUS
BELGIUM
CZECH REP.
UKRAINE
LUX.
SLOVAKIA
MOLDOVA
FRANCE
SWITZ.
AUSTRIA
HUNGARY
SLOV.
ROMANIA
CROATIA
B-H
SERBIA
BULGARIA
MONT.
KOSOVO
ALBANIA
MACEDONIA
ITALY
GREECE
RUSSIA
KAZAKHSTAN
GEORGIA
UZBEKISTAN
KYRGYZSTAN
ARMENIA
AZER.
TURKMEN.
TURKEY
TAJIKISTAN
JAPAN
SOUTH KOREA
CHINA
TUNISIA
MALTA
CYPRUS
SYRIA
LEB.
IRAQ
IRAN
ISRAEL
JORDAN
MOROCCO
KUWAIT
PAKISTAN
LIBYA
EGYPT
BAHRAIN
QATAR
UAE
NEPAL
Hong Kong SAR
TAIWAN
SAUDI ARABIA
INDIA
MAURITANIA
MALI
OMAN
BURMA
LAOS
NIGER
PHILIPPINES
SENEGAL
CHAD
SUDAN
ERITREA
YEMEN
THAILAND
VIETNAM
GUINEA
BURKINA FASO
DJIBOUTI
CAMBODIA
SIERRA LEONE
CÔTE D'IVOIRE
GHANA
TOGO
BENIN
NIGERIA
LIBERIA
C.A.R
South Sudan
ETHIOPIA
BRUNEI
MALDIVES
MALAYSIA
EQUATORIAL GUINEA
CAMEROON
SINGAPORE
UGANDA
SÃO TOME & PRINCIPE
GABON
DEM. REP. OF CONGO
KENYA
RWANDA
CONGO
BURUNDI
SEYCHELLES
INDONESIA
TANZANIA
COMOROS
ANGOLA
MALAWI
ZAMBIA
MADAGASCAR
FIJI
NAMIBIA
ZIMBABWE
MAURITIUS
BOTSWANA
MOZAMBIQUE
AUSTRALIA
SWAZILAND
SOUTH AFRICA
LESOTHO
NEW ZEALAND
Global debt grew by
140%
2000–11
Net debt
2010
3 billion people
live in countries owed over $1 billion more than they owe
400 million people
live in countries that are roughly in balance
3.5 billion people
live in countries owing over $1 billion more than they are owed

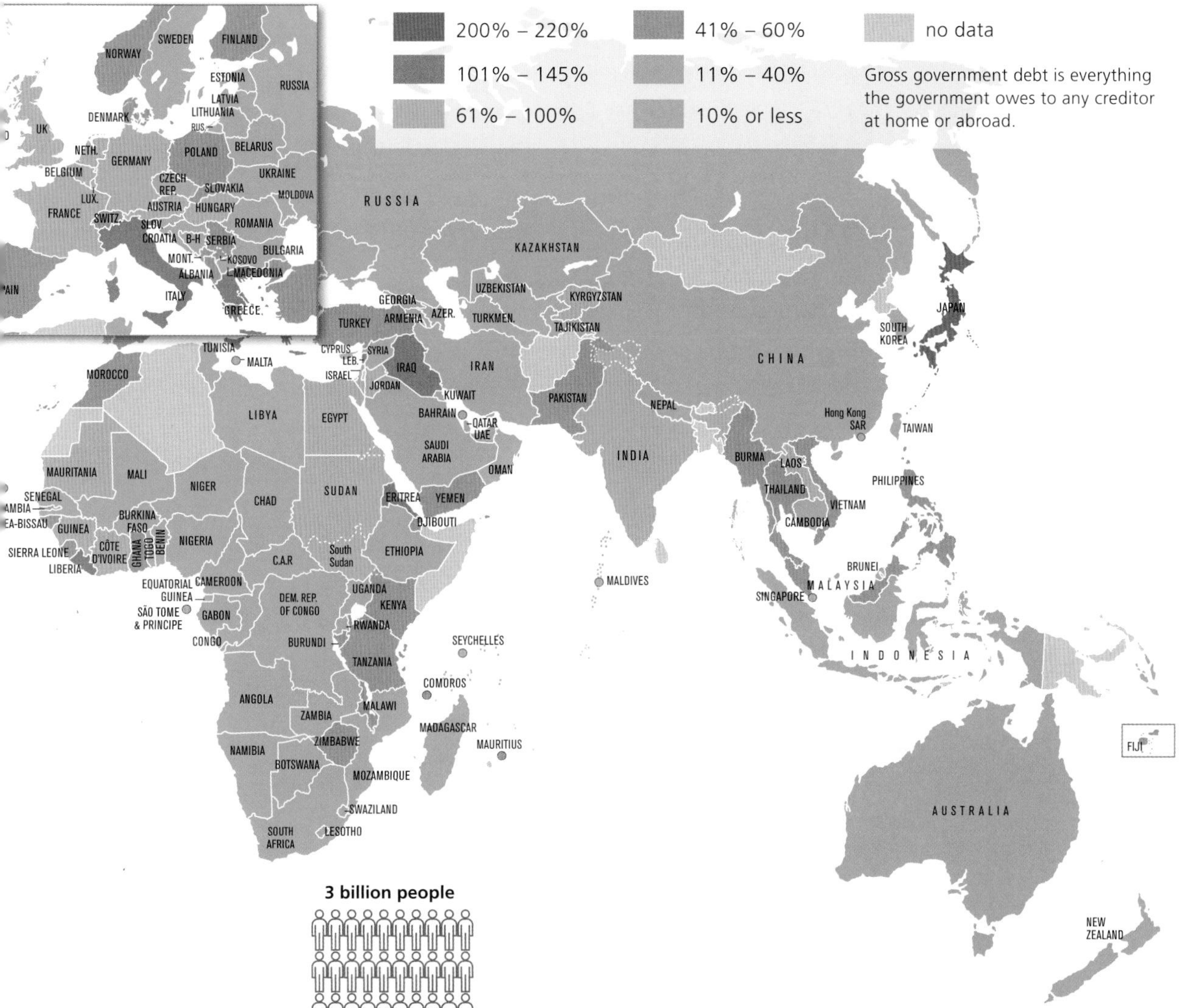

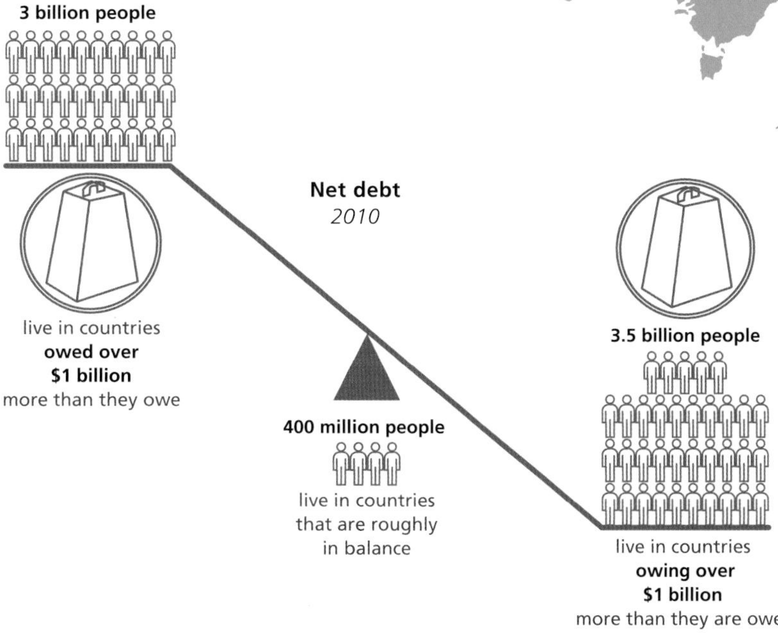

Tourism

2000:
723
million
tourist trips

Tourism is a sorely needed source of income for many countries. In the Middle East and North Africa, a third of export income is earned through tourism. And for many Caribbean and Pacific islands, the tourist dollar represents more than 40 per cent of the country's income. Tourism often threatens the natural and architectural beauty that attracts the visitors. It is a potent form of cultural invasion, and in extreme circumstances armed groups have declared tourists to be legitimate targets for attack.

Economic significance of tourism
2010 or latest available data

Countries where earnings from overseas visitors as percentage of export earnings is:

more than 40%

21% – 40%

BAHAMAS
DOMINICAN REPLUBIC
JAMAICA
ANTIGUA & BARBUDA
BELIZE HAITI
DOMINICA
ST KITTS & NEVIS
ST LUCIA
GRENADA
BARBADOS
ARUBA
ST VINCENT & GRENADINES

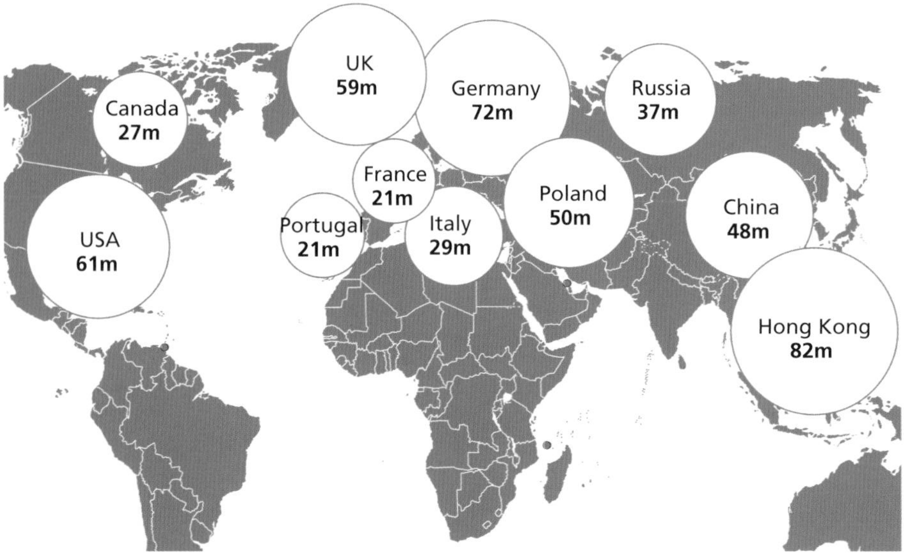

Departures
Countries generating highest number of overseas trips
2010 or latest available data

◄ 34 Diversity of Cities

2010:
940
million
tourist trips

2030
projected:
1,800
million
tourist trips

CROATIA
ALBANIA
ARMENIA
GREECE
SYRIA
MOROCCO
LEBANON
JORDAN
PALESTINIAN TERRITORIES
CAPE VERDE
EGYPT
GUINEA-BISSAU
LIBERIA
SÃO TOME & PRINCIPE
ETHIOPIA
UGANDA
RWANDA
TANZANIA
SEYCHELLES
MADAGASCAR
MAURITIUS
NEPAL
Macau SAR
CAMBODIA
MALDIVES
SOLOMON ISLANDS
SAMOA
VANUATU
FIJI
TONGA
FRENCH POLYNESIA

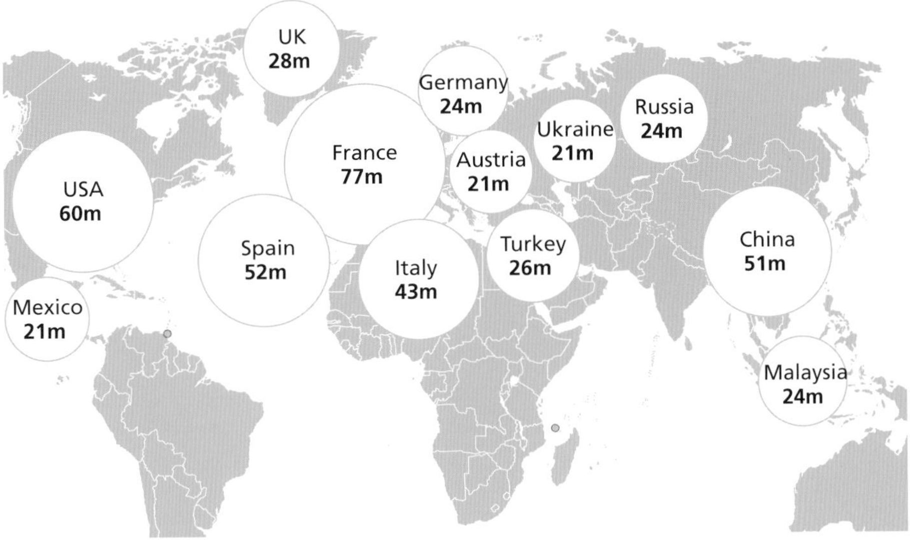

Arrivals
Countries attracting highest number of overseas trips
2010 or latest available data

20 million

Goals for Development

In 2000, the UN summit agreed the Millennium Declaration – aspirations for the new century. The following year the narrower, measurable Millennium Development Goals (MDGs) set out what the grand ambitions meant in practice, with 2015 as a target date for achieving them.

The MDGs have encouraged increased aid for development (though its continued growth is put in doubt by the tough economic environment), and have helped focus international effort onto important goals in health and education. But the record is mixed, partly because the MDGs are not equally applicable in all countries with widely differing circumstances. Conflict-affected countries have needs the MDGs do not address. And success in reducing global poverty is not due to the MDGs but to China's spectacular economic growth.

Millennium Development Goals
Progress achieved 2001–11 compared to targets whose benchmark is 1990

- target already met or expected to be met by 2015
- progress insufficient to reach target if prevailing trends persist
- no progress, or deterioration
- missing or insufficient data

Goal 1 Eradicate extreme poverty and hunger
Selected target: Reduce $1 a day poverty by half

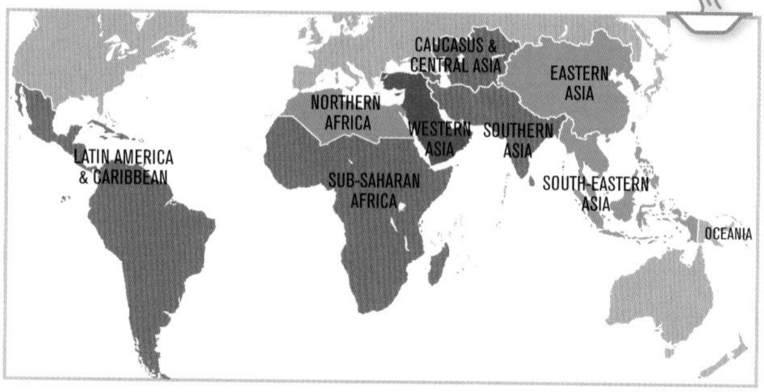

World poverty is falling mainly due to Chinese economic growth. In a troubled global economy, progress in Africa, South Asia, and Latin America is behind. ◄ 40 *Inequality;* ► 92 *Malnutrition*

Goal 2 Achieve universal primary education
Target: Universal primary schooling

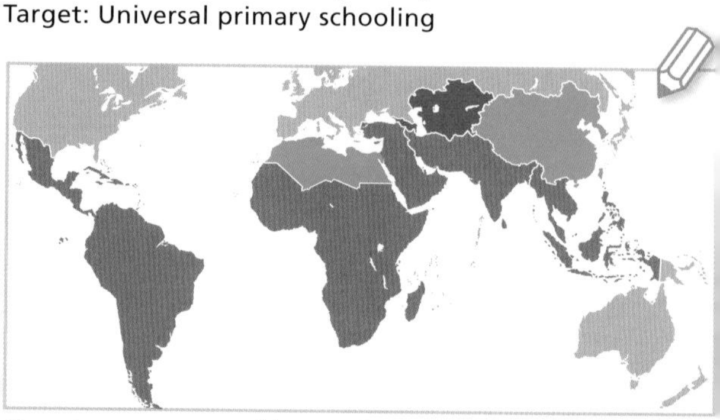

There is progress overall but much too slow to meet the target. There have been dramatic increases in Africa but the situation is static elsewhere. ◄ 30 *Literacy & Education*

Overseas aid
Total aid disbursed *1990–2009* and breakdown by donor *2009*

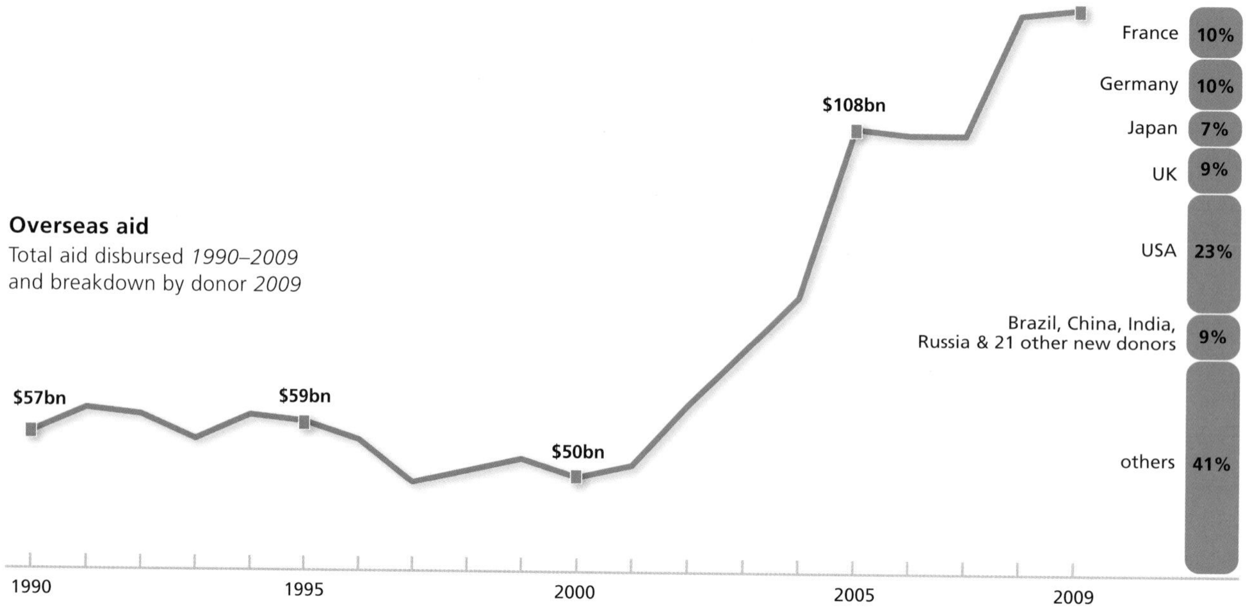

◄ *30 Literacy & Education; 40 Inequality*

Goal 3 Promote gender equality and empower women
Selected target: Increase women's paid employment

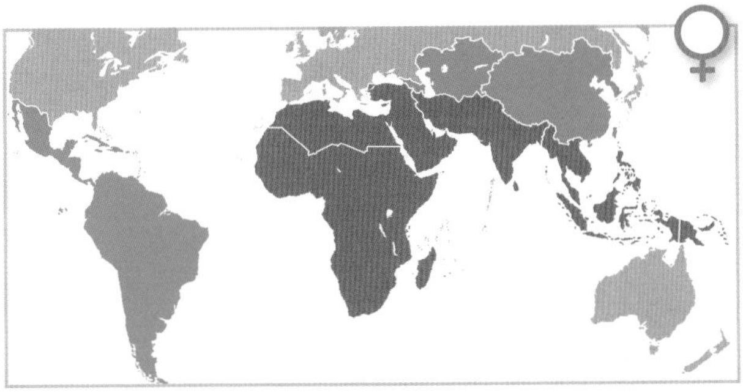

There have been significant gains in girls' education (and this target will be met on time) and slow improvements in women's economic and political participation. ▶ 84 *Women's Rights*

Goal 4 Reduce child mortality
Target: Reduce mortality of under-five-year-olds by 66%

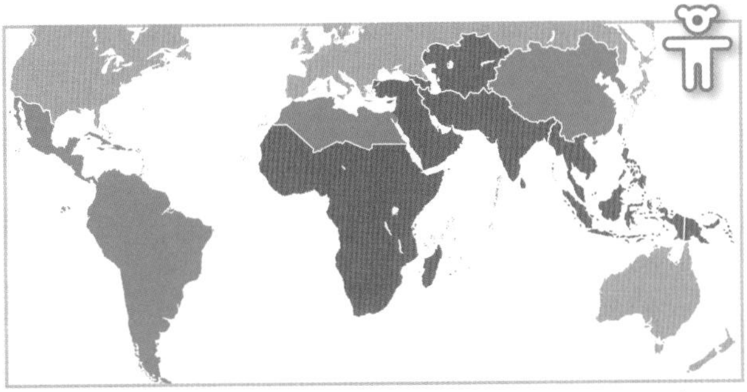

There has been progress everywhere, and global child mortality has fallen by one third; children in rural areas face much higher risk than urban children.

Goal 5 Improve maternal health
Selected target: Reduce maternal mortality by 75%

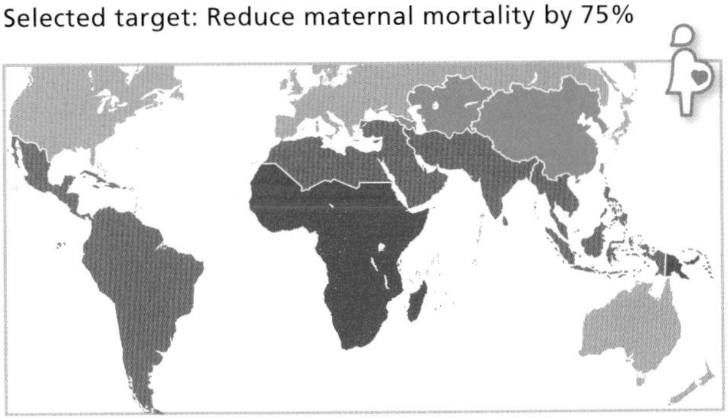

Based on very vague data, maternal mortality seems to be reducing (34% down by 2008) except in Africa, but even as a global average the goal looks unachievable.

Goal 6 Combat HIV/AIDS, malaria, and other diseases
Target: Halt and reverse spread of tuberculosis

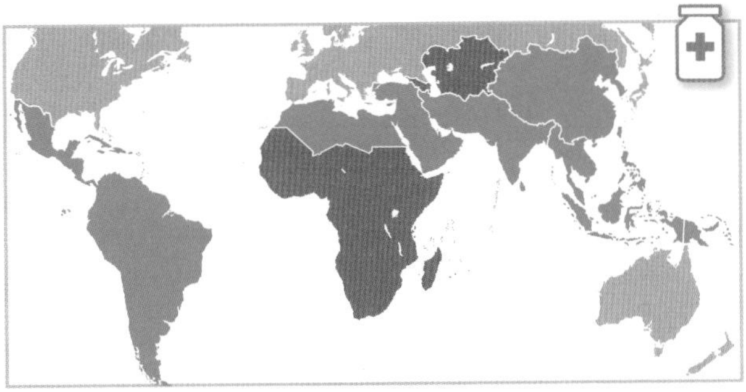

New HIV infections are declining – especially in Africa. Malaria deaths are 20% down. The incidence of tuberculosis is falling in Africa, and treatment is increasingly available. ▶ 98 *HIV/AIDS*

Goal 7 Ensure environmental sustainability
Selected target: Reduce forest loss

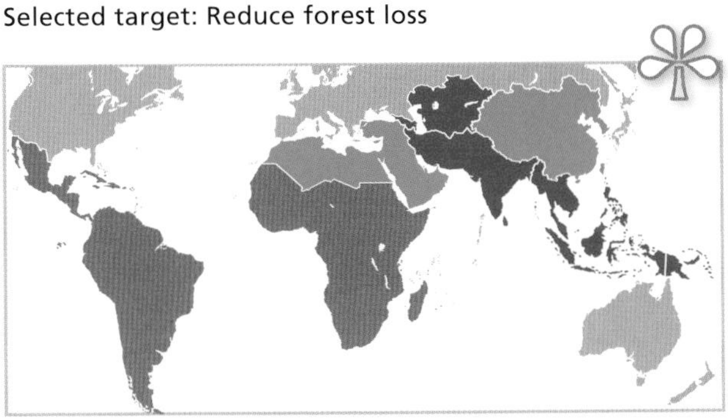

Despite progress, the world faces an environmental crisis. It has gone beyond safe margins on some key issues, and there is little sign of world agreement on a new course. ▶ 110 *Water Resources*; 114 *Waste*

Goal 8 Develop a global partnership for development
Selected target: Make internet widely accessible

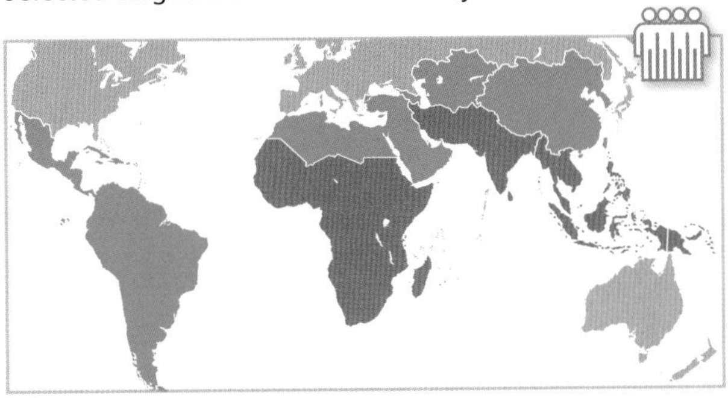

There has been increased aid, reduced debt burdens, and more transfer of technology – but terms of trade remain unfavourable to poorer countries.

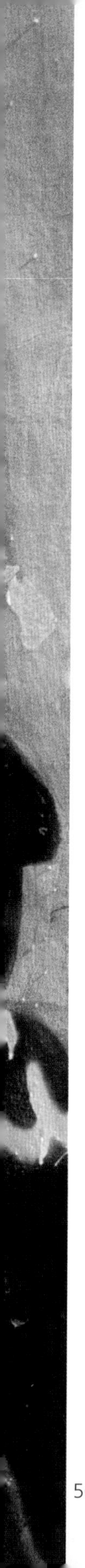

PART THREE

WAR & PEACE

Peace is one of the great but quiet good news stories of our time though it is a long way from being a smooth or perfect picture. Using consistent definitions, there were 50 armed conflicts in 1990 and 30 in 2010; a brief upsurge of wars in the early 1990s was followed by a sustained downward trend in the number of armed conflicts each year. It was fairly consistent until about 2006 but now seems to have bottomed out.

Though there is no certain information about war deaths, it does also seem true that while war remains one of the major causes of death worldwide, there is not only less war, but it is also less lethal than before. Nonetheless, the human costs remain extremely high, as 30 million refugees may attest, with long-term economic damage and, as one of the major after-effects of armed conflict, an increased risk that it will happen again.

The decline in armed conflict worldwide reflects a general pattern of being less inclined to inflict cruelty on fellow human beings, and less inclined to accept it when it happens. A much smaller proportion of people die violent deaths than a few hundred years ago. The decline in the number of wars has not just happened as part of a long historical trend, however; it is the result of an enormous effort. One study records a total of 646 peace agreements signed between 1990 and the end of 2007, considerably more in less than two decades than had been arrived at in the previous two centuries.

The benefits of the peace-making enterprise since 1990 are clear, but what is less obvious is whether it has addressed the underlying causes of armed conflict, or succeeded only in addressing symptoms without going further.

The situation in a country can be described as peaceful when people are able to have their conflicts without violence. Conflict is not only an apparently inevitable part of life, it is also often necessary, productive, and progressive. Many improvements in the conditions of ordinary people and almost all increases in political rights and freedoms were gained only by conflict. But if change is available only through violence, it is all too often tainted by the very acts that win it. The problem, in short, is not conflict – it is violent conflict.

Being able to have conflicts without threat of violence is what many of our most important institutions are for – courts, parliaments and assemblies, laws and government. When these are backed by other institutions that make it possible for people to be consulted about decisions that directly affect their lives, the whole builds into an implicit contract of accountable authority.

To achieve this, ordinary people need to be able to participate in shaping the way we are governed – primarily through elections to representative bodies. We need enough income and assets for a dignified life, and we need freedom from fear of physical or psychological threat. We need a fair and efficient justice system based on equality before the law and we need the agents of security such as the police to work with and for the people rather than to prey on us. And finally we need our well-being to be upheld and advanced through access both to services such as clean water, education, and health care, and to common goods, such as a sense of community. Lying behind these factors of a peaceful society are values of inclusivity and fairness. This is a view of society in which the greatest good is served by a balance between the collective good and the individual's well-being, and thus between the rights and responsibilities of individuals. Peace agreements offer an opportunity for countries afflicted by violent conflict to find a way towards this process of self-sustaining peace.

This is the direction of travel in some parts of the world. But there are also reasons for concern. Though the number of armed conflicts has declined, 1.5 billion people live in countries experiencing political and social instability and large-scale criminal violence. In these countries, not a single Millennium Development Goal has been achieved, and probably none will be by 2015, the MDG target date. The intersection of crime, politics, and business leads to intractable violent conflicts for which current international institutions are not really suited, neither in mandate, skills, nor mind-set. It is rarely possible for the International Red Cross to find humanitarian space between a state and a criminal. The UN's high representatives and other potential mediators have no mandate there either. Yet the scale of death and destruction inflicted in such cases may be as bad as in any armed conflict.

Furthermore, the decline in the number of armed political conflicts should not lead anyone to think something irreversible has happened. Potentially competing and clashing demands for natural resources could lead, especially against a background of social instability, to a resurgence in the number of civil wars. If that happens while the economic depression retains its grip, it is an open question whether the international organizations and governments that have hitherto been willing to fund peace-making, peacekeeping, and peacebuilding, will still have the energy and resources to continue.

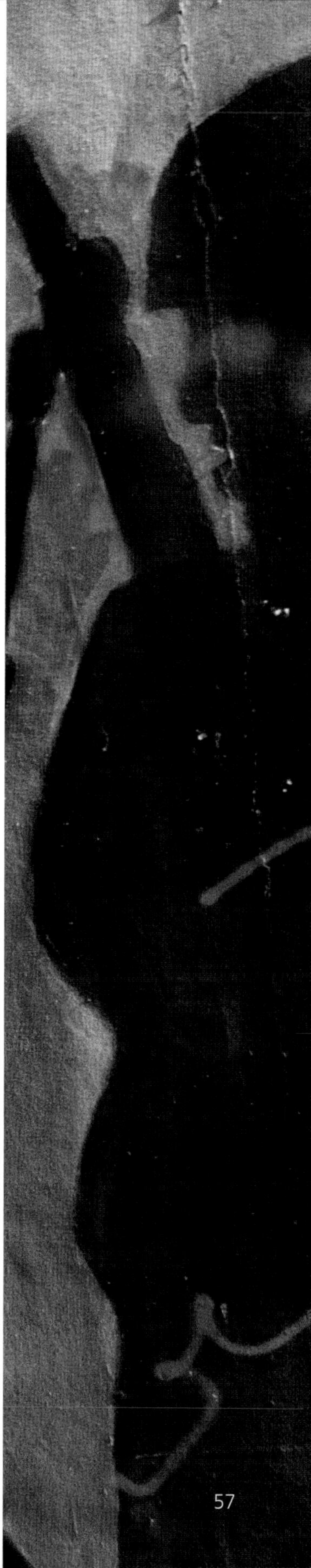

War in the 21st Century

The period since the end of the Cold War in 1989 is an era of growing peace – yet there has never been more global awareness of the problem of armed conflict. The war horrors in Afghanistan, Iraq, Sudan, Syria, and elsewhere have grabbed international attention; even when international intervention does not happen it is discussed. There is a feeling abroad that something has to be done.

Less widely noticed has been a gradual, uneven, but over time unmistakeable, decline in the number and ferocity of armed conflicts. It is no comfort to those who suffer amidst some of the most appalling brutality humans can devise, but the fact is that overall the world has been getting safer. The tougher economic times that have followed the financial crash of 2008 suggest it may get harder to sustain that progress.

Beyond national borders

Most war-fighting by states outside their borders was done in just three wars.

location of war

participating states

Dem Rep Congo, early 2000s:
Angola, Burundi, Chad, Namibia, Rwanda, Sudan, Uganda, Zimbabwe

Afghanistan from 2001:
Australia, Belgium, Canada, Denmark, France, Georgia, Germany, Italy, Netherlands, Norway, Turkey, UK, USA

Iraq from 2003:
Australia, Poland, UK, USA

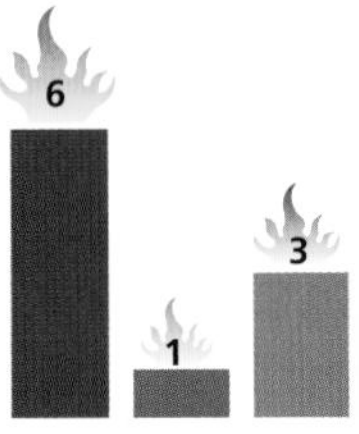

The Americas

◄ 26 Ethnicity & Diversity

At war

Presence of open armed conflict for political goals with continuity between clashes
2000–mid-2012

- has experienced armed conflict within national borders 2000–11
- armed conflict active within national borders during first half of 2012
- has *also* fought war outside national borders 2000–12
- has *only* fought war outside national borders 2000–12
- has not experienced armed conflict within national borders 2000–12

NORWAY
UK
DENMARK
NETH.
POLAND
BELGIUM
GERMANY
FRANCE
ITALY
MAC.
RUSSIA
GEORGIA
ARMENIA
AZER.
UZBEKISTAN
TAJIKISTAN
TURKEY
SYRIA
LEB.
IRAQ
IRAN
AFGHANISTAN
ISRAEL
PALEST. TERR.
PAKISTAN
NEPAL
INDIA
BURMA
THAILAND
PHILIPPINES
ALGERIA
LIBYA
MAURITANIA
MALI
NIGER
CHAD
SUDAN
ERITREA
YEMEN
DJIBOUTI
GUINEA
LEONE
CÔTE D'IVOIRE
LIBERIA
NIGERIA
C.A.R.
SOUTH SUDAN
ETHIOPIA
SOMALIA
UGANDA
SRI LANKA
D.R. CONGO
CONGO
RWANDA
BURUNDI
INDONESIA
ANGOLA
ZIMBABWE
NAMIBIA
AUSTRALIA

Two decades of growing peace

Number of wars

	1990	2000	2010
Europe	3	1	1
Africa	13	15	9
Middle East	7	3	5
Asia	21	17	12

52 Military Muscle; 66 Casualties of War; 68 Refugees; 80 Human Rights ▶

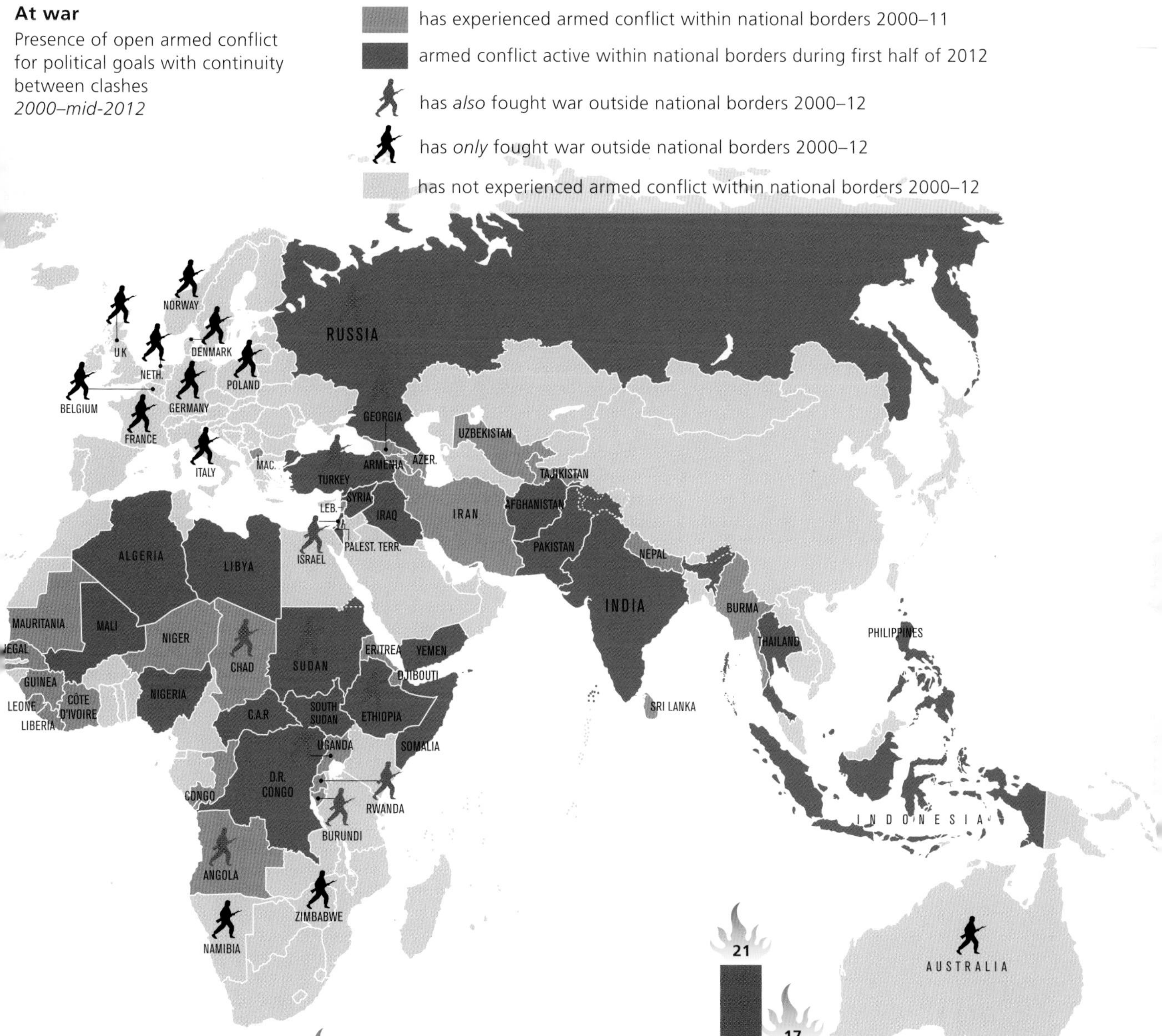

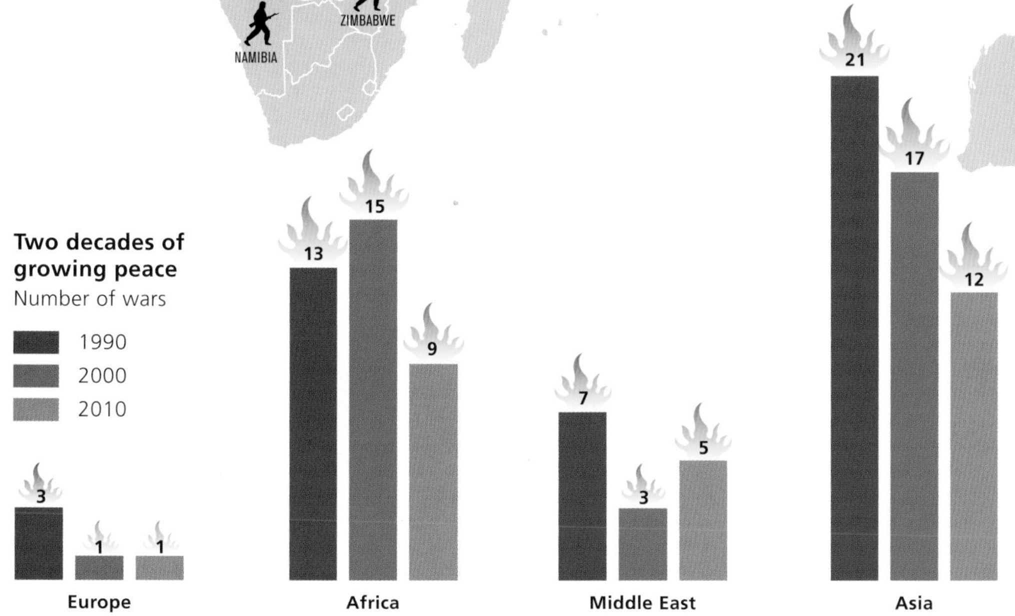

Warlords, Ganglords, & Militias

While the number and intensity of wars between states have declined, new problems have come into view – the proliferation of non-state armed forces and the number of armed conflicts in which the state has no part.

The power of private armies and the risk of non-state wars grow when and where the state's ability to impose order is weak – and in some parts of some countries the state is essentially absent for extended periods. This may happen because of the impact of war, or through the corruption of the state, or because it simply cannot afford to obtain the equipment and train the forces it would need in order to control its territory. Many militias continue to operate long after the war is over.

In those circumstances, local leaders emerge, often enriching themselves by controlling key economic activities – small-scale mining, as in eastern DRC, or the narcotics trade, as in Colombia, Mexico, and Central Asia. If the state does reappear with a campaign to restore its authority, its soldiers all too often become part of the problem, terrorizing civilians with theft, rape, and other human rights abuses.

One common abuse in which militias lead the way is recruiting children to fight, often forcibly, always with a brutal, traumatizing impact on the children's lives – even if they survive the war.

Child soldiers
Used by non-state armed forces
mid 2000s

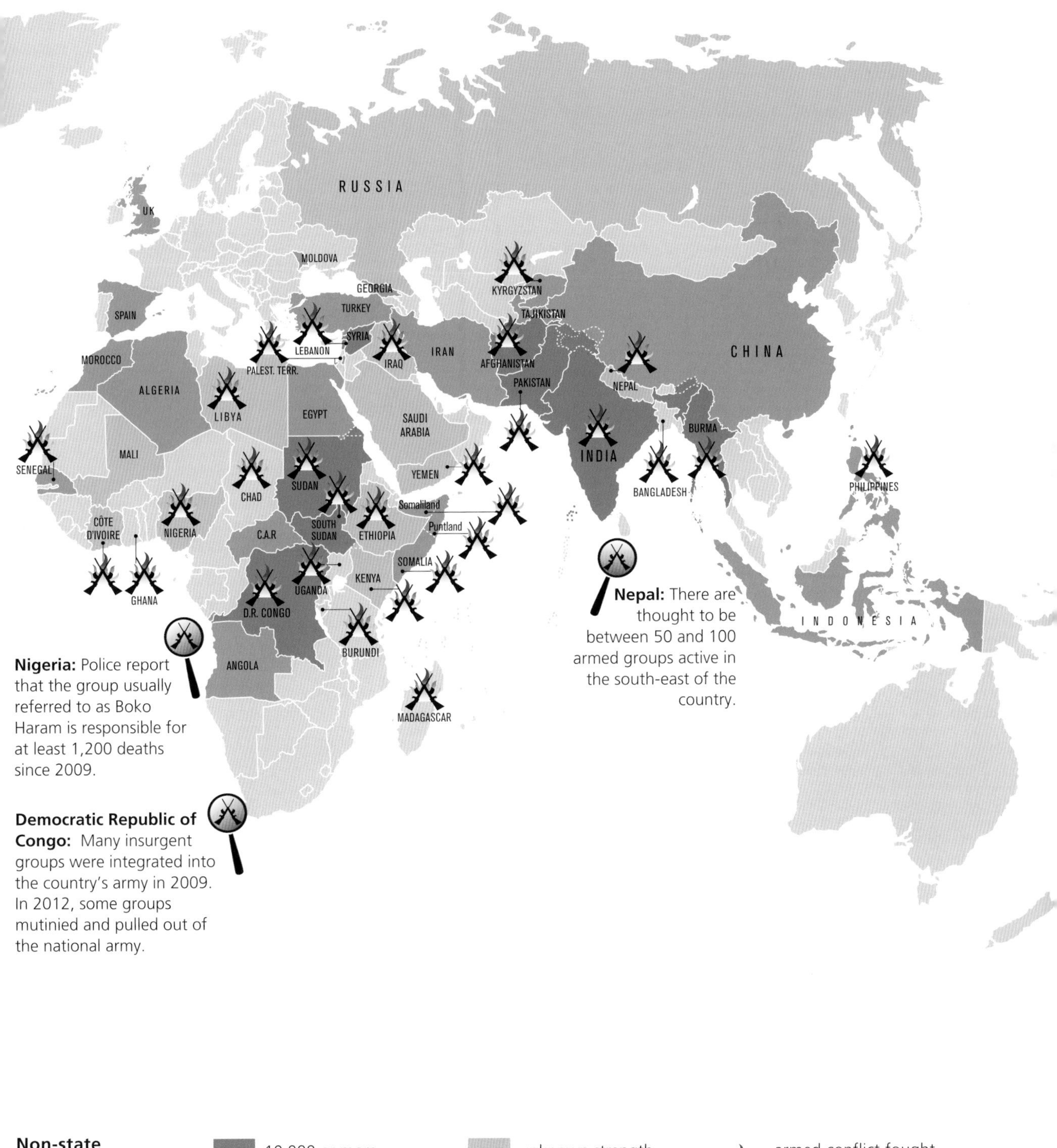

Nepal: There are thought to be between 50 and 100 armed groups active in the south-east of the country.

Nigeria: Police report that the group usually referred to as Boko Haram is responsible for at least 1,200 deaths since 2009.

Democratic Republic of Congo: Many insurgent groups were integrated into the country's army in 2009. In 2012, some groups mutinied and pulled out of the national army.

Non-state armed forces

Estimated strength

2010–12

- 10,000 or more
- fewer than 10,000
- unknown strength
- no known non-state armed force
- armed conflict fought between non-state forces *2002–12*

66 Casualties of War; 68 Refugees; 80 Human Rights; 82 Children's Rights ▶

Military Muscle

World military spending in 2011 was approximately $1.5 trillion. Regular armed forces had just over 20 million personnel. About 20,000 nuclear warheads were stockpiled.

With the end of the Cold War, many people believed there would be a major peace dividend. Military spending did indeed decline, but was protected against deeper cuts in the 1990s by several factors. Zones of political tension and military rivalry persisted; military spending was supported by entrenched interests and justified by residual security fears. And some Western states were attracted by the paradoxical idea of enforcing peace – using armed force against states such as Yugoslavia and Iraq, whose leaders' regional ambitions destabilized peace and security.

With the turn of the century, hopes of a renewed peace dividend were swamped by the US response to 9/11 – and by the response of other states to the renewed US willingness to project force. The global economic crisis has tightened the public purse strings, but interests, fears, and rivalries still combine to keep military spending buoyant.

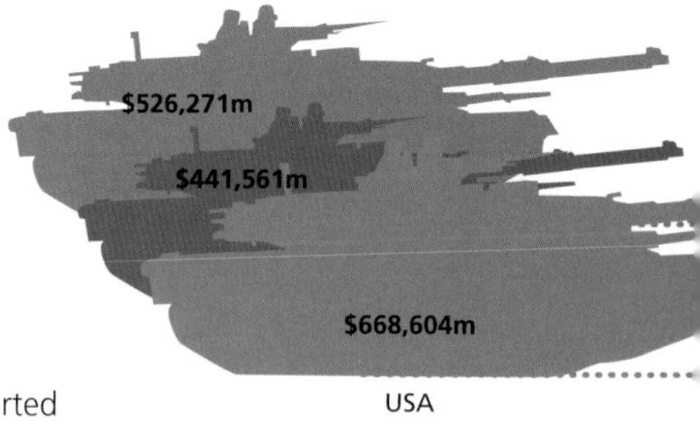

Armed forces top ten
Largest regular armed forces
2011

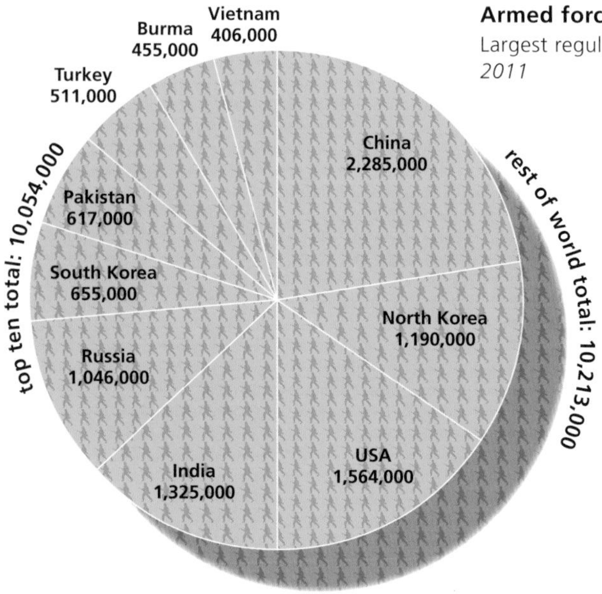

Military spending
As a percentage of GDP
2009

- 4.0% or more
- 3.0% – 3.9%
- 2.0% – 2.9%
- 1.0% – 1.9%
- less than 1.0%
- no data

Nuclear weapons

- first became nuclear-weapon state (where known)
- first held nuclear test (date of first weapon uncertain)

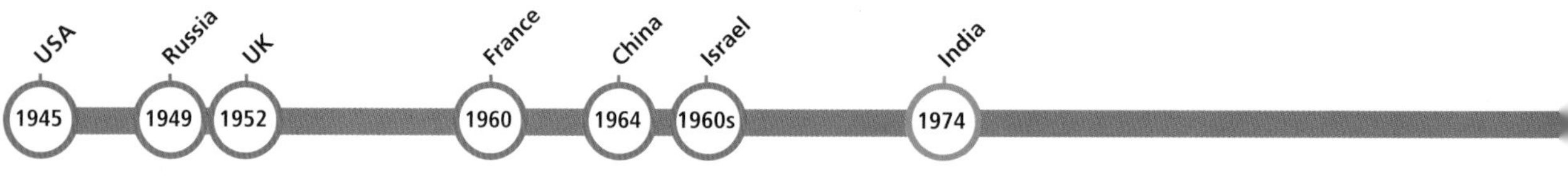

◀ 58 War in the 21st Century

Top military spenders

US$

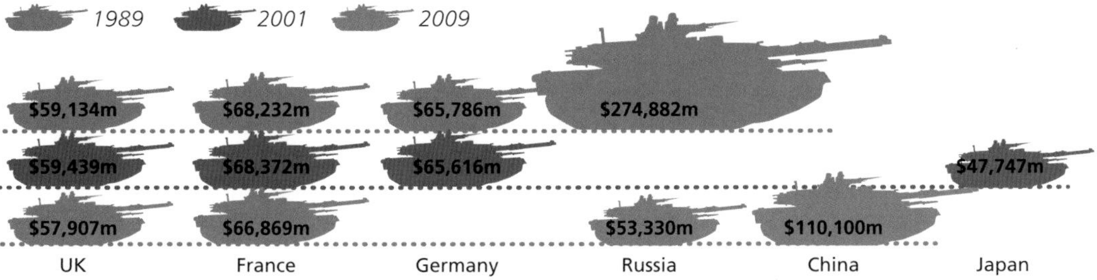

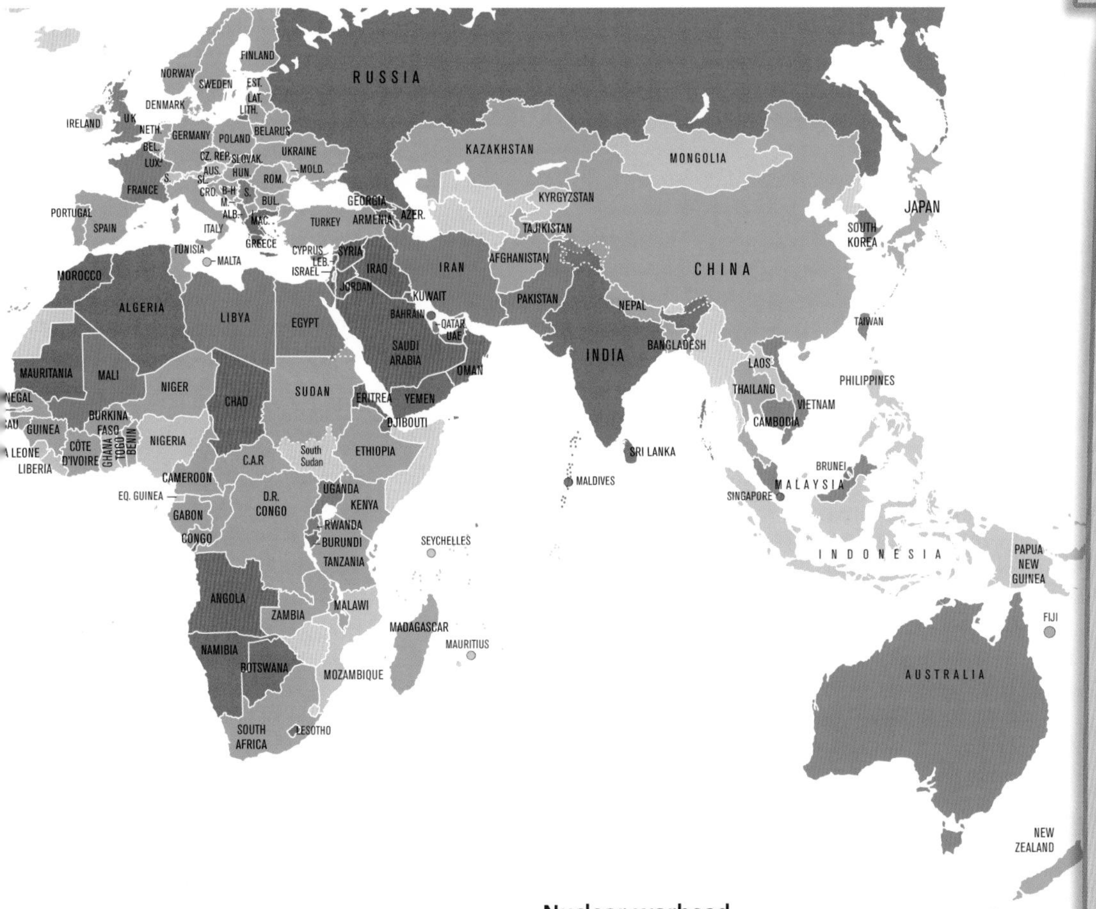

Nuclear warhead stockpiles

2011

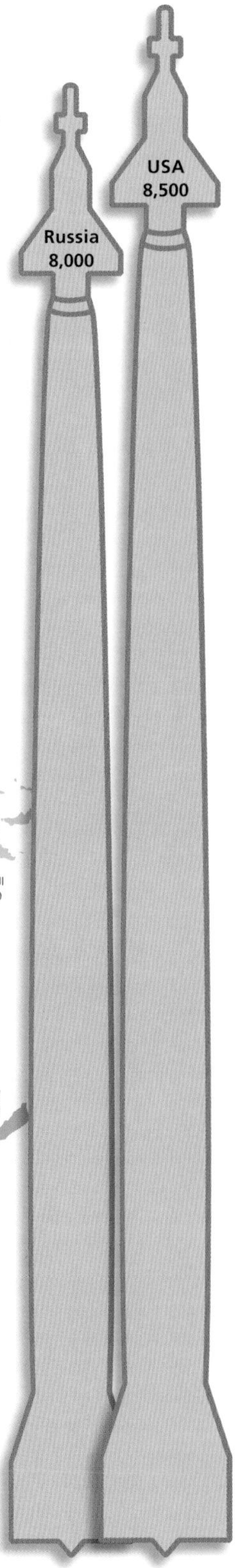

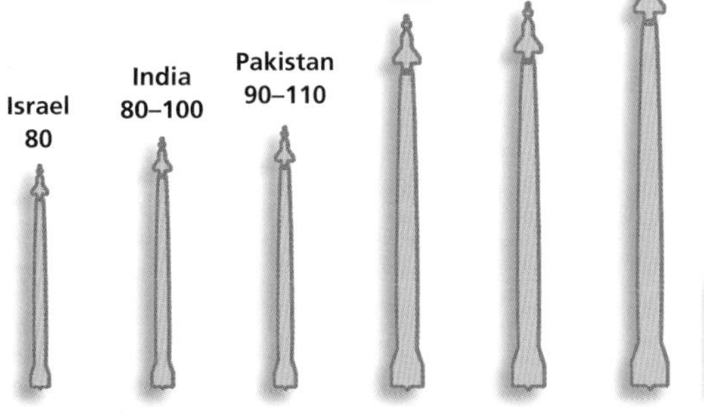

*There is no public information to verify that North Korea possesses operational nuclear weapons.

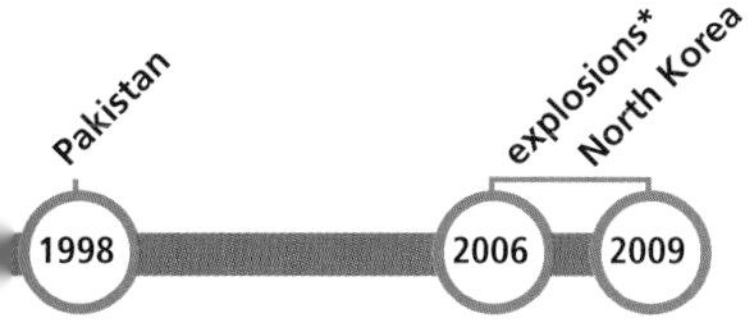

64 The New Front Line; 86 Gay Rights ▶

The New Front Line

Warfare constantly evolves. Global travel and communications allow different kinds of attack and response. Drones and special forces are now the instruments of choice for the most powerful, terror attacks remain the top tactical option for the less powerful but determined, and a race is on for cyber supremacy.

- drones
- special forces
- cyber
- terrorism/piracy

Global cyber attack, 2011: The biggest reported series of cyber attacks to date hit 72 organizations including:

- The governments of Canada, India, S. Korea, Taiwan, Vietnam, USA
- The UN secretariat in Geneva
- The Association of South-East Asian Nations
- The International Olympic Committee and the World Anti-Doping Agency
- Defence contractors and hi-tech companies

Estonia, 2007: A series of a "distributed denial of service" (DDoS) attacks originating from Russia disrupted government departments and interrupted access to emergency services.

USA, 9/11: Al-Qaeda terrorists crash three airliners into the World Trade Center and the Pentagon, killing 2,973 people of more than 50 nationalities.

London, UK, 2005: Four suicide bombers on public transport kill 52 people.

Terror and the economy: Each act of terror costs the country where it takes place about 0.4% of annual GNI.

London, UK, 2012: UK's counter-intelligence director illustrated cyber threat by reference to an unnamed major UK company that lost around $1.35bn in a hostile cyber attack.

USA, 9/11: Estimated cost to al-Qaeda of attack on the World Trade Center and Pentagon: $0.5m. Estimated cost to USA of responding, including rebuilding and counter-terror measures, approximately $3.3tn. Cost ratio: 1:7,000,000

Piracy global cost: Including theft, insurance, damage, preventive measures, and response: approximately $2bn a year.

Madrid, Spain, 2004: Bombs on four trains kill 191 people.

Piracy around the globe, 2012: The International Maritime Bureau warned shipmasters about the following piracy hotspots: coasts of Ecuador and West Africa; Red Sea, Gulf of Yemen; Indian Ocean from Oman to Madagascar as far east as the Maldives; coasts of Bangladesh and Indonesia; Malacca Straits, Singapore Straits.

Cyber Command, 2010: USA appoints first general in charge of cyber warfare. 30,000 US troops reassigned to cyber warfare missions.

Libya, 2011: Former UK special forces soldiers fought with rebels to topple the Gaddafi regime.

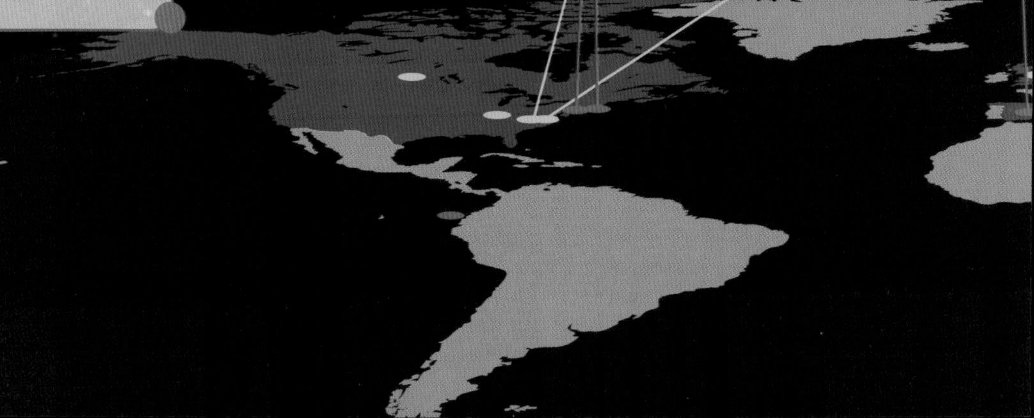

Beslan, Russia, 2004: Chechen fighters hold children and parents hostage in school. 336 hostages and 30 Chechens killed when Russian security forces storm school.

Georgia, 2008: As the Russian–Georgian war started, Russian nationalists mounted a "distributed denial of service" (DDoS) attack on Georgia – flooding government websites with bogus enquiries so as to overwhelm and crash them.

US military, Middle East, 2008: At a US military base in the Middle East, memory sticks containing a self-propagating worm were deliberately left in a washroom. One or more soldiers broke regulations by putting one in a military laptop. US Central Command was infected; the clean up took 14 months.

Somalia: Piracy has grown into a local "industry". In 2000, Somali pirates were responsible for 5% of global attacks; by 2009 this had risen to 52%. In June 2012 they were holding 13 vessels and 185 hostages.

Somalia, 2007–12: Up to 169 civilians killed by US drone strikes.

Kampala, Uganda, 2010: Ethiopian group al-Shabab detonated bombs in a bar where people were watching the football World Cup, killing 76 people.

Abbottabad, Pakistan, 2011: US Special Forces assassinated Osama bin-Laden 9½ years after 9/11.

Pakistan, 2007: Karachi, October: Bomb kills 140 supporters of ex-Prime Minister Benazir Bhutto. Rawalpindi, December: Bhutto and 28 supporters killed in further attack.

Pakistan, 2004–12: 332 reported US drone strikes, with a total death toll estimated at about 3,000, including 300 to 800 civilians and as many as 175 children.

Afghanistan, 2012: 30 US drone attacks on civilian homes in first 6 months of the year.

Iran, 2010: 30,000 government computers and some centrifuges in Iran's nuclear enrichment plant were deactivated by Stuxnet virus, widely believed to originate from USA and Israel.

Iran, 2012: Flamer, the most sophisticated cyber worm yet created, was allegedly designed in Israel. Targeted Iranian officials' computers, wiping out hard drives, and forcing some oil terminals to go offline. Bluetooth capability allowed it to leap from an infected laptop to other devices.

Virtual manoeuvres, 2011, 2012: US and Chinese officials jointly played cyber war games.

Mumbai, India, 2008: 10 terrorists mount three-day attack, focusing on two hotels, the main train station and a Jewish centre, killing 166 people.

North Korea, 2012: A senior US officer is reported saying that US and South Korean special forces have parachuted into North Korea to gather intelligence about underground military installations. Report is officially denied.

Xinjiang, China, 2008: Separatists reportedly attacked a group of around 70 policeman on a training run with machetes and grenade, killing 16 people. **2011:** 18 people died in a series of alleged terrorist attacks in the city of Kashgar.

China, 2009: China's special forces join a public military parade for first time.

China, 2010: China claimed it was hit by nearly 500,000 cyber attacks, almost half originating overseas: 15% from the USA and 8% from India.

Bali, 2002: 200 holidaymakers killed in al-Qaeda bomb attack.

Casualties of War

We have less certain knowledge about casualties than about almost any other aspect of war. Figures for battle deaths are concocted for propaganda – to claim success or blame, and to argue for or against outside intervention. Strip that away and uncertainties remain, caused by the power of rumour and the rudimentary systems of information in many war-torn zones.

About 600,000 deaths have been recorded as directly caused by violent conflicts from 2000 through 2010. That is almost certainly well below the real total. Statistical methods vary, and as a result the Peace and Conflict Research Department at Uppsala University, generally regarded as authoritative on global figures, includes an estimate for deaths in Iraq that is only 10 to 15 per cent of that provided by Iraq Body Count, usually regarded as authoritative on Iraq. One group of research centres proposed figures for 2004 to 2007 about double Uppsala's global estimates.

The confusion is even greater about indirect deaths caused by disease as health facilities are destroyed in war, or by the crime that erupts out of the chaos. One reasonable estimate is that, on average, indirect deaths are about four times as high as direct deaths – but there is no certain information.

The effects of war are long lasting. An average of 30 years of economic growth is lost through a civil war, and the country's international trade takes on average 20 years to recover. People who might otherwise have grown up healthy are born into poverty, malnutrition, and ill health. And one effect of war is war itself; 90 per cent of contemporary armed conflicts are old conflicts coming back.

1.5 billion people live in countries under the threat of large-scale organized violence

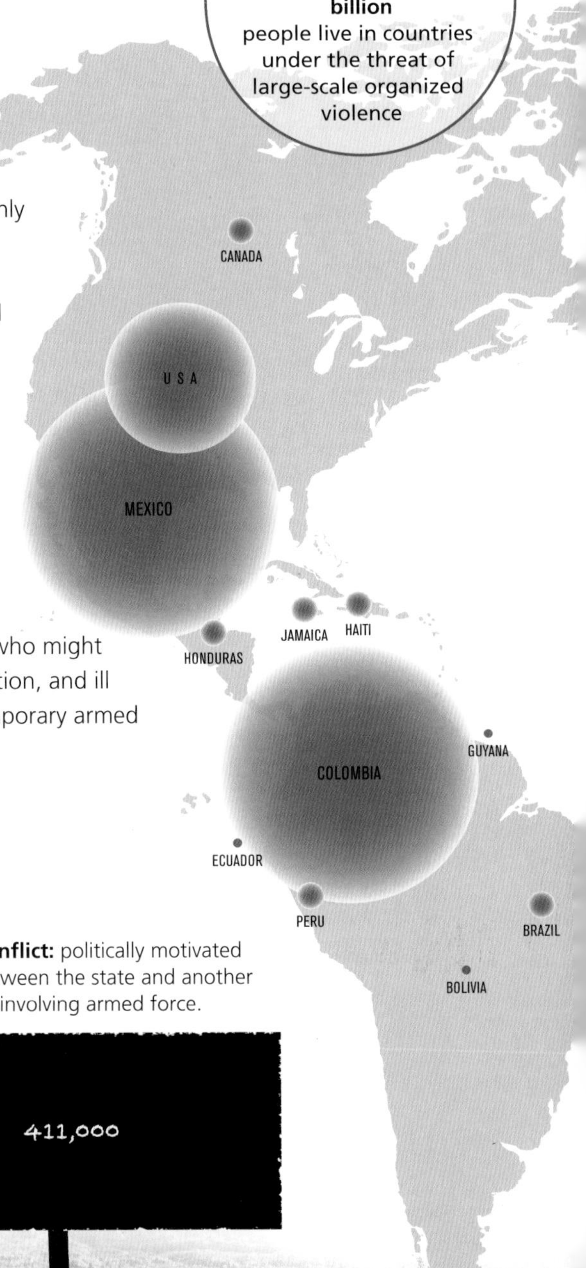

Death toll
By type of conflict
2000–10

Non-state conflict: an armed conflict that does not actively involve the state but other, non-state groups.

One-sided violence: organized and sustained attacks on defenceless civilians by the state or an armed group.

Armed conflict: politically motivated violence between the state and another party, involving armed force.

◄ 58 War in the 21st Century; 60 Warlords, Ganglords, & Militia

The 21st-century toll
Estimate of deaths from violent conflict
2000–10
more than 100,000
10,001 – 100,000
5,001 – 10,000
1,001 –5,000
101 – 1,000
1 –100
RUSSIA
NORWAY
UK
NETH.
DENMARK
BELGIUM
GERMANY
POLAND
FRANCE
SPAIN
ITALY
MACEDONIA
TURKEY
GEORGIA
UZBEKISTAN
ARMENIA
AZER.
KYRGYZSTAN
TAJIKISTAN
AFGHANISTAN
IRAQ
LEBANON
ISRAEL & PALEST. TERR.
IRAN
ALGERIA
EGYPT
SAUDI ARABIA
ERITREA
PAKISTAN
NEPAL
CHINA
CHAD
NIGER
SENEGAL
MALI
SUDAN & South Sudan
BURMA
LAOS
SIERRA LEONE
GUINEA
LIBERIA
CÔTE D'IVOIRE
GHANA
NIGERIA
YEMEN
DJIBOUTI
ETHIOPIA
INDIA
BANGLADESH
THAILAND
PHILIPPINES
C.A.R
UGANDA
KENYA
SOMALIA
SRI LANKA
D.R. CONGO
RWANDA
TANZANIA
CONGO
BURUNDI
INDONESIA
ANGOLA
ZIMBABWE
MADAGASCAR
NAMIBIA
AUSTRALIA
Regional toll
Estimate of deaths from violent conflict
2000–10
58,700 Americas
Europe 15,400
175,400 Middle East & North Africa
220,000 Sub-Saharan Africa
129,000 Asia & Oceania

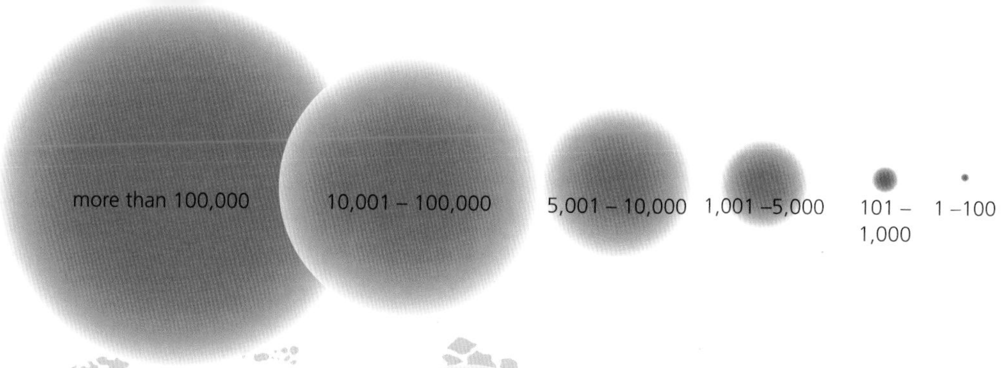

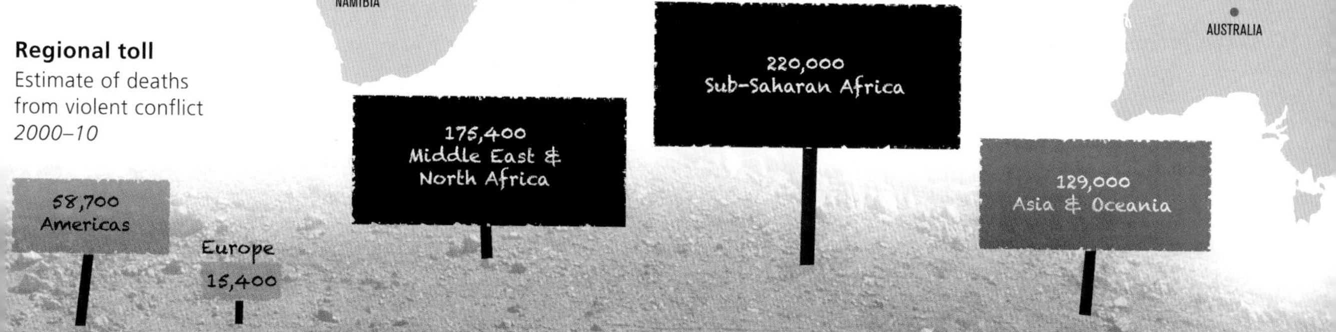

Refugees

30 million people are unable to return to their homes because of war or repression. Many have been made refugees more than once. Some refugee populations now include the grandchildren of those who originally fled.

Major refugee populations
Origin and current location
end 2010 or latest available data
= 10,000 refugees

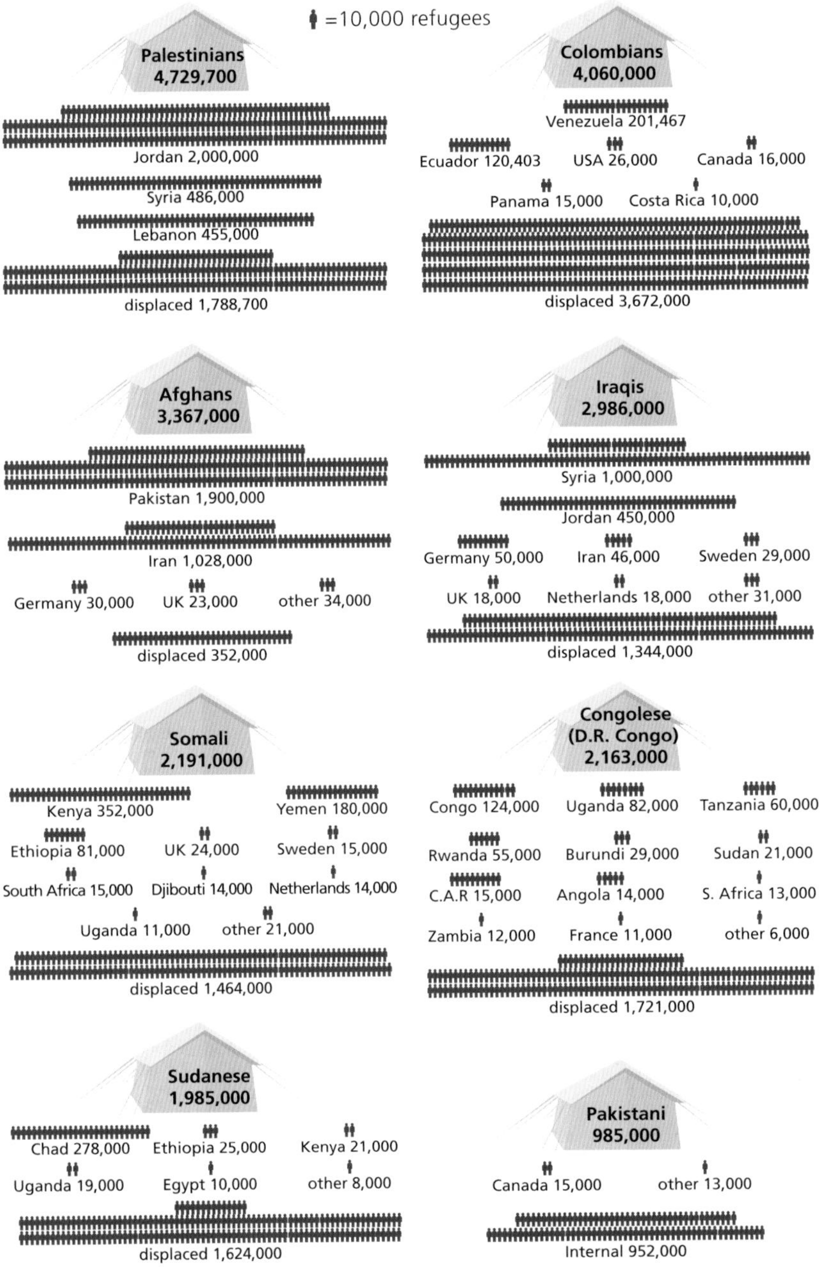

Displaced
Number of people who have fled their homes but remain in their own country
end 2010

Some **14 million** people are **internally displaced**.

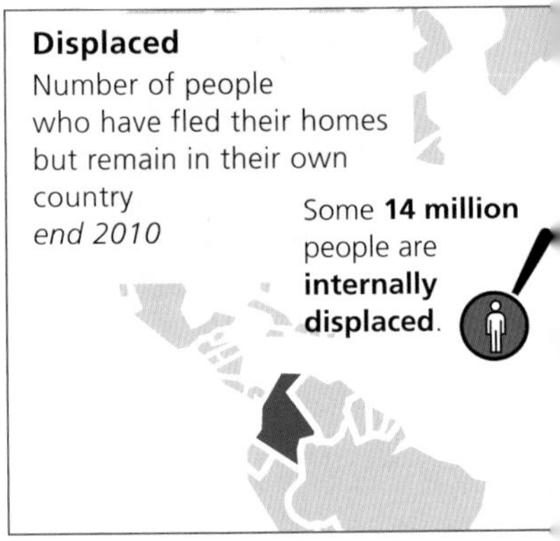

◄ 58 War in the 21st Century; 60 Warlords, Ganglords, & Militia

Flight
Number of international refugees hosted by country
end 2010
Worldwide, there are about **12 million refugees**.
Over
85%
of refugees, displaced, and stateless people come from
8
countries
1 million or more
500,000 – 999,999
100,000 – 499,999
10,000 – 99,999
1,000 – 9,999
fewer than 1,000
no data
ICELAND
NORWAY
SWEDEN
FINLAND
EST.
LAT.
LITH.
DENMARK
IRELAND
UK
NETH.
BEL.
LUX.
GERMANY
POLAND
BELARUS
UKRAINE
MOLD.
LIECHT.
CZ. REP.
SL.
AUS.
HUN.
ROM.
FRANCE
S.
SL.
CRO.
B-H
S.
M.
ALB.
MAC.
BUL.
GREECE
ITALY
PORTUGAL
SPAIN
TUNISIA
MALTA
MOROCCO
ALGERIA
LIBYA
EGYPT
RUSSIA
KAZAKHSTAN
MONGOLIA
UZBEKISTAN
KYRGYZSTAN
TAJIKISTAN
TURKMEN.
GEORGIA
ARMENIA
AZER.
TURKEY
CYPRUS
SYRIA
LEB.
ISRAEL
JORDAN
IRAQ
IRAN
AFGHANISTAN
PAKISTAN
KUWAIT
BAHRAIN
QATAR
UAE
SAUDI ARABIA
OMAN
YEMEN
CHINA
JAPAN
SOUTH KOREA
NEPAL
INDIA
BANGLADESH
Hong Kong SAR
THAILAND
VIETNAM
CAMBODIA
PHILIPPINES
SRI LANKA
MALAYSIA
SINGAPORE
INDONESIA
EAST TIMOR
PAPUA NEW GUINEA
VANUATU
FIJI
AUSTRALIA
NEW ZEALAND
MAURITANIA
MALI
NIGER
CHAD
SUDAN
ERITREA
DJIBOUTI
SENEGAL
GAMBIA
GUINEA-BISSAU
GUINEA
SIERRA LEONE
LIBERIA
BURKINA FASO
CÔTE D'IVOIRE
GHANA
TOGO
BENIN
NIGERIA
C.A.R
South Sudan
ETHIOPIA
SOMALIA
CAMEROON
GABON
CONGO
D.R. CONGO
UGANDA
KENYA
RWANDA
BURUNDI
TANZANIA
ANGOLA
ZAMBIA
MALAWI
ZIMBABWE
NAMIBIA
BOTSWANA
MOZAMBIQUE
SWAZILAND
SOUTH AFRICA
Stateless
Number of stateless people within country
end 2010
Close to **4 million** people are **stateless**.

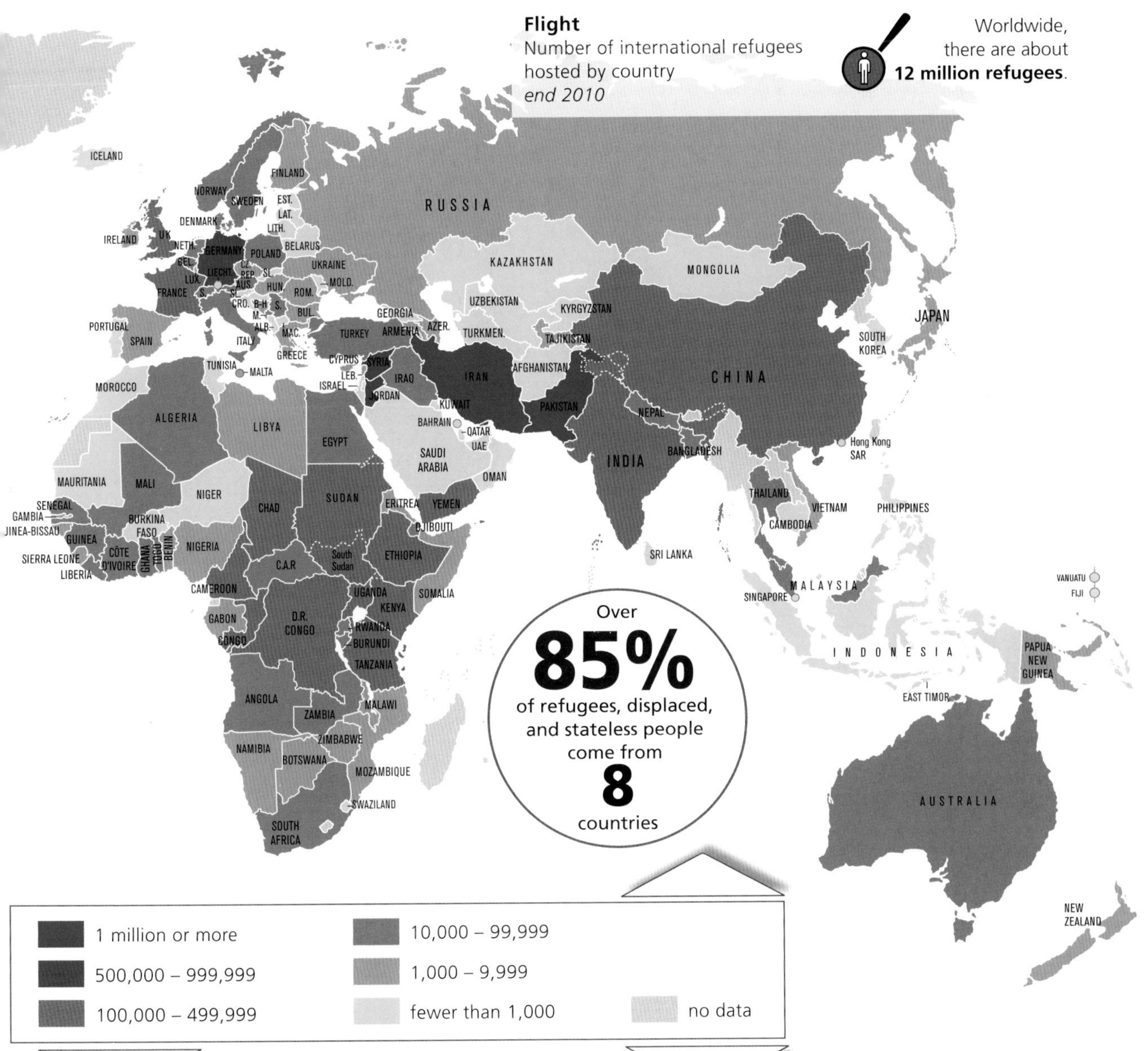

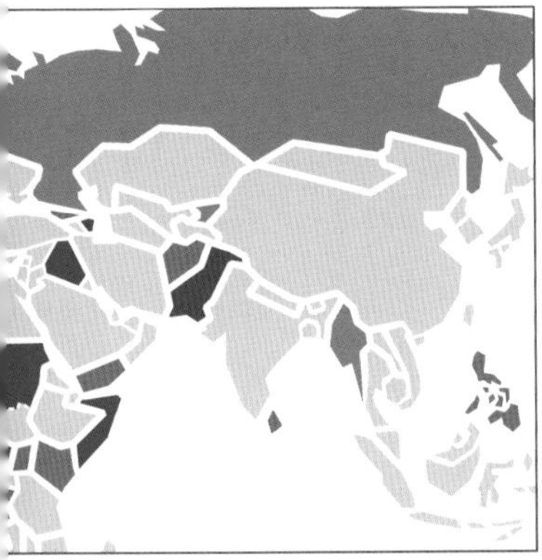

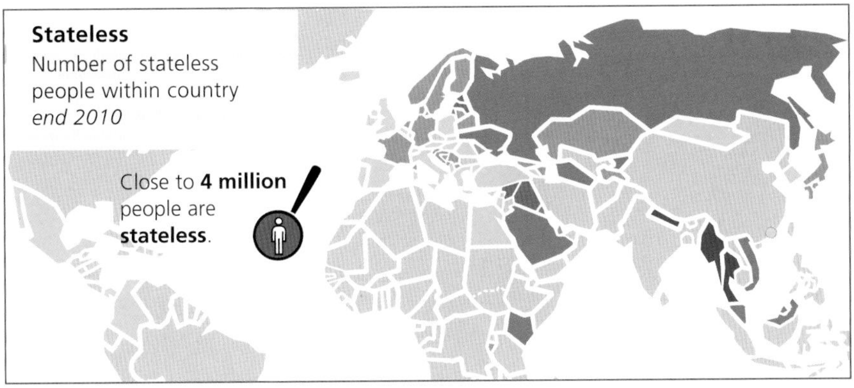

Peacekeeping

There are nearly 100,000 UN peacekeepers, counting police as well as military personnel. The number of missions increased rapidly following the end of the Cold War in 1990, not because there were suddenly more wars (although the number did increase in the early 1990s), but because the end of the confrontation between the USA and the Soviet Union freed the United Nations to do more.

For the same reason, there were more agreements for peacekeeping forces to support. A UN study found that in the first 12 or so years after the end of the Cold War, as many peace agreements were signed as in the previous 200 years.

The number of peacekeeping missions plateaued in the mid-2000s and, although the trend is not yet clear, it looks as though it is now tailing off. This is partly an indication that several peacekeeping missions have been successfully accomplished – but may also be a sign that rich states are less willing to pay for peacekeeping in tougher economic times.

Forces for peace
Number of military and police personnel committed to UN peacekeeping operations
2012

- 5,000 or more (numbers shown)
- 1,000 – 4,999
- 500 – 999
- 1 – 499
- none

Locations of missions

- UN peacekeeping missions
- UN political and/or peacebuilding missions
- Non-UN peacekeeping operations

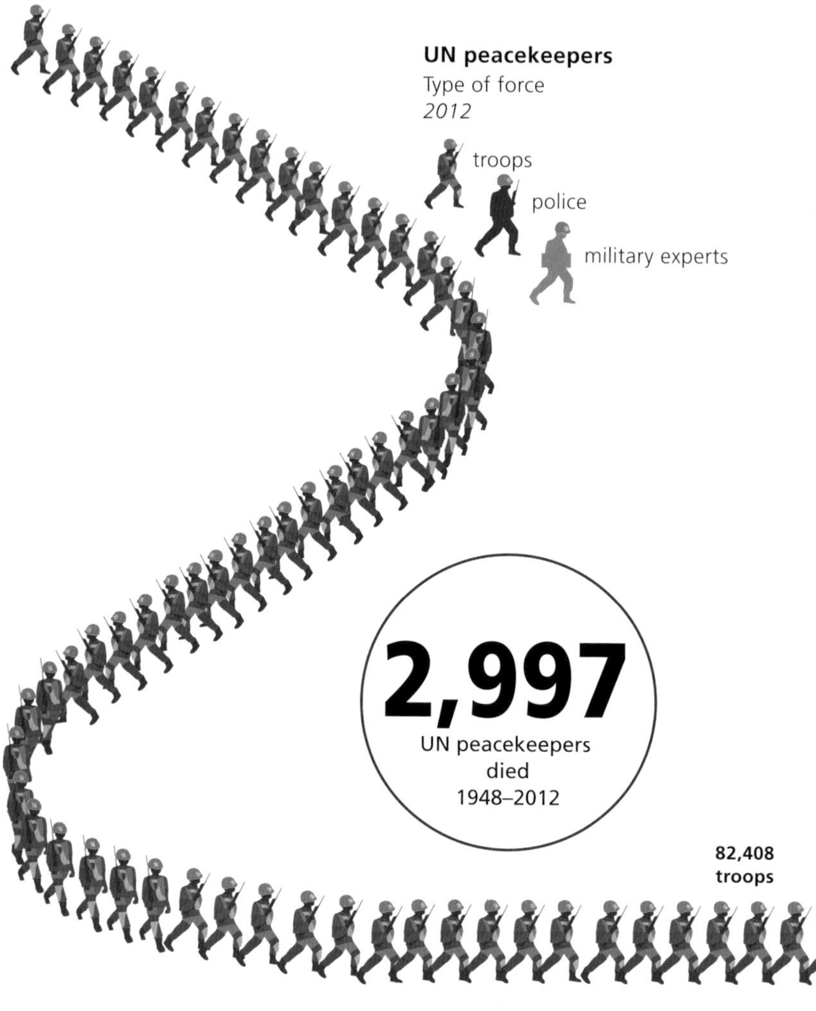

UN peacekeeping missions

Number active

1950–2010

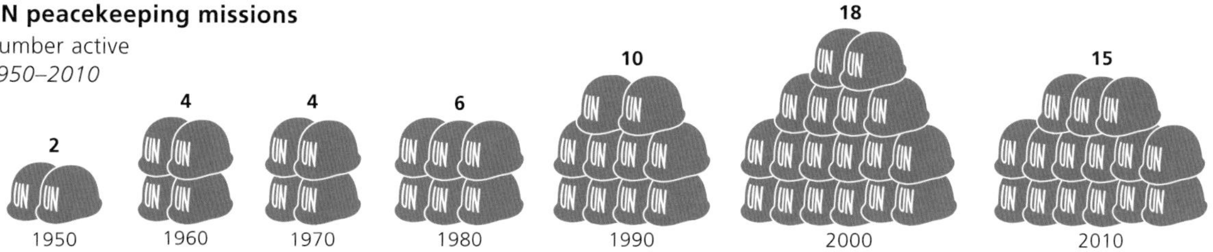

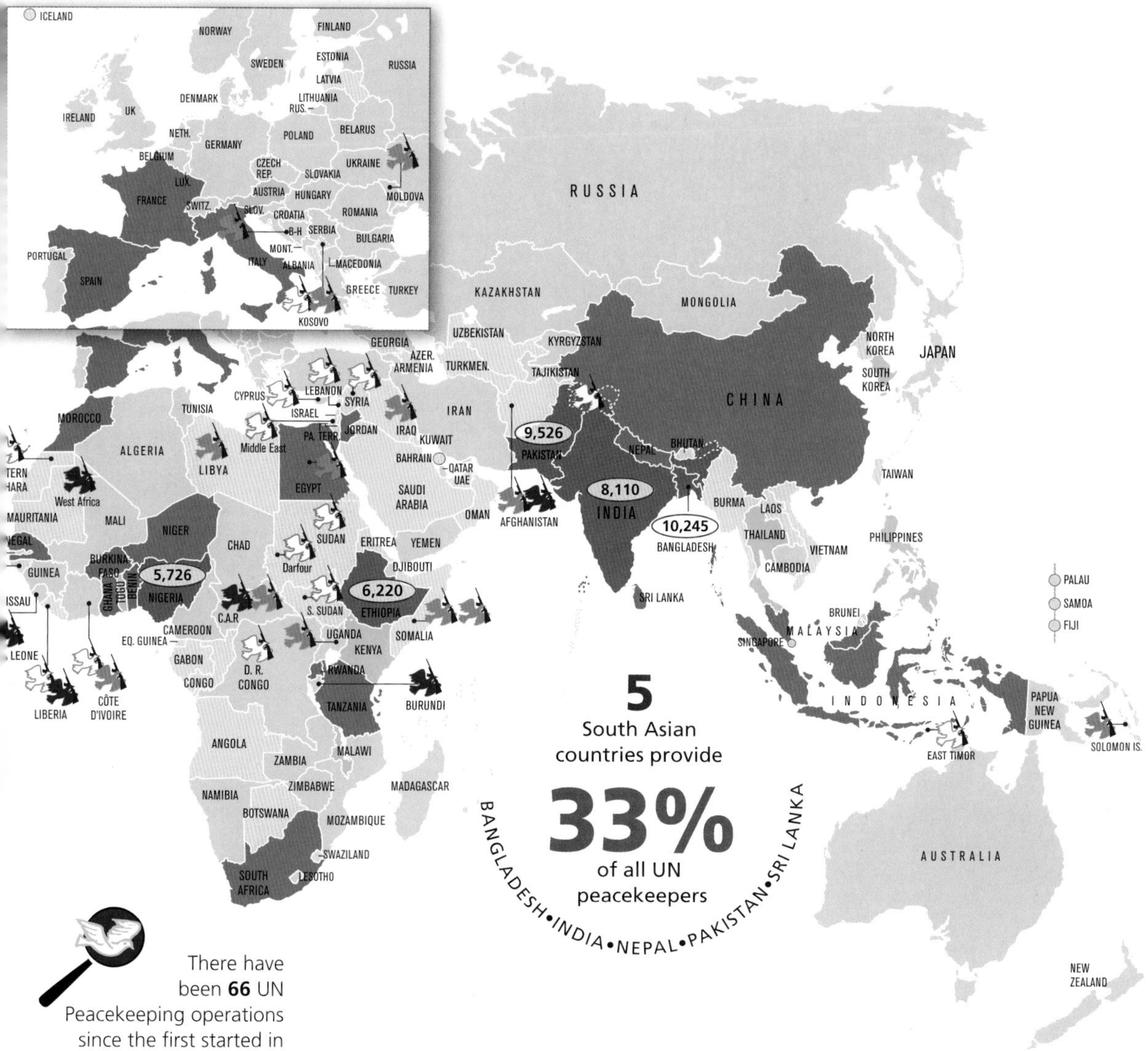

There have been **66** UN Peacekeeping operations since the first started in the Middle East in 1948. It is still going.

72 Global Peacefulness ▶

Global Peacefulness

Discussion of armed conflict and peace almost always focuses heavily on what goes wrong and why. The Global Peace Index is an independent attempt to make sense of the other, too often neglected, part of the discussion – what goes right and why. The Index ranks countries according to their peacefulness, looking both at peace at home (government stability, democratic values, community relations, and trust between citizens) and peace in foreign relations (propensity to war, military spending, commitment to UN operations).

The Index is based on the idea that helping people and governments to understand what creates peaceful relations is a significant step towards making it possible for the world to be more peaceful.

If the USA were as peaceful as Canada, it would save $360 billion of public and private spending.

Direct and indirect costs of violence:

$8 trillion in 2010

Reducing worldwide violence by just **25%**

would release enough resources to pay for:

The annual costs of:

avoiding the worst effects of climate change

achieving the Millennium Development Goals

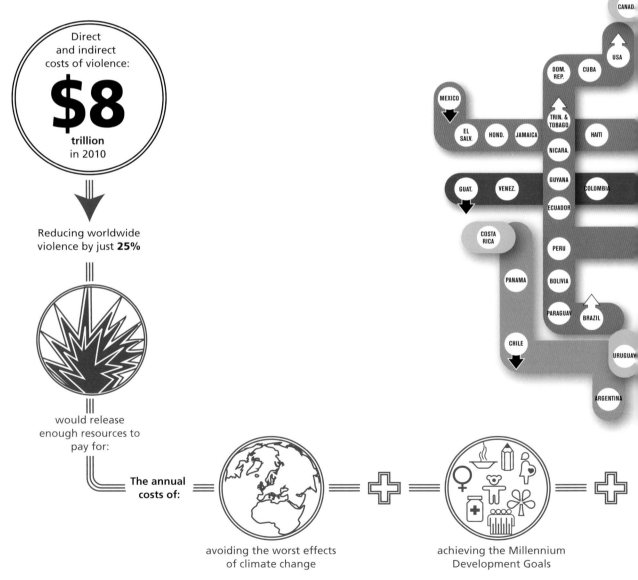

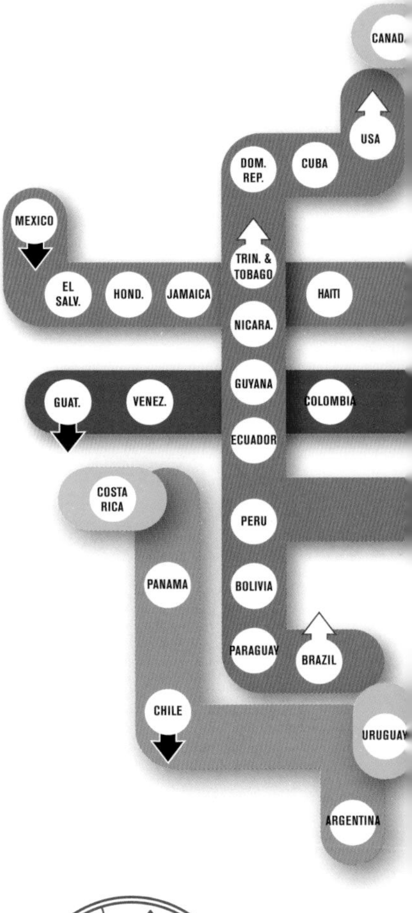

◄ *42 Quality of Life; 70 Peacekeeping*

Level of peacefulness
According to Global Peace Index (GPI) 2011
very high
high
medium
low
very low
Changes 2008–11
climbed 15 or more places
fell 15 or more places
Fastest riser: Malawi rose 34 places 2008–11
Fastest faller: Libya fell 82 places 2008–11
NORWAY
SWEDEN
FINLAND
POLAND
ICELAND
HUNGARY
ESTONIA
LATVIA
RUSSIA
NETH.
DENMARK
GERMANY
SLOVAKIA
UK
BELGIUM
LITHUANIA
KAZAKH.
IRELAND
SWITZ.
AUSTRIA
SLOVENIA
CZ. REP.
MOLDOVA
GEORGIA
UZBEK.
FRANCE
ITALY
CROATIA
BOSNIA-HERZ
BULGARIA
ROMANIA
TURKEY
TURKMEN.
SPAIN
NORTH KOREA
PORTUGAL
ALBANIA
MACED.
SERBIA
UKRAINE
BELARUS
ARMENIA
AZER.
KYRGYZ.
TAJIK.
NEPAL
MONG.
TUNISIA
SOUTH KOREA
MONTENEGRO
BHUTAN
MOROCCO
IRAQ
SYRIA
GREECE
EGYPT
CYPRUS
JORDAN
BANGLA-DESH
JAPAN
CHINA
ALGERIA
LIBYA
NIGERIA
CHAD
C.A.R
BAHRAIN
ISRAEL
LEBANON
IRAN
AFGHAN-ISTAN
PAKISTAN
INDIA
SRI LANKA
BURMA
PHILIPPINES
SUDAN
GUINEA
LIBERIA
MALI
YEMEN
SOUTH SUDAN
CAMEROON
UAE
MAUR.
NIGER
SAUDI ARABIA
EQUIT. GUINEA
ETHIOPIA
D.R. CONGO
SOMALIA
OMAN
LAOS
THAILAND
CAMBODIA
CÔTE D'IVOIRE
ERITREA
KUWAIT
CONGO
GABON
KENYA
QATAR
SINGAPORE
MALAYSIA
VIETNAM
TAIWAN
GAMBIA
BURKINA FASO
SENEGAL
RWANDA
UGANDA
MADAGASCAR
INDONESIA
PAPUA NEW GUINEA
GHANA
ANGOLA
BURUNDI
SIERRA LEONE
ZIMBABWE
AUSTRALIA
TANZANIA
NAMIBIA
SWAZILAND
NEW ZEALAND
ZAMBIA
BOTSWANA
MOZ.
MALAWI
The total costs of:
paying off the public debt of Greece, Portugal, and Ireland
rebuilding after the 2011 Japanese earthquake and tsunami
Total amount redirected: $2 trillion

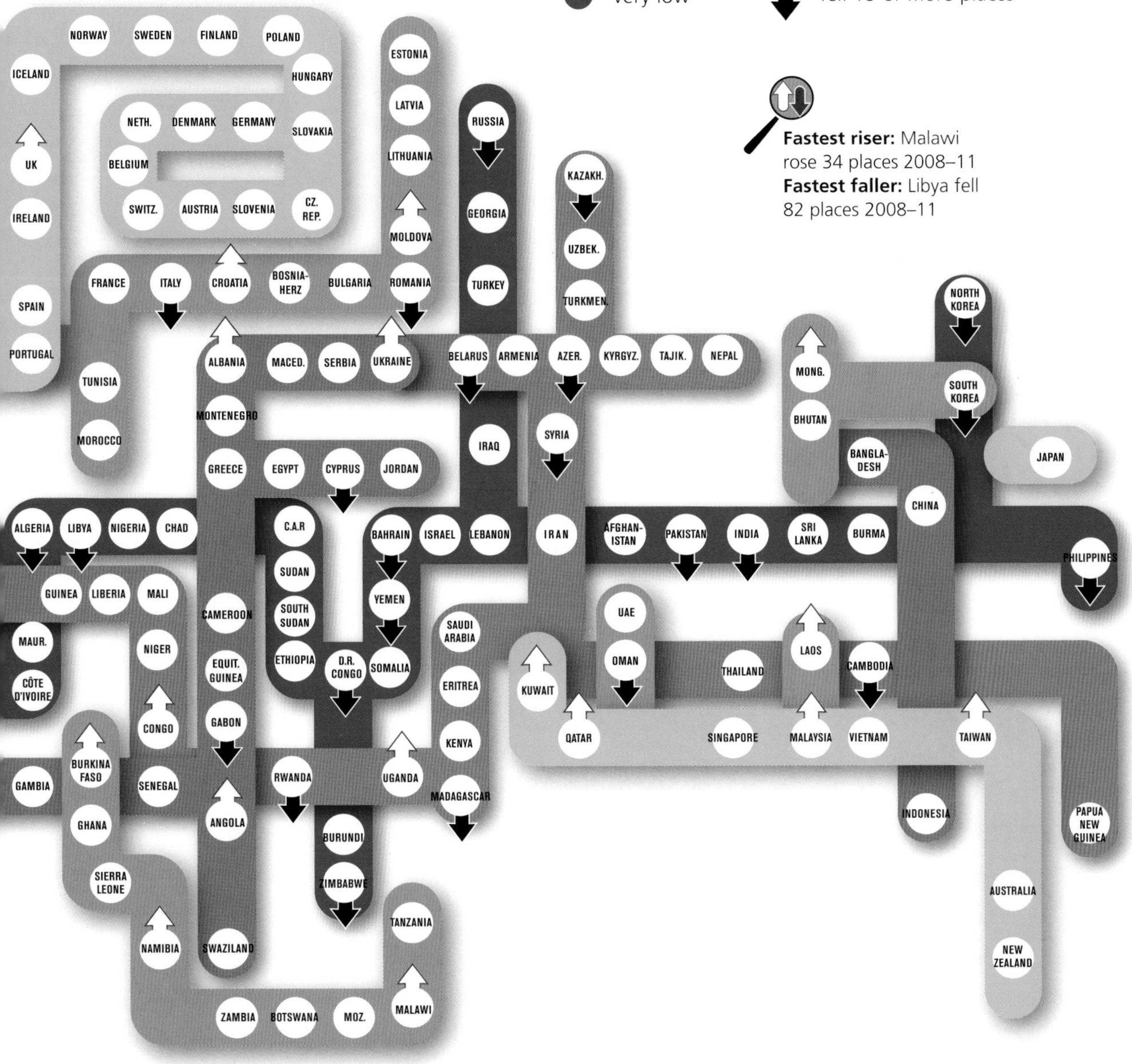

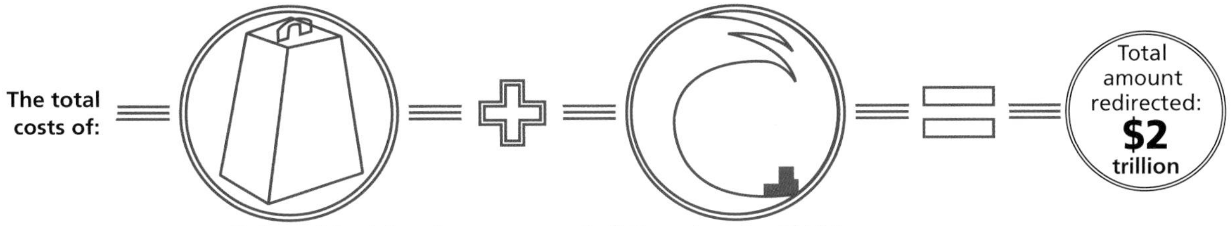

PART FOUR

RIGHTS & RESPECT

Protection from both economic depredation and the threat of violent conflicts derives from laws developed on the basis of the common good. When laws are made by a process that represents and responds to the interests of the majority, and are therefore accepted rather than imposed, then it can be said that social order is based on the rule of law. Then the contract between citizen and state upholds accountable authority. Such societies are more resilient, and the majority of people fare better, than when power is arbitrary and laws are made by an elite minority for their own interests.

Ours is an age of growing democracy – at least when measured by the number of countries that are now established democracies, and the percentage of the world population that lives in them. Governing in this way is a relatively new development in human history. The trend of history has only been moving in that direction for one or two centuries, and until the last 20 to 25 years it would have been impossible to think of democratic government as the global norm.

The transition from dictatorship to democracy is perilous. The upsurge of wars in the early 1990s came at the same time as the states that emerged out of the former Soviet Union and ex-Yugoslavia were making their way – some of them – towards democracy. Those who expect to be disadvantaged by that transition almost always resist the change if they can. It is hard for there to be any peaceful way of pursuing the ensuing conflict when the institutions that might keep it peaceful are themselves being fought over. The democratic wave that swept the Middle East in 2011 and into 2012 was accompanied everywhere by violence, with open civil war in Libya and Syria.

But it is not only the transition to democracy that is of concern. Even today, in countries that are established democracies, it is not certain that it is irreversibly entrenched. Democratic countries in the years since 2008, most notably in Europe, have witnessed a fragmentation of political norms and social consensus. This is in large part a direct result of the economic problems of the day, with unemployment on the increase, especially for young people, and the economic future looking bleak. It also builds on a much longer and slower erosion of the vitality of democracy. In many established democracies, though there continue to be surges of political energy on major, mobilizing issues, political participation is not at all high. Exercising the vote is as far as the vast majority of citizens' political participation goes, and there is not always a solid majority of people who go out and vote.

Democracy is a system that says to the holders of government power, "You might be wrong – so we reserve the right to check on you every few years and replace you if need be." And in some systems it says to the highest holders of government power, "Regardless of whether you get it right or wrong, you'll be out in a few years." This must generate a degree of humility compared to holders of power under other systems. And it is that humility among the leaders that is the greatest and most precious characteristic of not just a democratic system but of democratic culture.

When that humility seems to diminish and the arrogance of power takes hold in elected leaders and on a whole governing class, that is when it is time to take care. That is when the strength and the authenticity of democratic institutions may start to be eroded by stealth.

A good litmus test of the rule of law is respect for human rights. Beyond law as a system of justice, of controls and constraints, human rights law upholds fairness in society, based on mutual respect. In order to work, it has to be universal – fairness for all, mutual respect among all.

When some people are declared to be second-class citizens – whether on the basis of race, skin colour, ethnicity, gender, sexual preference, physical ability, faith, regional or national origin, age, or any other marker of identity – the consequences are serious. Fairness and mutual respect corrode, the rule of law suffers, democracy if nominally present is weakened, and the interests of ordinary people are inevitably treated as disposable compared to those of a narrow elite – *even if the majority collude in the unfairness.*

There is said to be wisdom in numbers but at times the majority can head in very unwise directions, carried away by fear, heated political rhetoric, the distractions of political charisma, ignorance, and a host of other profoundly human reasons. The framework of law is often needed to protect us against ourselves.

The web of international agreements and laws that support human rights is steadily strengthening. There is increasing acceptance of international norms, and growing rejection of arguments that are made by this or that group or big power for exempting its actions from the law.

For rights to be real, the responsibility to respect them must also be embraced. In the best functioning communities, there is a balanced sense of rights and responsibilities. A society that respects human rights is one in which people not only have a clear sense of their rights but also of their duties to each other.

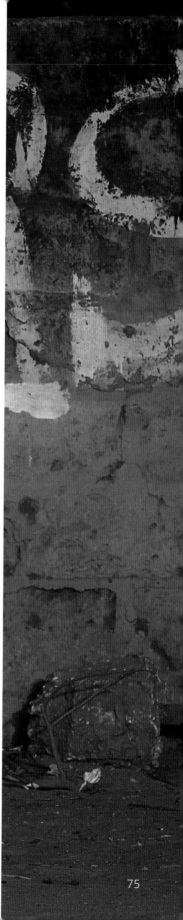

Political Systems

The global trend is democratic. Not without reverses, often at the cost of bloodshed and brutality, the number of democratic states has steadily increased since the end of the Cold War in 1990. That event itself set many states off on a democratic transition. At about the same time, democracy was consolidating in much of Latin America, and there was a wave of democratization in Africa.

In 2011 a democratic wave started to sweep through the Middle East and North Africa as people mobilized against corrupt and authoritarian rule. In 2011 and 2012 there were changes in government in Tunisia, Egypt, Morocco, Libya (after Western military intervention), and Yemen, and a bloody civil war began in Syria. Exactly what direction the changes would eventually take was unclear.

Living politics

The share of the world's people living under different political systems *2012*

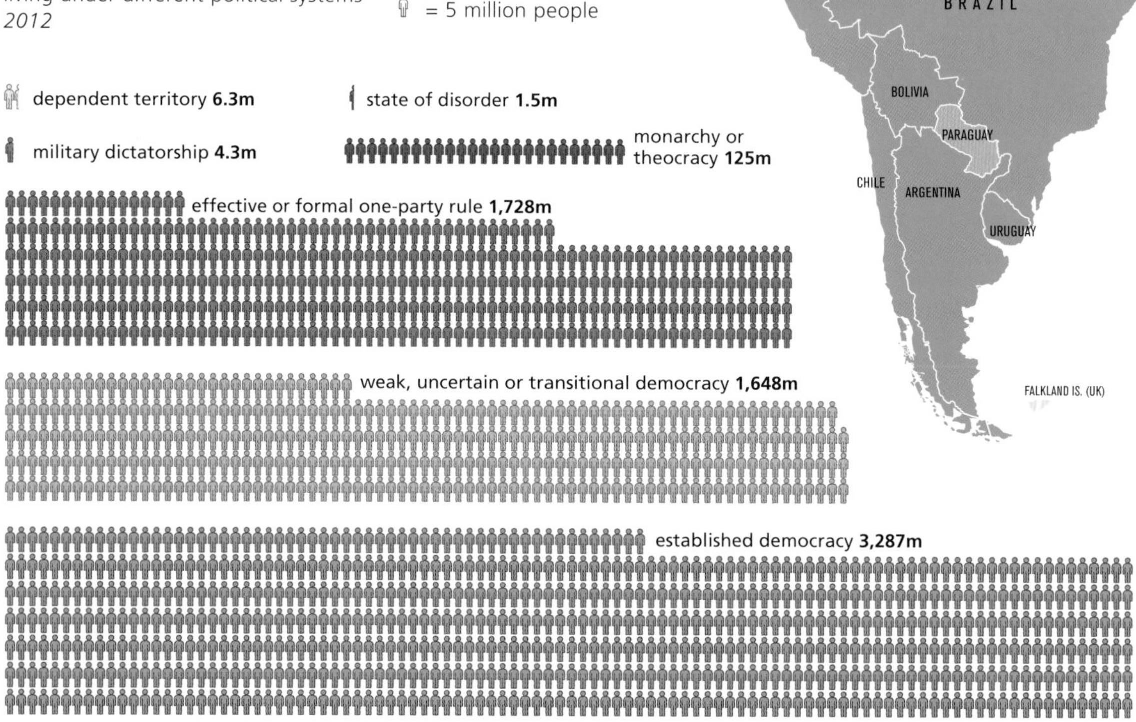

◄ *20 The States of the World; 48 Corruption*

Political systems

2012

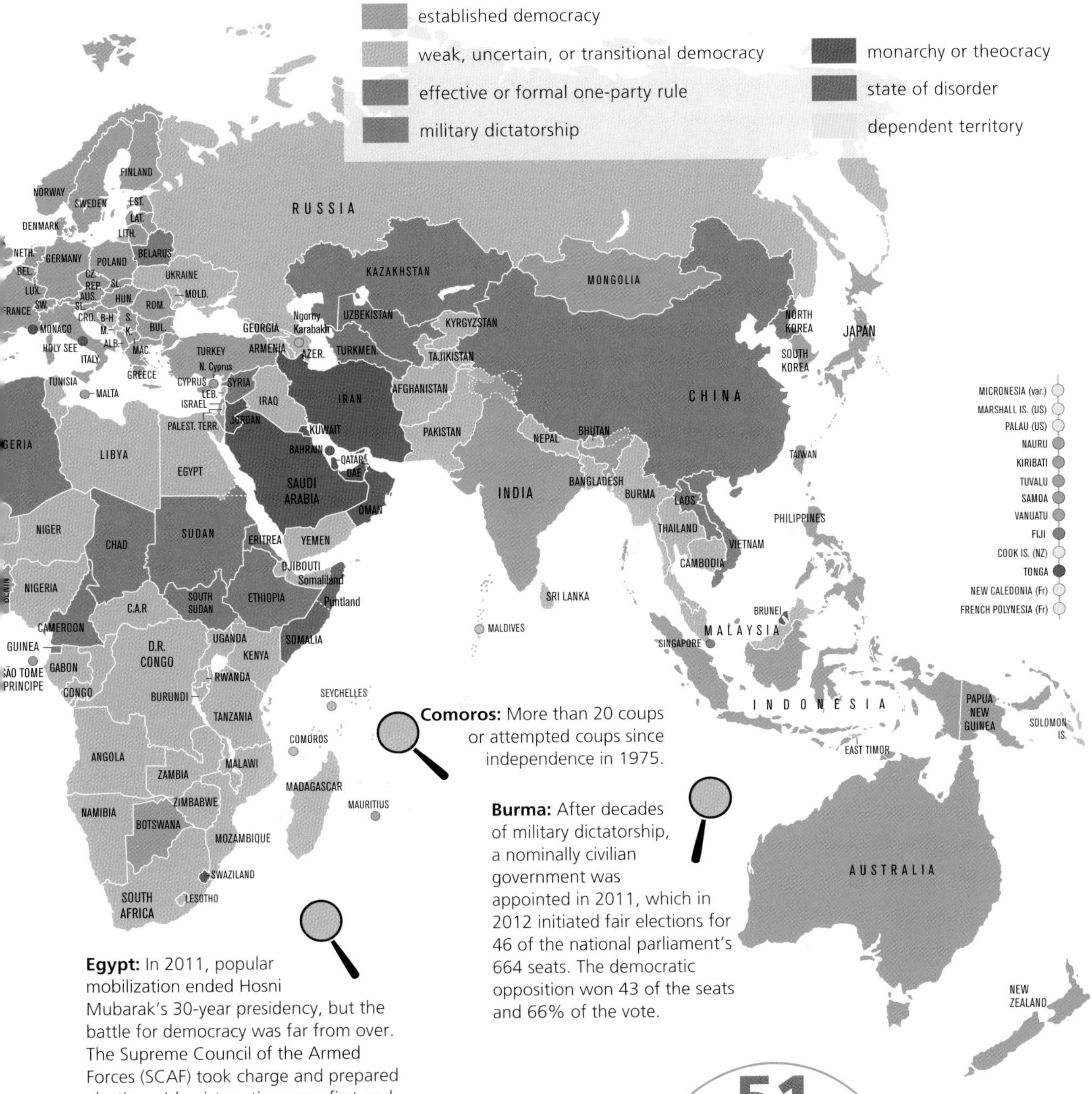

Comoros: More than 20 coups or attempted coups since independence in 1975.

Burma: After decades of military dictatorship, a nominally civilian government was appointed in 2011, which in 2012 initiated fair elections for 46 of the national parliament's 664 seats. The democratic opposition won 43 of the seats and 66% of the vote.

Egypt: In 2011, popular mobilization ended Hosni Mubarak's 30-year presidency, but the battle for democracy was far from over. The Supreme Council of the Armed Forces (SCAF) took charge and prepared elections. Islamist parties came first and second in the 2011–12 parliamentary elections, but six months later the supreme court dissolved parliament. At the same time, SCAF took extra powers for itself, but the presidential elections went ahead, resulting in a win for Mohamed Morsi, candidate of the Muslim Brotherhood, which had previously been banned from politics for decades.

51 established democracies in 1990;

88 in 2012

Religious Rights

Faith is often a matter of government policy, and in some countries is the cornerstone of the state. Almost a quarter of the world's states have a formal link to a religion enshrined in their constitution or laws. What that means in practice varies widely. An official religion can mean intolerance, discrimination, or repression for other faiths – but a state-backed religion has also proved to be compatible with secularism in the state and tolerance in society. The greatest intolerance and violence can spring from religious groups that are, or were at one time, marginalized by the state.

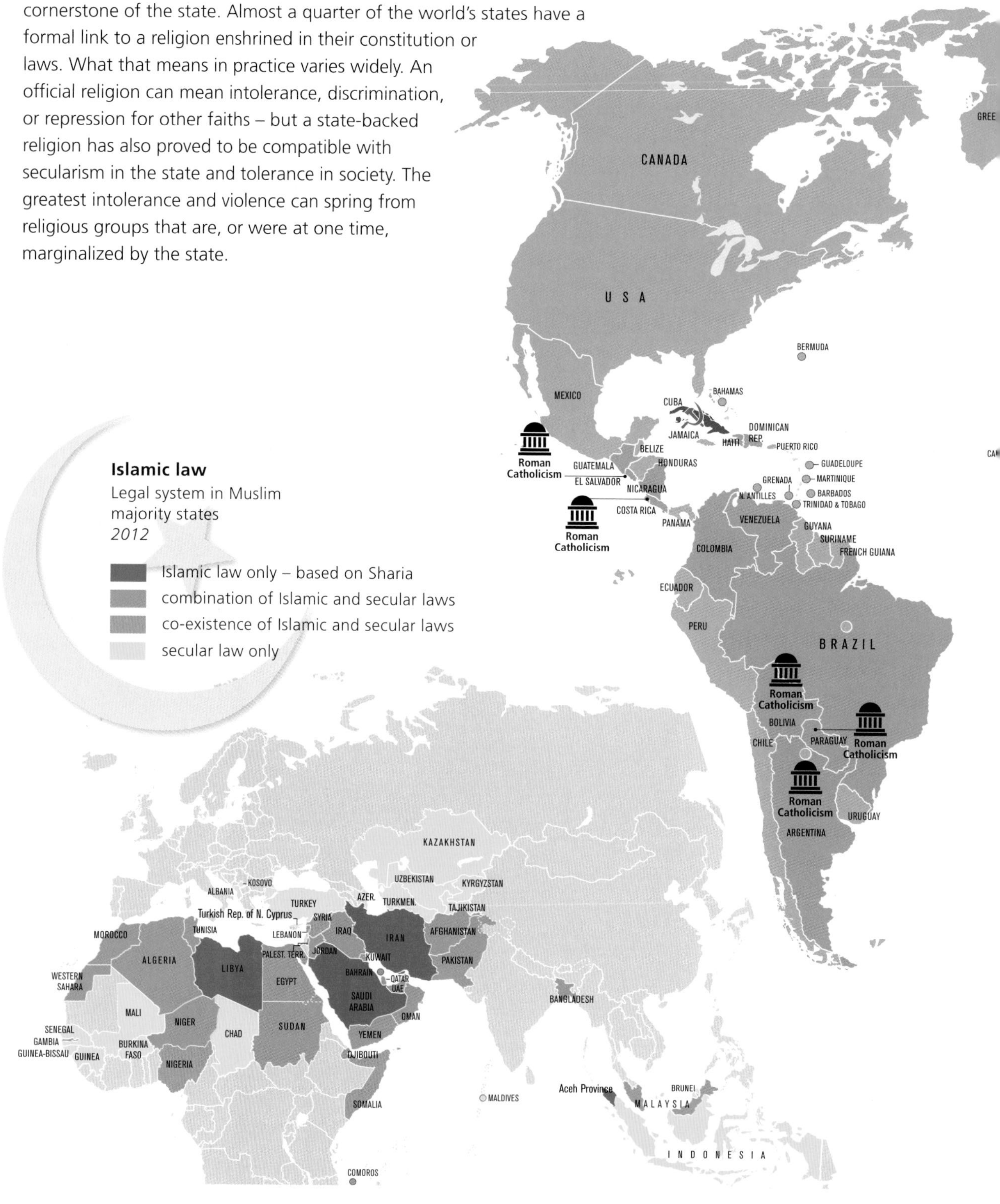

◄ 26 Ethnicity & Diversity; 76 Political Systems

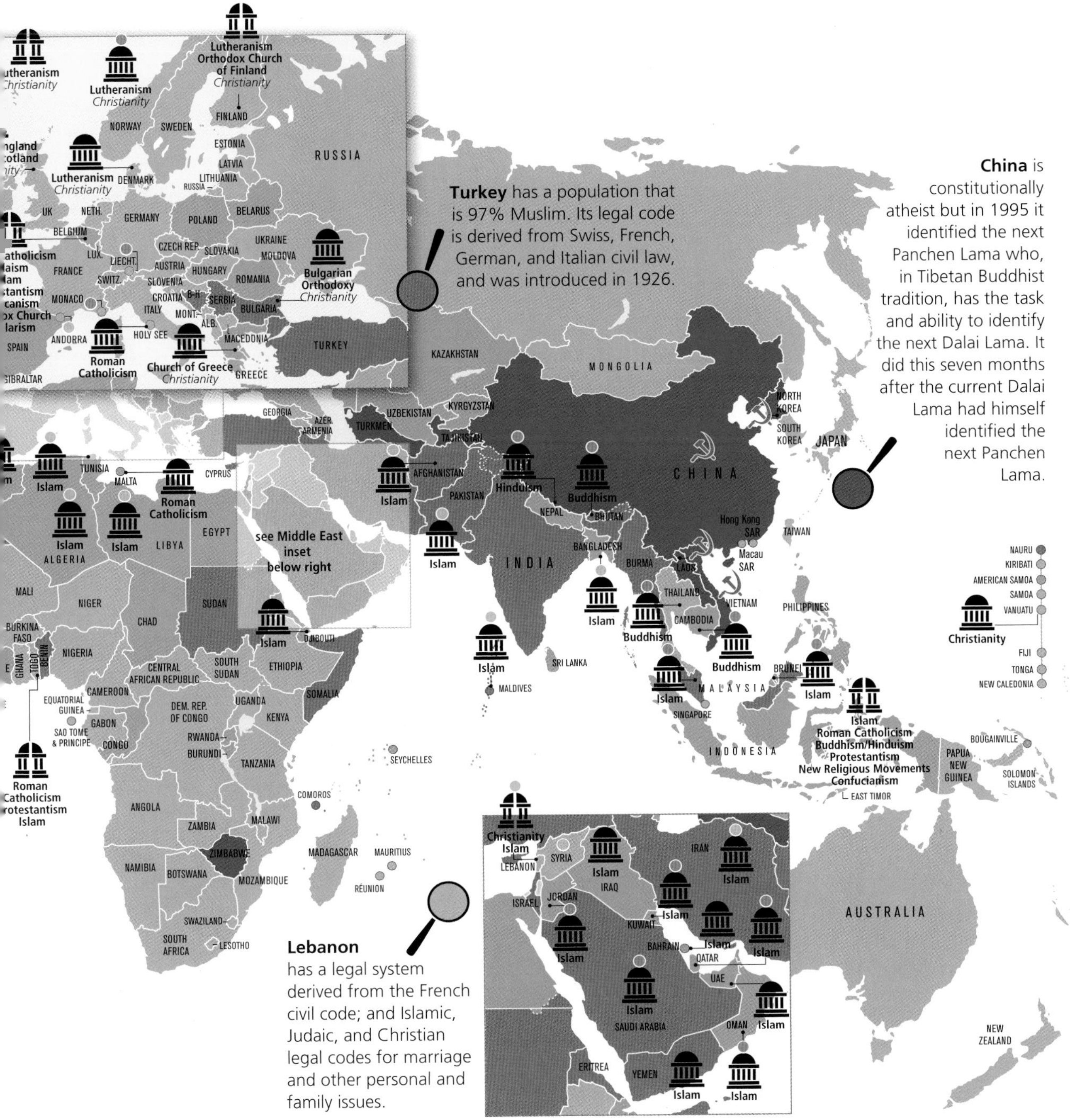

Turkey has a population that is 97% Muslim. Its legal code is derived from Swiss, French, German, and Italian civil law, and was introduced in 1926.

China is constitutionally atheist but in 1995 it identified the next Panchen Lama who, in Tibetan Buddhist tradition, has the task and ability to identify the next Dalai Lama. It did this seven months after the current Dalai Lama had himself identified the next Panchen Lama.

Lebanon has a legal system derived from the French civil code; and Islamic, Judaic, and Christian legal codes for marriage and other personal and family issues.

State attitudes to religion

2012 or latest available data

- discriminates against all religions and interferes with religious freedom
- favours religion of majority and interferes with or limits freedom of other religions
- favours religion of majority but tolerates other religions
- tolerates all religions

- state declared atheist in law
- state religion established in law
- state recognizes more than one religion or religious group
- monarch must be of given religion
- head of state or government must be of given religion

Human Rights Abuses

In some countries the contract of accountable authority between the state and the citizen is missing, and the greatest menace that citizens face comes from the state that should represent, empower, and guard them. In 34 countries, there are credible reports of extra-judicial execution. As with other abuses, the state has not always authorized the actions and may even be trying to stamp them out. Forces within the state often regard themselves as above the law they should staunchly uphold. And non-state groups – militias, gangs, private security guards – are also responsible for extreme abuses in many countries.

The foundational idea of human rights is that there is something special and deserving of respect about every person. Killing people, whether done according to that country's laws or illegally and arbitrarily, reveals an erosion of that respect. Reducing people to commodities, enslaving and trading them reveals something equally malign. Among trafficked women and girls, 95 per cent have been violently assaulted or threatened in order to force them to perform sexual acts.

Extreme abuse of human rights

2011

Worst form of abuse for which there are credible reports:

- extra-judicial executions & other lethal force
- torture
- arbitrary arrest and detention
- mistreatment by police and/or prison authorities
- violent and/or abusive treatment of refugees, asylum seekers, or immigrants
- no human rights abuses recorded
- no data available

Amita, Middle East to UK: Domestic servant, took new job, passport stolen, no pay, no liberty, 16–18 hour working day, raped. Escaped.

Josephine, eastern Congo: Kidnapped by the Lord's Resistance Army, her grandfather killed in front of her, forced labour and sexual services, saw further murders, escaped when sent out to find food and walked 40km to find safety.

Sabine, 23, France: Given by her parents in part payment for a car, used as domestic servant and hired out to men for sex, tortured and beaten, identification papers stolen. Dumped at a hospital when she fell ill. Parents were sentenced to 30 years in prison.

Mylee, Philippines to Saudi Arabia: Went to Saudi Arabia to work as maid, raped repeatedly, escaped after several months.

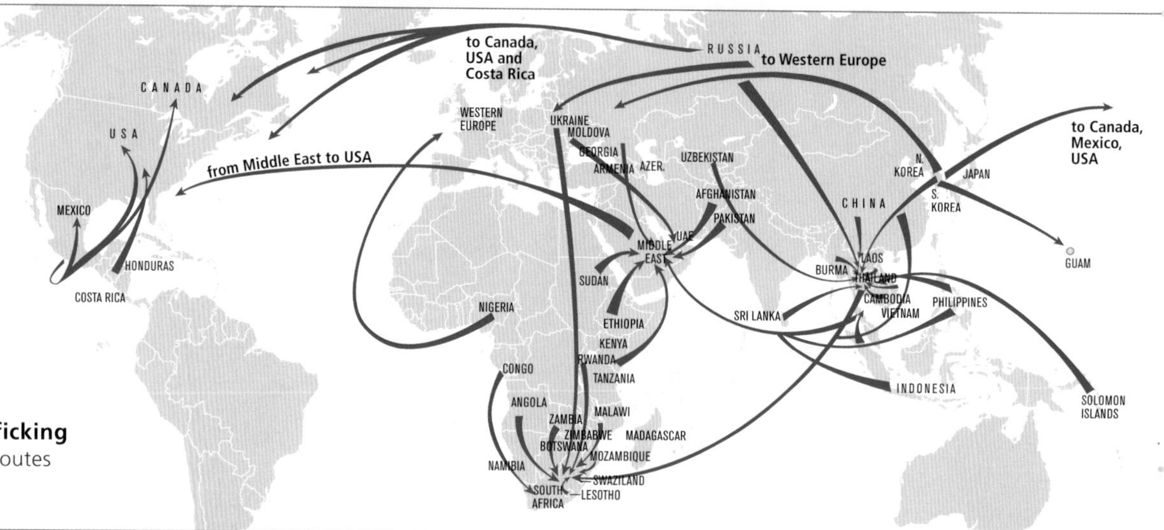

Sex trafficking

Selected routes

2012

Karina, 19, Lima, Peru: Moved to city to work as waitress and fell in love with a man who forced her into sex with men in nightclubs. Escaped after two years.

Maira, 15, Honduras: Recruited with two other girls with offer of work in Houston. Held captive, beaten, raped, and forced to work in cantinas that doubled as brothels. Escaped after six years. Her two friends remain missing.

Alissa, 16, Dallas, USA: Dated and moved in with an older man who persuaded her to work as escort. Tattooed her with his nicknames to brand her as his, and advertised her on internet. Assaulted and threatened her. She escaped.

Olga, 23, Moldova: Went to Dubai for a job. Met at airport by a couple who forced her into prostitution with beatings and threats. She escaped.

◄ 58 War in the 21st Century; 60 Warlords, Ganglords, & Militias

GREENLAND
ICELAND
NORWAY
SWEDEN
FINLAND
EST.
LAT.
LITH.
RUSSIA
DENMARK
IRELAND
UK
NETH.
GERMANY
POLAND
BELARUS
BEL.
LUX.
FRANCE
UKRAINE
MOLD.
ROM.
BUL.
PORTUGAL
SPAIN
HOLY SEE
ITALY
MAC.
ALB.
GREECE
TURKEY
N Cyprus
CYPRUS
MALTA
TUNISIA
S. Ossetia
Abkhazia
GEO.
ARM.
AZER.
KAZAKHSTAN
UZBEKISTAN
TURKMEN.
KYRGYZSTAN
TAJIKISTAN
MONGOLIA
N. KOREA
S. KOREA
JAPAN
CHINA
SYRIA
LEB.
ISRAEL
PALEST. TERR.
JORDAN
IRAQ
IRAN
KUWAIT
BAHRAIN
QATAR
UAE
AFGHANISTAN
PAKISTAN
NEPAL
BHUTAN
INDIA
BANGLADESH
BURMA
LAOS
THAILAND
CAMBODIA
VIETNAM
TAIWAN
PHILIPPINES
MOROCCO
ALGERIA
LIBYA
EGYPT
SAUDI ARABIA
OMAN
YEMEN
WESTERN SAHARA
MAURITANIA
MALI
NIGER
CHAD
SUDAN
ERITREA
DJIBOUTI
Somaliland
Puntland
CAPE VERDE
SENEGAL
GAMBIA
GUINEA-BISSAU
GUINEA
SIERRA LEONE
LIBERIA
CÔTE D'IVOIRE
B.F.
GHANA
TOGO
BENIN
NIGERIA
C.A.R.
SOUTH SUDAN
ETHIOPIA
SOMALIA
CAM.
EQ. GUINEA
SÃO TOME & PRINCIPE
GABON
CONGO
D.R. CONGO
UGANDA
KENYA
RWANDA
BURUNDI
TANZANIA
SEYCHELLES
COMOROS
ANGOLA
ZAMBIA
MALAWI
ZIMBABWE
NAMIBIA
BOTSWANA
MOZAMBIQUE
MADAGASCAR
MAURITIUS
SWAZILAND
LESOTHO
SOUTH AFRICA
SRI LANKA
MALDIVES
BRUNEI
MALAYSIA
SINGAPORE
INDONESIA
EAST TIMOR
PNG
PALAU
AUSTRALIA
NEW ZEALAND
MICRONESIA
MARSHALL IS.
NAURU
KIRIBATI
TUVALU
SAMOA
VANUATU
FIJI
TONGA
NEW CALEDONIA
FRENCH POLYNESIA
SURINAME
FRENCH GUIANA
BARBADOS
ST VINCENT & GREN.
URUGUAY

Slavery in the fishing fleet
Most crew members on Thai-owned long-haul fishing vessels off Indonesia and the Philippines are Burmese and Cambodians, many of whom are forced or conned into work and then imprisoned on the boats for months or even years.

MT
SD
WY
NE
UT
CO
AZ
OK
TX
MO
AR
LA
MS
ALA
GA
FL
SC
NC
TN
KY
IN
OH
PA
VA
MD
DE
USA
BAHAMAS
CUBA
BELIZE
JAMAICA
GUATEMALA
EL SALVADOR
ST KITTS & NEVIS
ANTIGUA & BARBUDA
DOMINICA
ST LUCIA
BARBADOS
ST VINCENT & G.
GREN.
TRINIDAD & TOBAGO
GUYANA
SURINAM
BRAZIL
BOLIVIA
CHILE
RUSSIA
LATVIA
BELARUS
KAZAKHSTAN
MONGOLIA
N. K.
S. K.
JAPAN
CHINA
TAJ.
AFGHANISTAN
PAKISTAN
IRAN
IRAQ
SYRIA
LEB.
ISRAEL
P. T.
JORDAN
KUWAIT
BAHRAIN
QATAR
UAE
SAUDI ARABIA
OMAN
YEMEN
TUNISIA
MOROCCO
ALGERIA
LIBYA
EGYPT
MAURITANIA
MALI
NIGER
CHAD
SUDAN
ER.
GAMBIA
GUINEA
B. F.
S. L.
LIBERIA
GHANA
BEN.
NIGERIA
CAM.
C.A.R.
S. SUDAN
ETHIOPIA
SOMALIA
EQ. G.
CONGO
D.R. CONGO
UGANDA
KENYA
TANZ.
COMOROS
ZAMBIA
MALAWI
ZIMBABWE
BOTSWANA
MADAGASCAR
SWAZ.
LESOTHO
INDIA
BANGLADESH
BURMA
LAOS
THAILAND
VIETNAM
TAIWAN
SRI LANKA
MALDIVES
BRUNEI
MALAYSIA
SINGAPORE
INDONESIA
PNG
MICRONESIA
MARSHALL IS.
NAURU
KIRIBATI
TUVALU
SAMOA
VANUATU
FIJI
COOK IS.
NIUE
TONGA
PALAU

Judicial killings
Status of death penalty
2011
retentionist
retains death penalty for ordinary crimes
abolitionist for ordinary crimes only
law provides for death penalty only for exceptional crimes such as crimes under military law or crimes committed in exceptional circumstances
abolitionist in practice
retains death penalty for ordinary crimes such as murder but has not executed anyone during past 10 years and is believed to have a policy or established practice of not carrying out executions
abolitionist for all crimes
law does not provide for the death penalty for any crime
no data

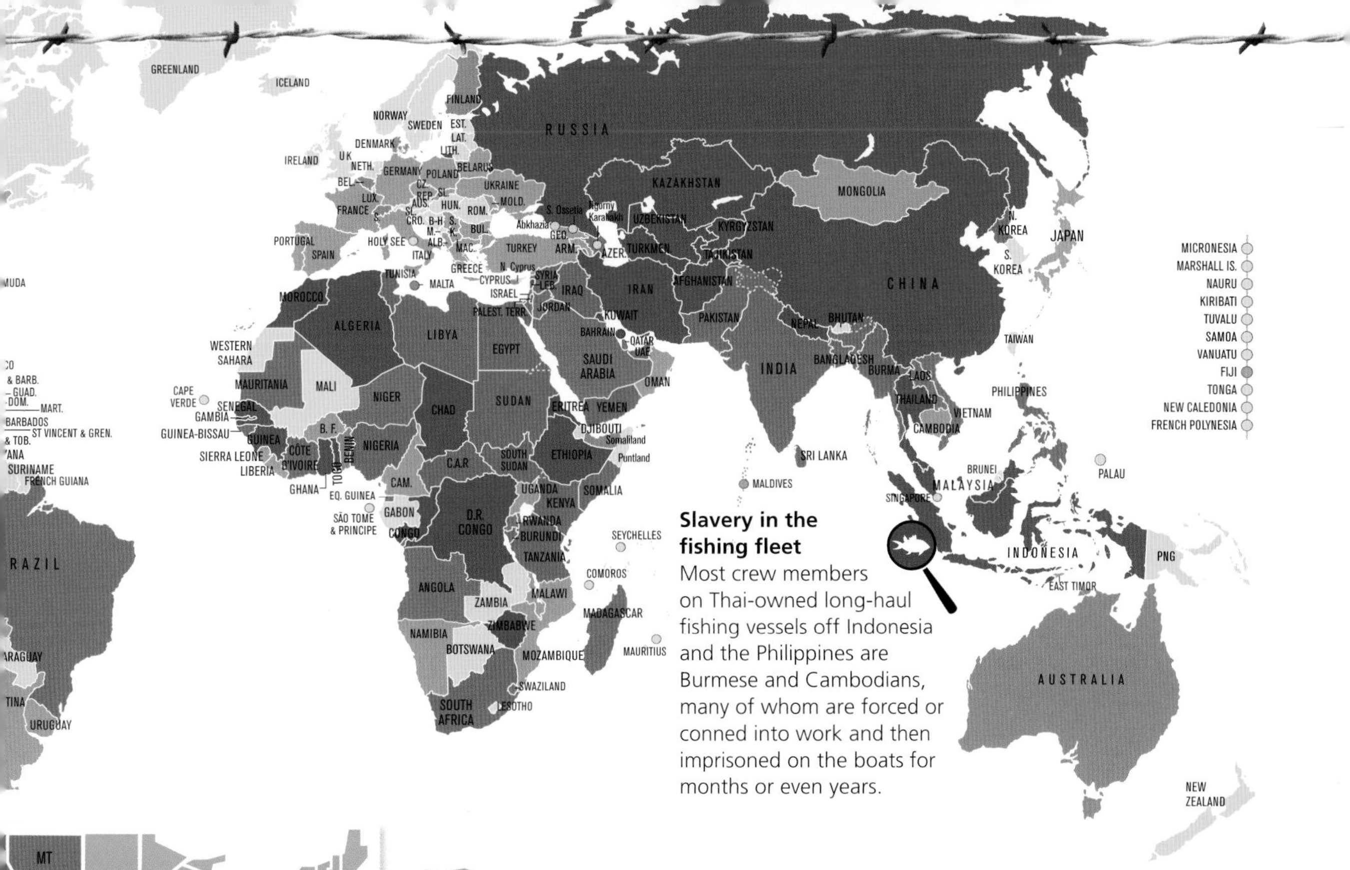

Children's Rights

As with other groups, respect for the rights of children is steadily improving – yet that only throws into starker relief the abuses that continue. Too many children are not registered at birth, which deprives them of the rights and recognition of citizenship before they even get started in life. In developing countries, one child in six between the ages of 5 and 14 is in work, often doing tasks that will cripple them in later years. One child in eight who should be attending primary school does not – a total of 67 million absentees between the ages of 5 and 11. And just over 40 per cent of them live in countries affected by violent conflicts.

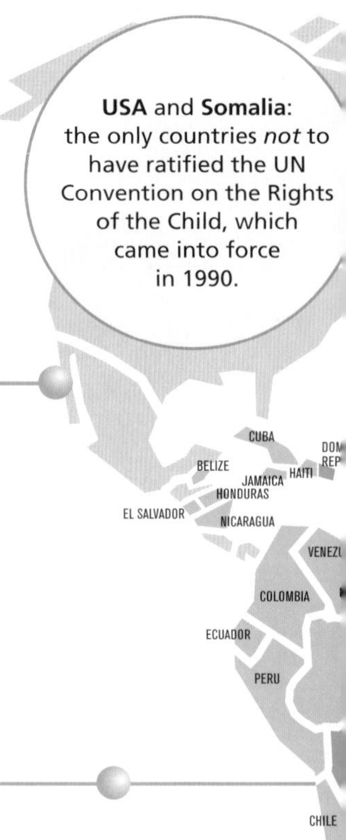

Where children are working
Economically active children aged 5–14 years as percentage of age-group
2008

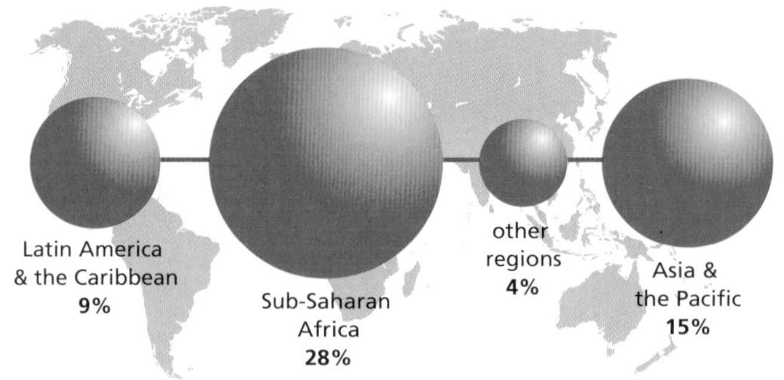

Children at risk
Number of children employed in hazardous work
2004 & 2008

Hazardous work includes any of the following: work underground, under water, high up, carrying heavy loads, exposure to hazardous substances, use of dangerous equipment, or physical, sexual or psychological abuse.

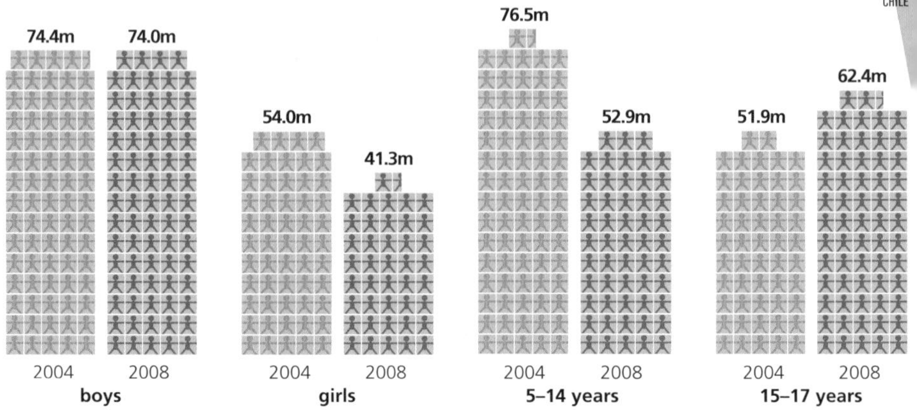

Children not in school
Percentage of school-age children not attending school by region
2009 or latest available data

● not in school
● in school

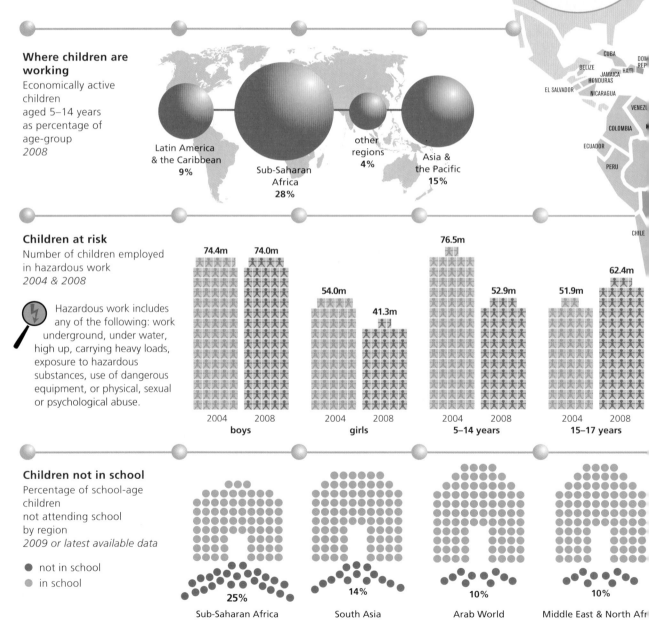

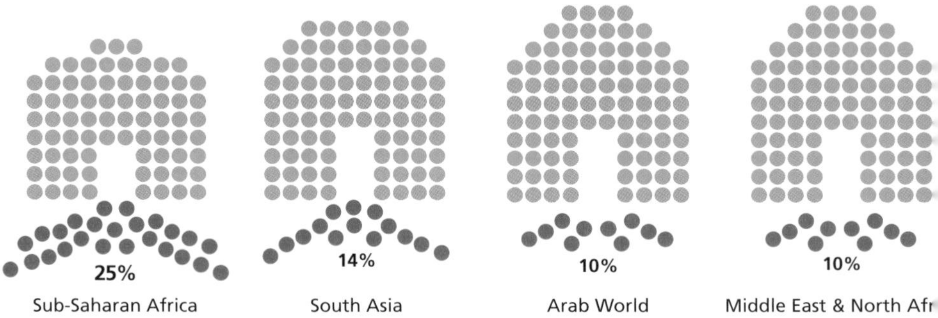

◄ *30 Literacy & Education; 60 Warlords, Ganglords, & Militias*

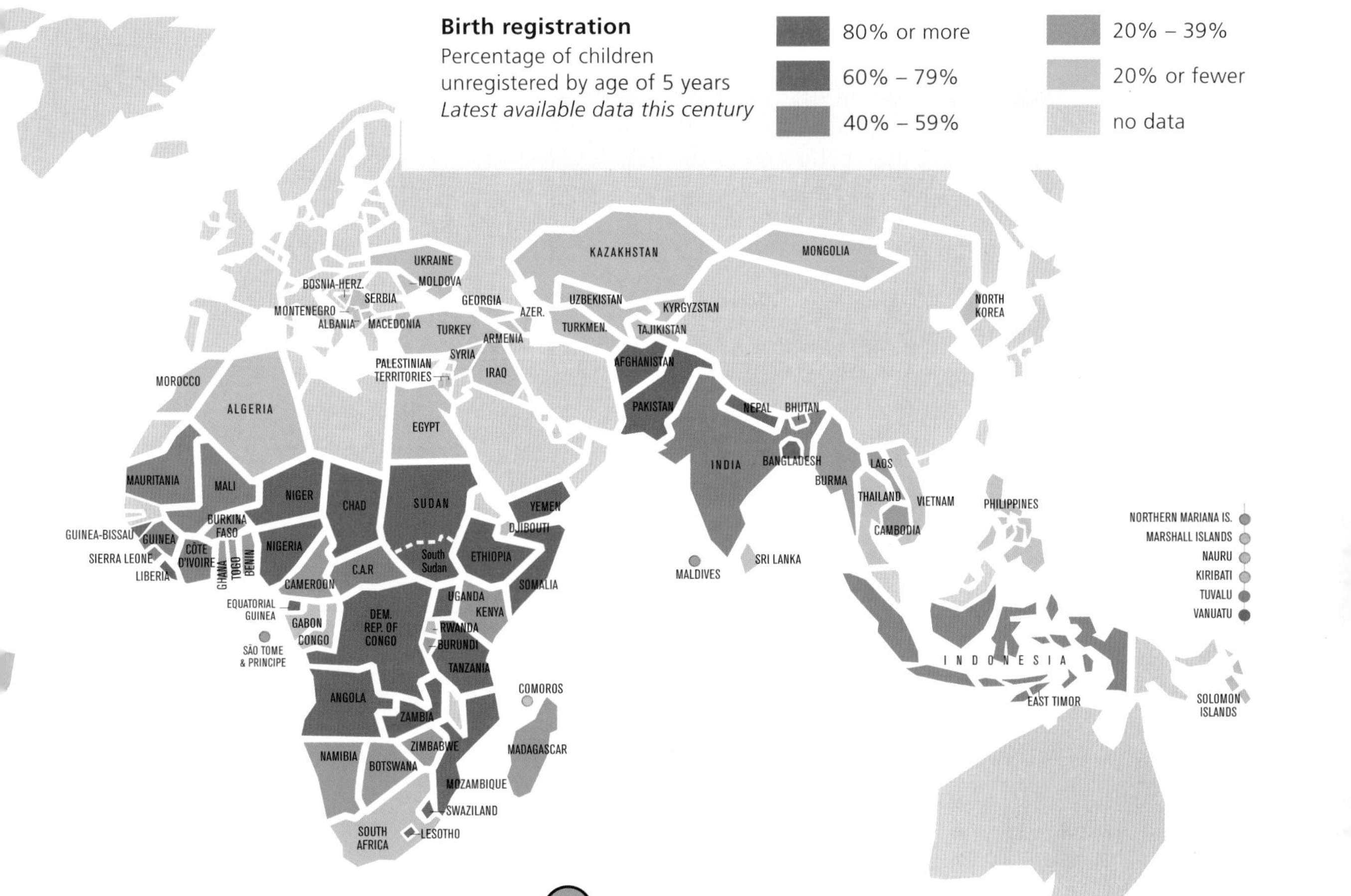

Afghanistan: 613 attacks on schools in 2009
Yemen: 220 schools destroyed, damaged or looted during fighting, 2009–10
Gaza: Israeli bombardment in 2008–09 damaged 280 schools, killed 350 children, injured 1,815.

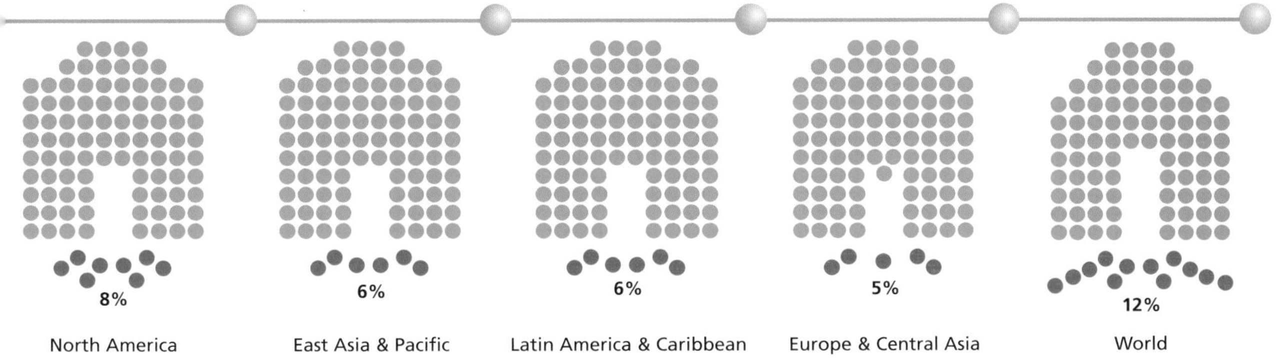

Women's Rights

Everywhere, recognition of the equal rights of women is advancing, but the pace is highly uneven. In the 1950s, women as heads of democratic governments were unknown; in the 1960s and 1970s, they were a rarity; in the 1980s and 1990s they were uncommon but getting steadily less so. Yet today the question remains, why so few? Only 49 democratic countries have ever had a woman head of government, even counting appointed prime ministers in presidential systems.

In business it's even more unusual to find a woman in charge: only 12 of the 500 largest corporations in the world have a female CEO. In the UK, the Equal Pay Act entered force in 1972; 40 years later, full-time working women still earn 15 per cent less an hour than their male counterparts. And some 600 million women – more than half the world's working women – have insecure jobs, often outside the purview of labour law.

Women in parliament
Proportion of seats in national parliaments held by women
2011

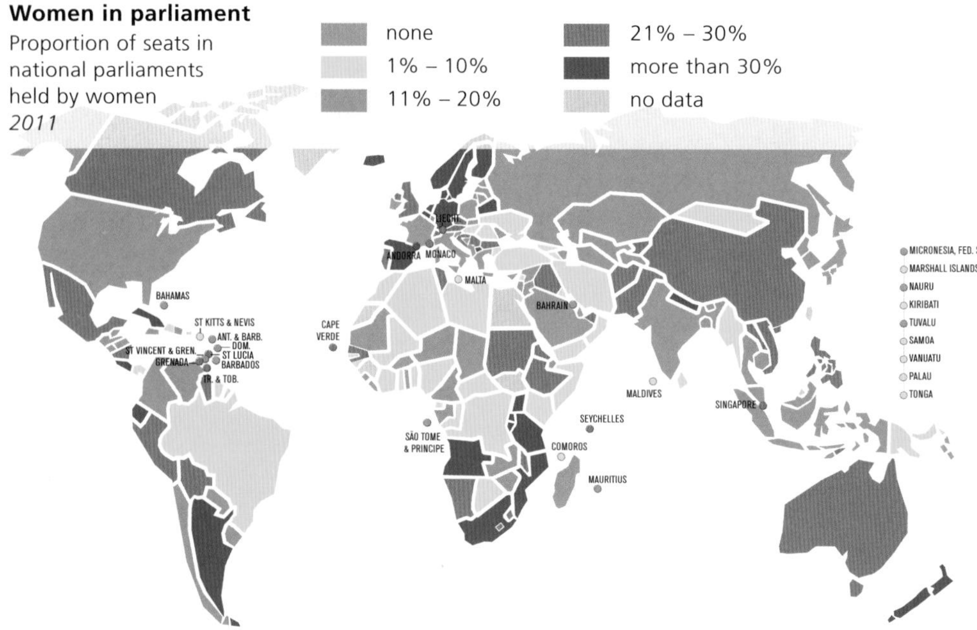

The first female head of government in a democratic country was Sirimavo Bandaranaike in Sri Lanka in 1960. Over the next 40 years she spent 17 and a half as Prime Minister, the last six of them serving under her daughter, President Kumaratunga.

Women in government
Number of countries with female heads of government each year since 1960s

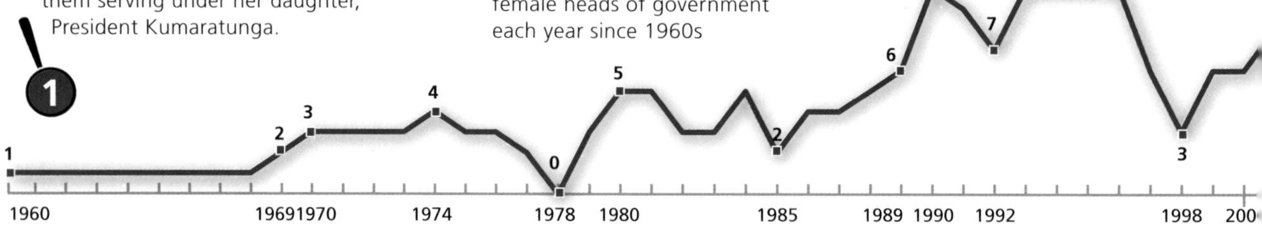

◀ 54 Goals for Development; 76 Political Systems

Equal rights

Gender Inequality Index score *2011*

- 0.71 or more *least equal*
- 0.51 – 0.70
- 0.31 – 0.50
- 0.11 – 0.30
- 0.05 – 0.10 *most equal*
- no data

Gender Inequality Index trends *2000–11*

- improvement in equality of 0.10 or more
- decline in equality

The Gender Inequality Index is a composite measure that reflects inequality in achievements between women and men in three dimensions: reproductive health, empowerment, and the labour market.

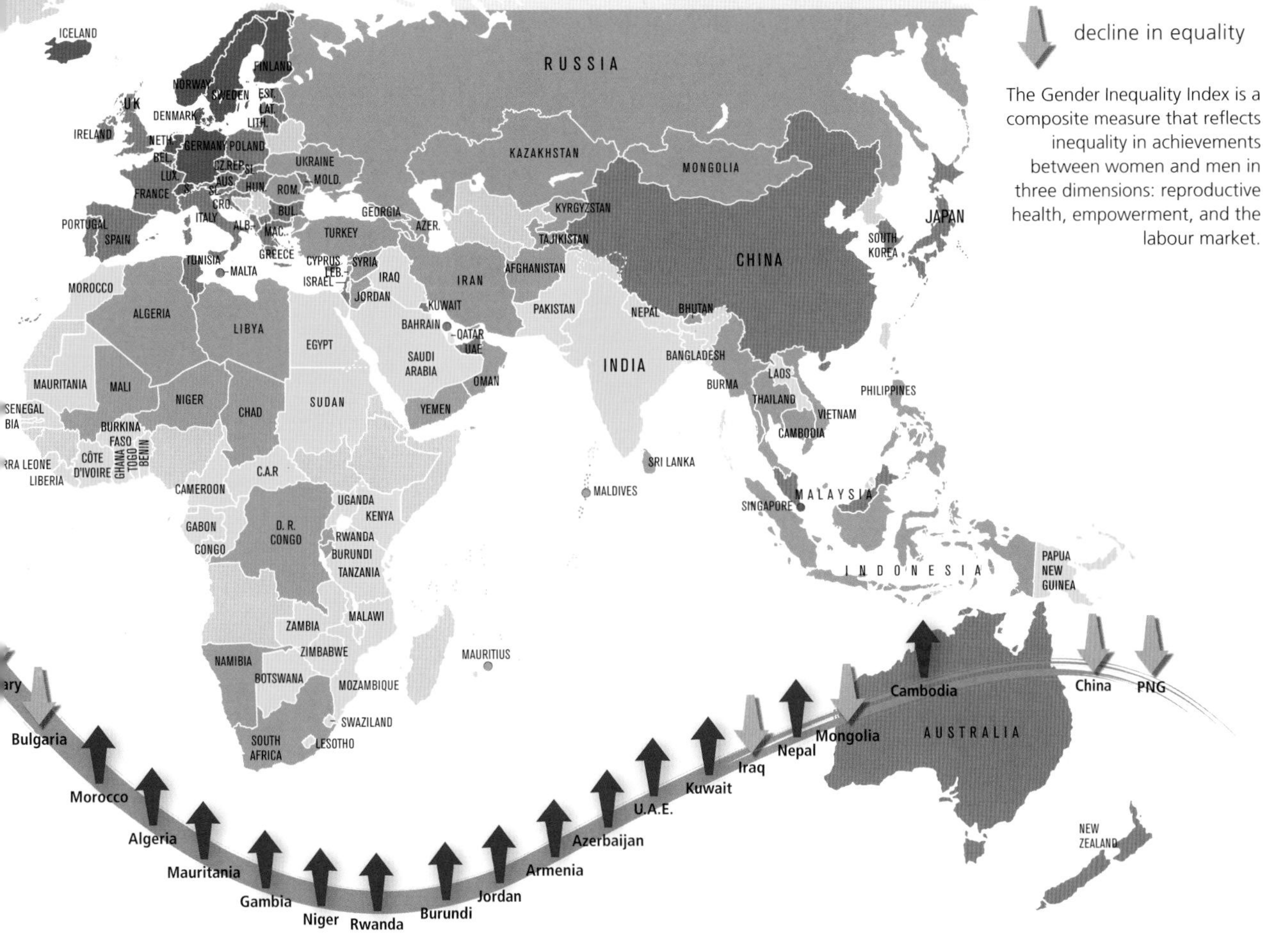

Women as head of government

In democratic countries

- in post early 2012
- at least one since 1960, but not in 2012
- never

Excluding ceremonial heads of state and short-term acting prime ministers. *Including* appointed prime ministers in a democratic presidential system and heads of governments attempting the transition to democracy.

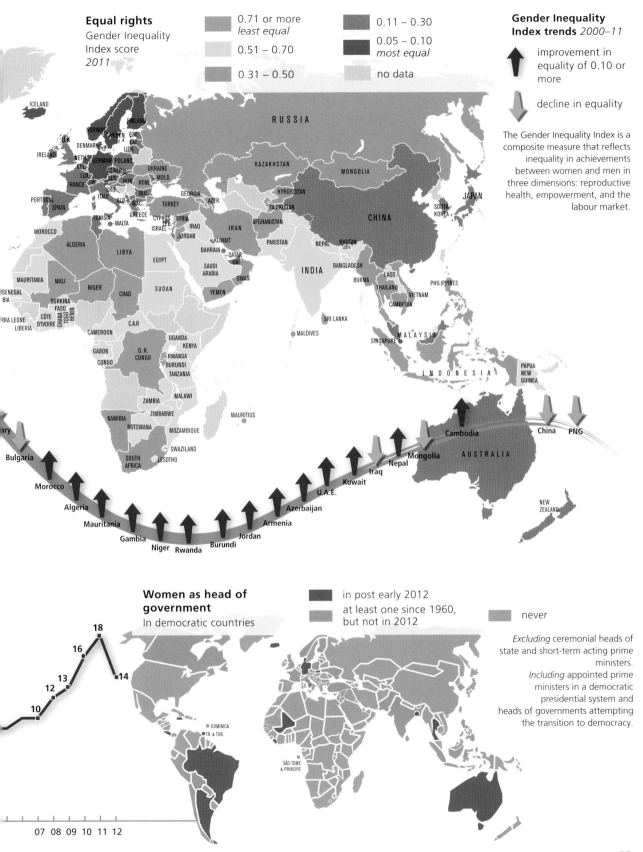

Gay Rights

There are 113 countries where sexual activity and relationships between people of the same sex are legally allowed, 76 where they are illegal. But the reality experienced by gay people is much more diverse than that implies. There remain many countries where same-sex relations are legal for women but not men, many countries where social reality is more oppressive than the law, and others where it is more liberal. The extent of legal rights varies considerably, even in countries where homosexuality is legal – just as the degree of punishment varies where it is illegal.

The acceptability or not of gays serving in the military is an interesting litmus test of the degree to which acceptance of homosexuality is normalized and people are treated as citizens – with the same rights, duties and choices – regardless of sexual preference.

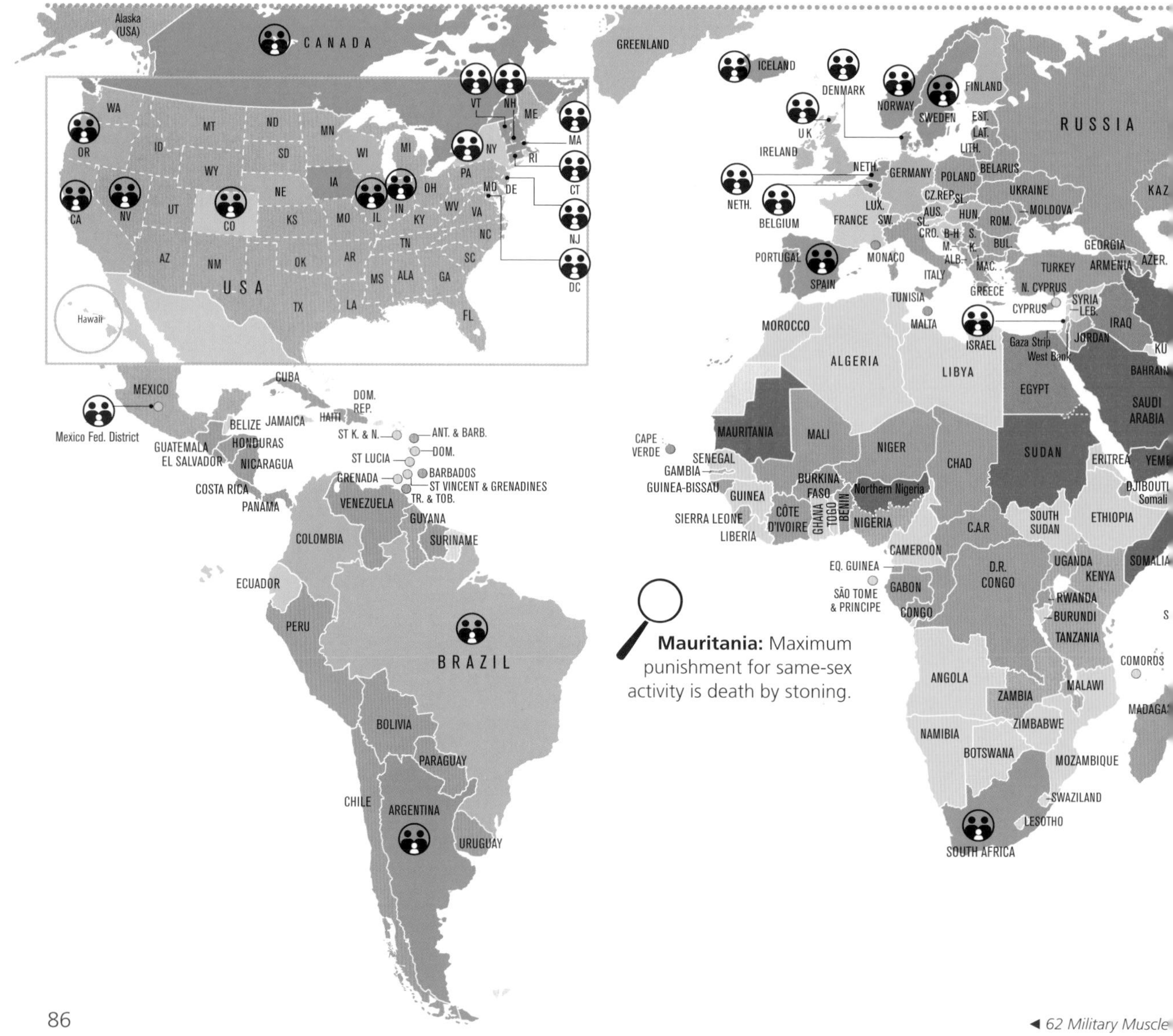

◄ 62 Military Muscle

The right to serve

2011

- gays may serve in the military
- gays may not serve in the military
- no data

Legal status of same-sex sexual acts and relationships

2011

Punishment where illegal:

- death penalty
- prison sentence over 10 years
- prison sentence up to 10 years

Extent of rights where legal:

- same-sex acts legal but no legal status for same-sex relationships
- same-sex couples have some rights of union/marriage
- civil partnership/union allowed
- full marriage rights for same-sex couples
- legal status unclear

The right to adopt

- joint adoption by same-sex couples allowed

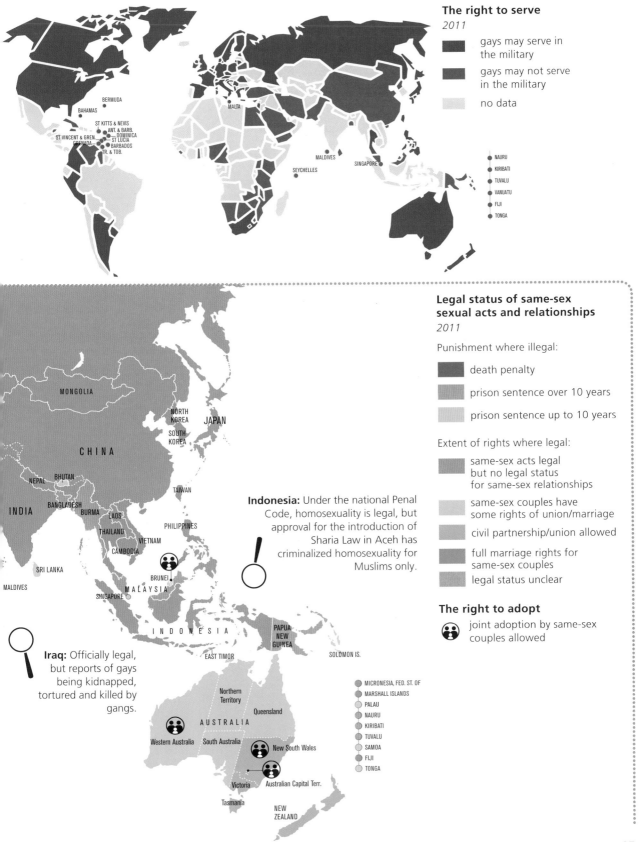

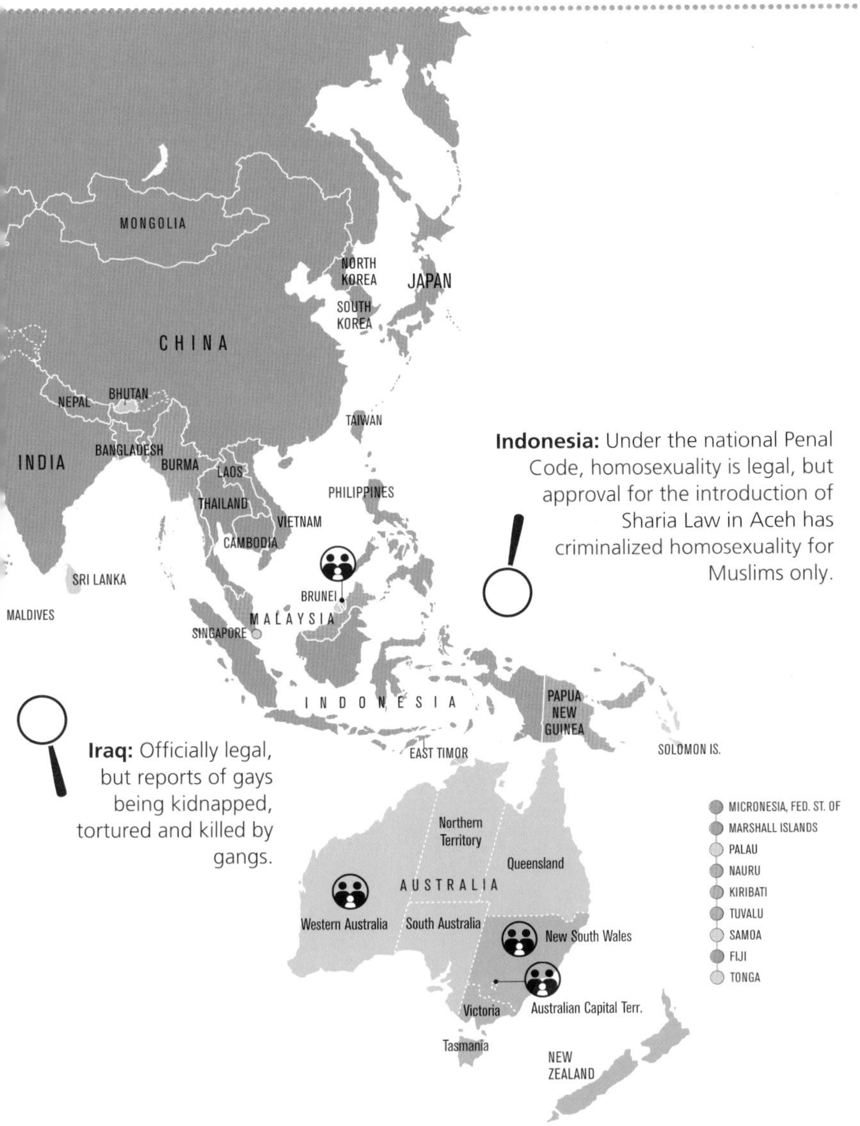

Indonesia: Under the national Penal Code, homosexuality is legal, but approval for the introduction of Sharia Law in Aceh has criminalized homosexuality for Muslims only.

Iraq: Officially legal, but reports of gays being kidnapped, tortured and killed by gangs.

PART FIVE

HEALTH OF THE PEOPLE

The health of the people is in many ways a reflection of the health of a society. Good health is a basic need, and access to good health care is a basic right. It is acknowledged as a central part of the contract between state and citizen in many countries, even if in much of the world it has no traction and no reality. The ability to provide proper health care is a sign that at least part of the energy of the society is put towards caring for its members. So in many countries, the inability – or in some, the refusal – to provide proper health care is a sign of how far society has to go before it is really upholding ordinary citizens' well-being.

The other side of this coin is less about collective action and more about the individual. For good health is not only a result of the care that people receive from properly trained personnel in properly equipped clinics and hospitals, it is also a result of the care we take of ourselves. Care for ourselves and care for others, when balanced, are intimately bound together. Even where large-scale provision for health care is possible and achieved, people's health and longevity can still vary significantly. And countries that, if judged by wealth alone, have very different capacities for providing health care for their populations sometimes turn out to have very similar results, because of how resources are organized and how people take care of their own health.

Malnutrition persists, and the number of undernourished people in a world that steadily gets richer has remained stubbornly steady for two decades – albeit in a rising population so the proportion of undernourished is falling. But the opposite problem, obesity, is now a global epidemic. It is one of the life-style ailments of a changing world, contributing to serious diseases.

The deficiencies revealed by the persistence of undernourishment are largely about scarcity and inadequate resources to maintain a decent and healthy way of living. On the other side, part of the problem revealed by the obesity epidemic is the difficulty people have escaping the trap of their own appetites and patterns of consumption. These are often not just social habits but effective physiological dependence on the animal fats and sugars that cheap processed foods contain.

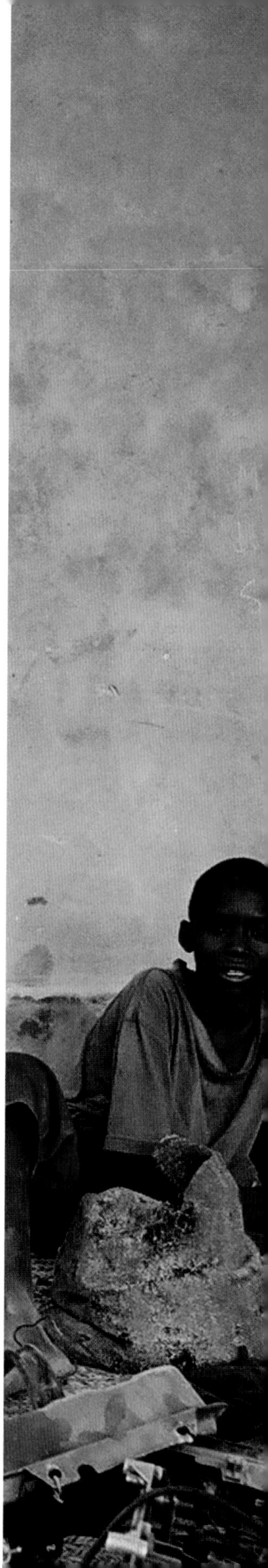

Even more is this the case with smoking. Tobacco is addictive and remains the only legal, mass-marketed consumable in which harm is inherent in the core function. It is not a side effect, nor a result of using it wrongly; use tobacco as advertised and harm ensues. It is one of the five main life-style causes of cancer.

But if a consideration of obesity and smoking leads us to think about human short-sightedness and capacity for self-harm, looking at health issues is also inspiring. Resources and knowledge have been mobilized that are capable of defeating diseases. There is no cure for HIV/AIDS but its spread has been stopped and numbers of deaths and new infections are declining. Likewise, many forms of cancer are treatable or preventable; the advance of medical science has opened the path towards eventually defeating it.

With health, however, as with almost everything, the distribution of resources and therefore of access to treatment and preventive education is unequal. Richer countries inevitably have better access to both. As a result, despite scientific advances, the estimated incidence of cancer is expected to double by 2030. For mental and behavioural disorders, the number of known sufferers is proportionately about the same in high-income and low-income countries, but the difference between *per capita* spending on medicines in high-and low-income countries respectively is over 1,500 to 1; for antipsychotic drugs, it is over 2,700 to 1.

Health is a development issue, not only because greater economic development tends to bring about better health care and better public health as clean water and sanitation facilities are provided, but also because a population weakened by illness is less economically productive. The relatively light disease burdens of the richer countries – and a few striking cases such as Libya (under Gaddafi, interestingly enough) and Cuba – are part of the benefits of their economic growth. And the heavy disease burdens of some other countries not only reflect but also contribute to their weaker economic performance.

Beyond a country's wealth, however, a considerable body of statistics shows that fairness and equality are good for public health. Among the richer countries, it is the more egalitarian that have the best health records – both in physical and mental health. The social fabric that contributes to even, friendly relations, eases health issues by encouraging people to help and take the pressure off each other. High levels of income inequality appear to inflict damage on that fabric by highlighting the divisions in society.

Overall, huge advances have been registered – and all other things being equal, will presumably continue to be registered – in the treatment of diseases including cancer. This brings enormous relief to millions of people. Meanwhile, alongside the ailments brought us by nature and by our natural physiology, the way we live and behave continues to generate the problems that medical science has to solve. The next step, surely, is to figure out how to live better.

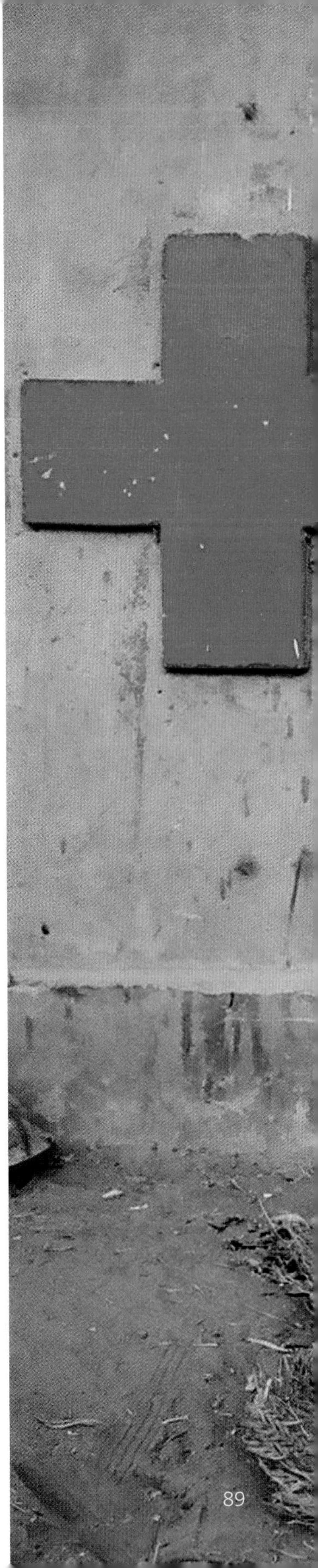

Malnutrition

For the past two decades the number of undernourished people worldwide has remained stubbornly steady, although undernourished people now represent a smaller proportion of an increased global population. Deficiencies in diet are as serious a problem as insufficiencies of food. The absence of vitamins in daily intake can lead to crushing ailments.

Food prices soared in 2007 to 2008, leading to serious violence in at least 30 countries. The economic crunch of 2008 to 2009 (and longer in some countries) raised fears that, even in some rich countries, hunger would return and undernourishment rise again. In 2012, the combined impact of severe drought in the USA – a major food supplier to the world – and floods and drought elsewhere was predicted to raise global food prices once more.

Food price rise
2007–08

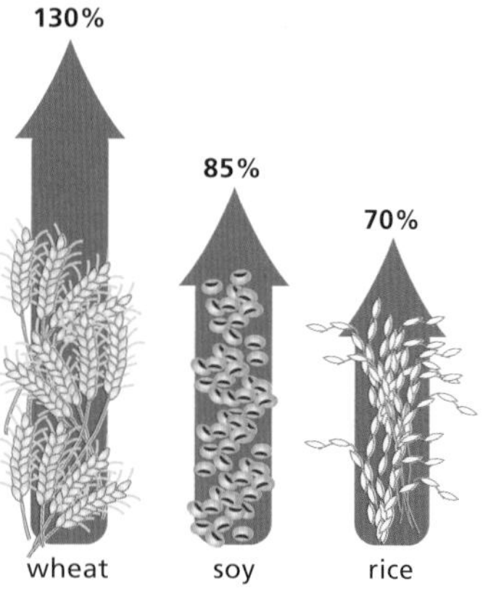

Trends in undernourishment
1990–2010

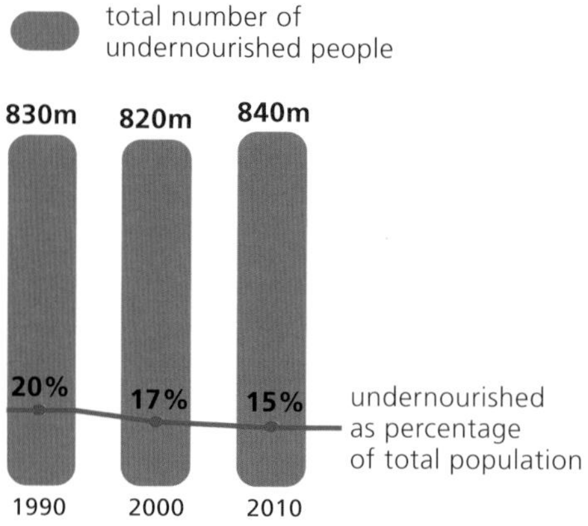

Vitamin A deficiency
2000s

Too little Vitamin A in the diet leads to the risk of blindness.

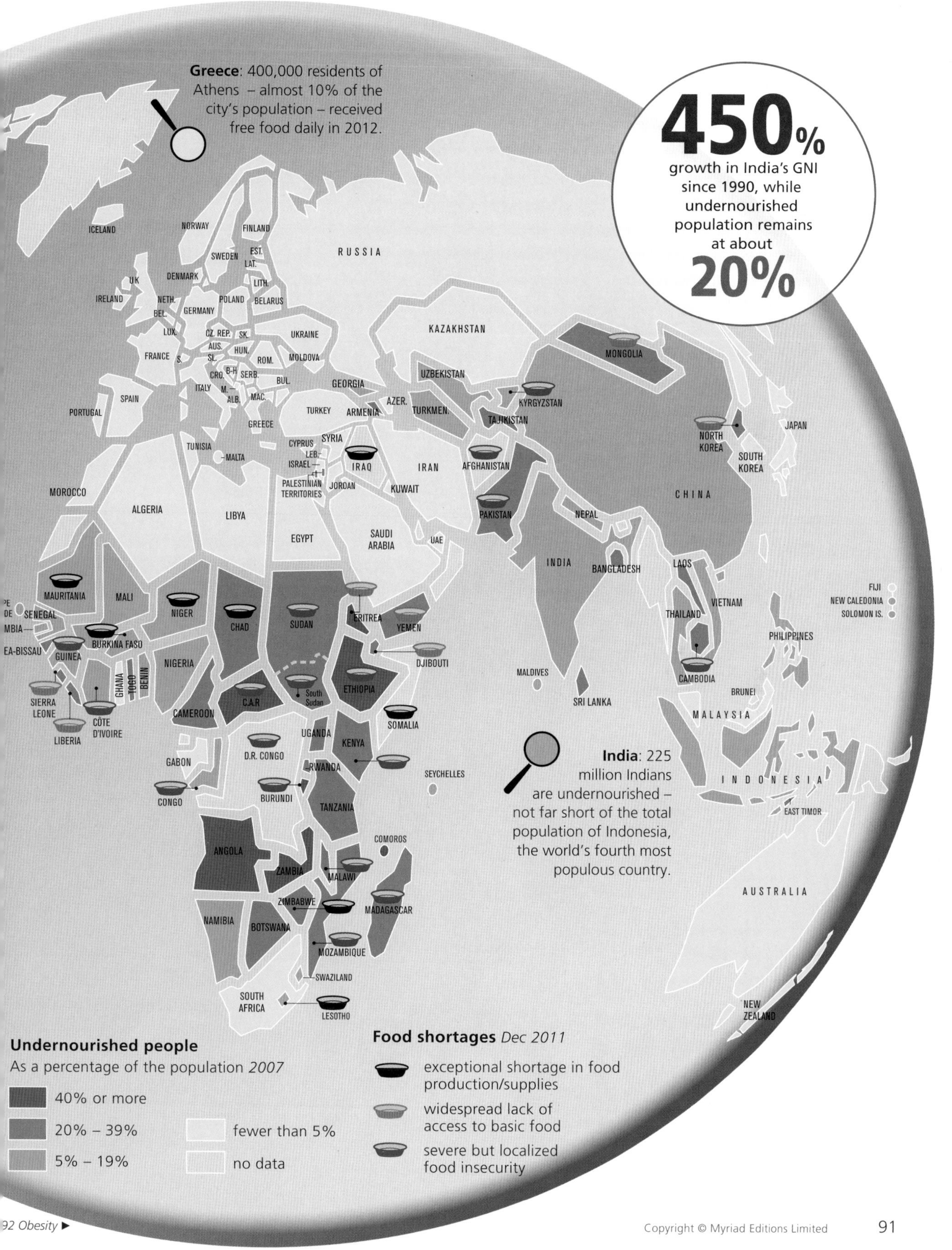

Greece: 400,000 residents of Athens – almost 10% of the city's population – received free food daily in 2012.

450% growth in India's GNI since 1990, while undernourished population remains at about **20%**

India: 225 million Indians are undernourished – not far short of the total population of Indonesia, the world's fourth most populous country.

Undernourished people
As a percentage of the population *2007*

- 40% or more
- 20% – 39%
- 5% – 19%
- fewer than 5%
- no data

Food shortages *Dec 2011*

- exceptional shortage in food production/supplies
- widespread lack of access to basic food
- severe but localized food insecurity

92 Obesity ▶

Obesity

With 1.5 billion adults – more than a fifth of the global population – overweight or obese, and the incidence of obesity more than double that of 1980, the World Health Organization has declared obesity a global epidemic.

Two-thirds of the world's population live in countries where there are more deaths from excess weight than from undernourishment. Cheap processed foods are particularly high in animal fats and sugars. In rich countries, the unhealthy diet of those on low incomes and in poverty is fuelling the obesity epidemic, which is in turn contributing to serious diseases. Health services are struggling to cope with the strain.

Increased risk of disease

Percentage of cases attributable to being overweight or obese
2008

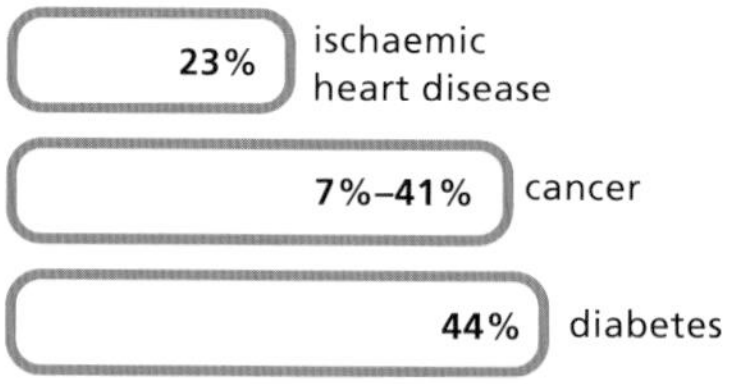

America growing obese

Obese adults in USA as percentage of total population
1990, 2000, 2010

30% or more
25% – 29%
20% – 24%
15% – 19%
10% – 14%
less than 10%
no data

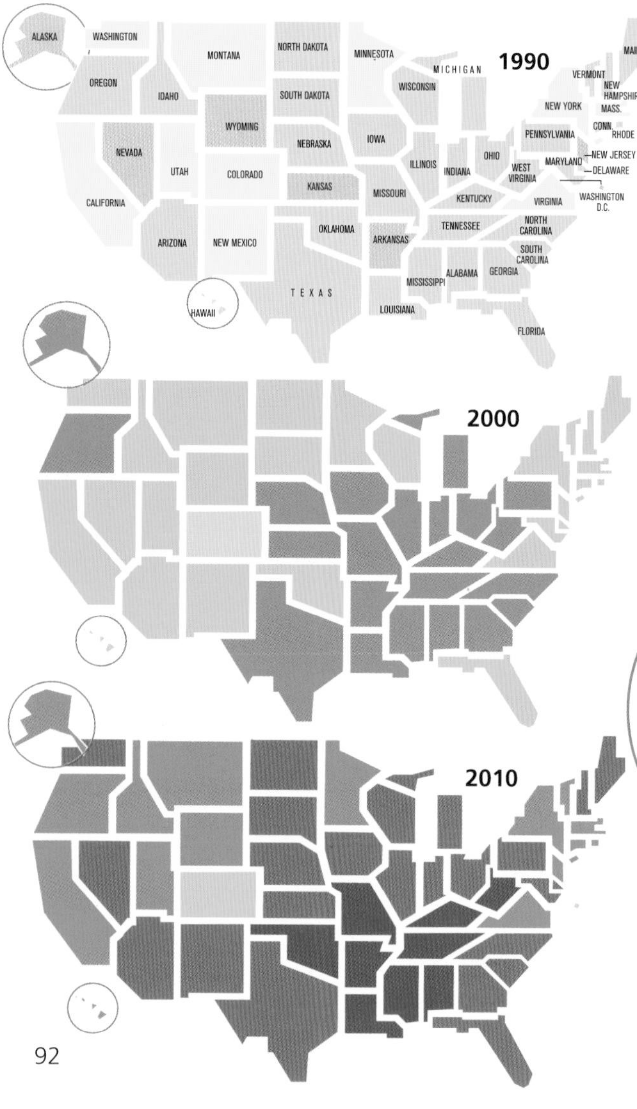

USA: By 2010, about 12.5 million children and adolescents – 17% of the population aged 2 to 19 years – were obese, over three times the rate in 1980.

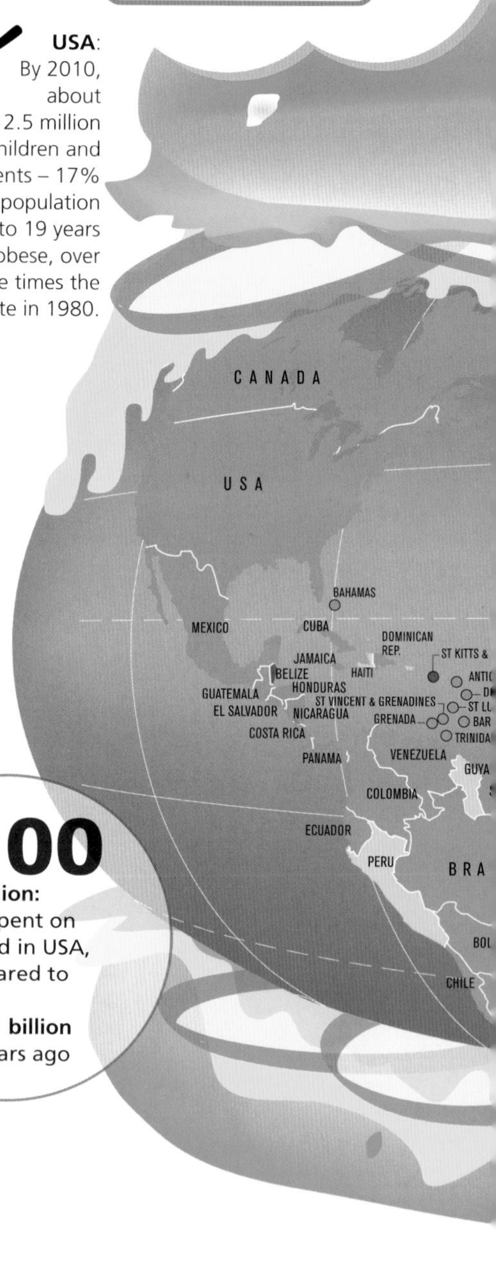

$100 billion:
total spent on fast food in USA, compared to
$3 billion
40 years ago

◀ 90 Malnutrition

Overweight adults

Percentage of people aged 20+ years with a BMI of 25 or more (overweight)
2008

- 70% or more
- 50% – 69%
- 25% – 49%
- 10% – 24%
- fewer than 10%
- no data

A BMI (Body Mass Index) score equals a person's weight (in kg) divided by their height (in metres) squared.
BMI scores are categorized as follows:
under 18.5: underweight
18.5 – 24.9: healthy
25.0 – 29.9: overweight
30.0 and over: obese

Smoking

Tobacco smoke contains 4,000 known chemicals, of which at least 250 are harmful and 50 cause cancers. Between a third and a half of smokers die from tobacco-related diseases, losing on average 15 years compared to life expectancy. Of the 6 million currently dying each year from tobacco-related causes, 600,000 are non-smokers, dying because of other people's smoking.

Tobacco causes a death every six seconds. Compared to 100 million deaths from tobacco in the 20th century, current trends are for up to 1 billion tobacco-related deaths by the end of the 21st.

Where cigarettes are being smoked
Share of total consumption by region
2007

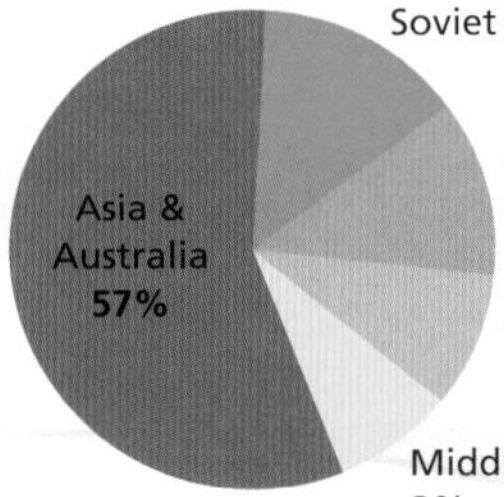

17 billion cigarettes are smoked each day **12 million** each minute

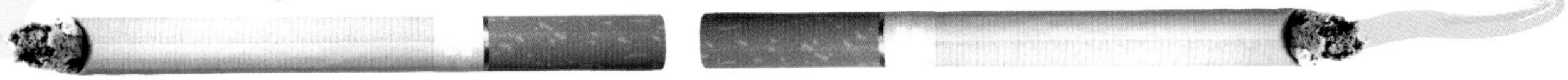

Deaths
Annual toll
2005–09, projected 2009–30
millions

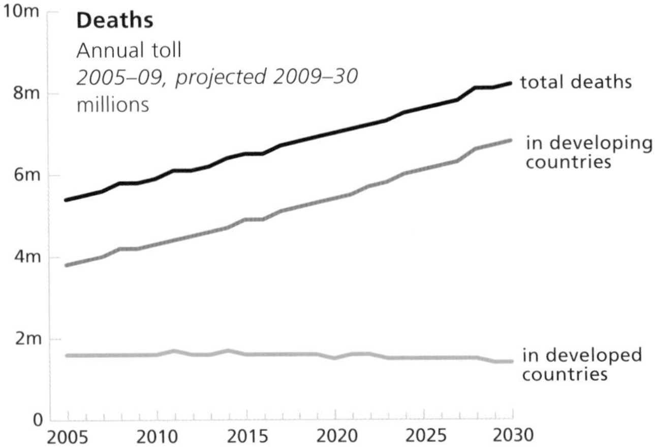

10%
of adult deaths are due to tobacco

Global cigarette consumption
Total number of cigarettes smoked each year
1880–2020 projected
billions

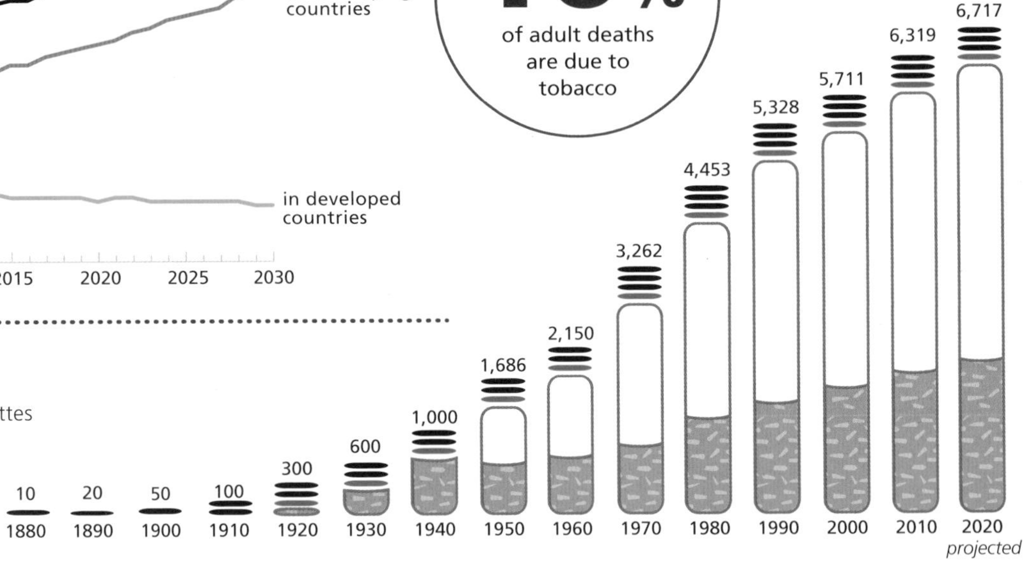

Spreading the word
Countries where there was at least one anti-tobacco national mass media campaign
2009–10

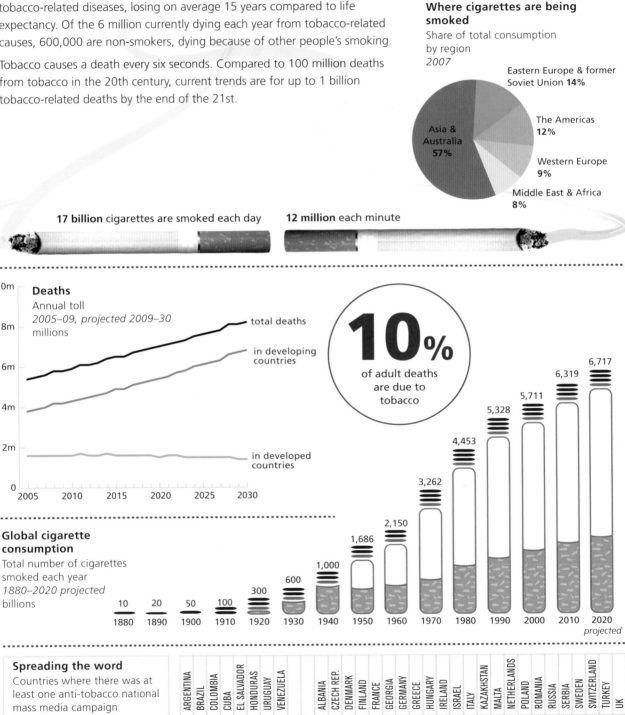

Smoking
Percentage of men and women who smoke cigarettes
2009

- 60.0% or more
- 50.0% – 59.9%
- 40.0% – 49.9%
- 30.0% – 39.9%
- 20.0% – 29.9%
- fewer than 20.0%
- no data

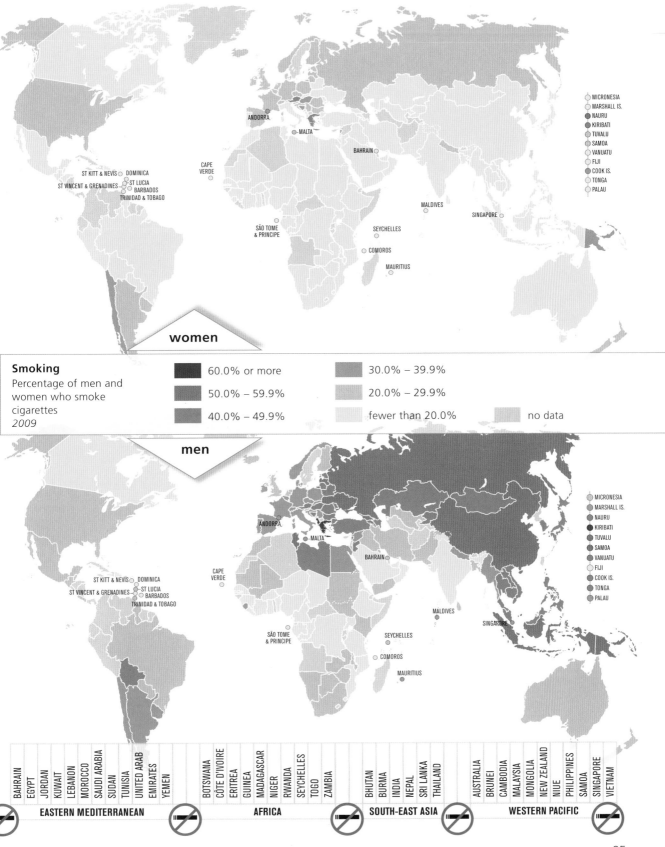

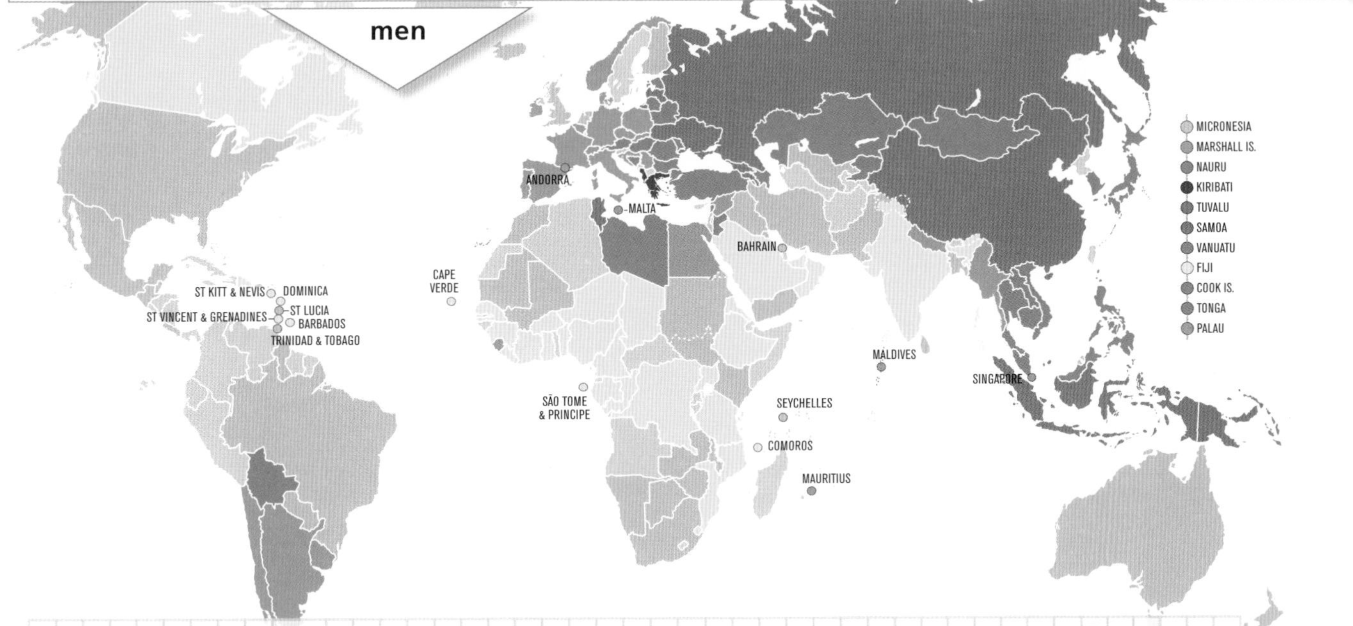

EASTERN MEDITERRANEAN: BAHRAIN, EGYPT, JORDAN, KUWAIT, LEBANON, MOROCCO, SAUDI ARABIA, SUDAN, TUNISIA, UNITED ARAB EMIRATES, YEMEN

AFRICA: BOTSWANA, CÔTE D'IVOIRE, ERITREA, GUINEA, MADAGASCAR, NIGER, RWANDA, SEYCHELLES, TOGO, ZAMBIA

SOUTH-EAST ASIA: BHUTAN, BURMA, INDIA, NEPAL, SRI LANKA, THAILAND

WESTERN PACIFIC: AUSTRALIA, BRUNEI, CAMBODIA, MALAYSIA, MONGOLIA, NEW ZEALAND, NIUE, PHILIPPINES, SAMOA, SINGAPORE, VIETNAM

96 Cancer ▶

Cancer

Cancer is a generic name for diseases characterized by the growth and spread of abnormal cells. It is believed to be the commonest cause of death worldwide, responsible for 13 per cent of all deaths. Though treatments and preventive strategies are improving, the estimated incidence of cancer more than doubled from 1975 to 2008, and it is expected to double again by 2030.

As the world's population grows, and improvements in general health mean that people live longer on average, cancer looms ever larger. In countries where prosperity is advancing, bringing with it changes in lifestyle, diet, and tobacco use, the incidence of cancer is rising. Although the rate of cancer is currently four times greater in high-income countries than elsewhere, rates in poorer countries are increasing rapidly.

Cancer is most treatable when caught early. On a large scale, early diagnosis requires education and active screening programmes as part of comprehensive health care – more likely prospects in richer than in poorer countries.

> Beating cancer now is a realistic ambition because, at long last, we largely know its genetic and chemical characteristics.

James Watson, 2009
Molecular biologist and geneticist, co-discoverer of structure of DNA

Unequal death rates
Once cancer has been contracted, the rate of death is five times higher in poorer than in richer countries.

7.6 million deaths from cancer worldwide in 2008

Unequal chances
2008

Childhood cancer-survival rates

Breast-cancer survival rate

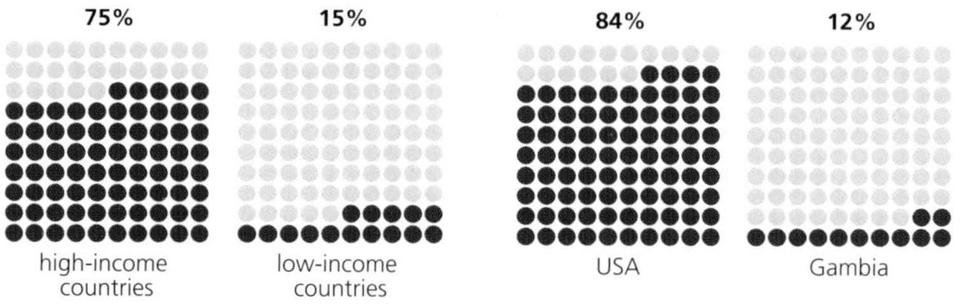

Increasing incidence
Number of new cases per annum
1975–2030 projected based on 1% per annum increase in incidence

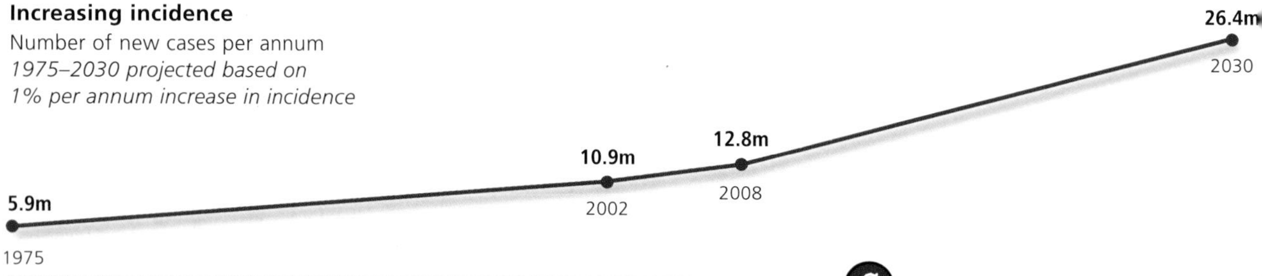

Cancer cases in poorer countries
As percentage of global total
2008 & 2030 projected

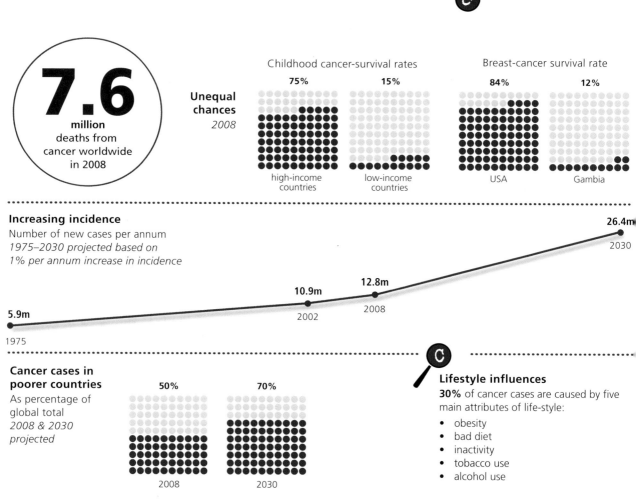

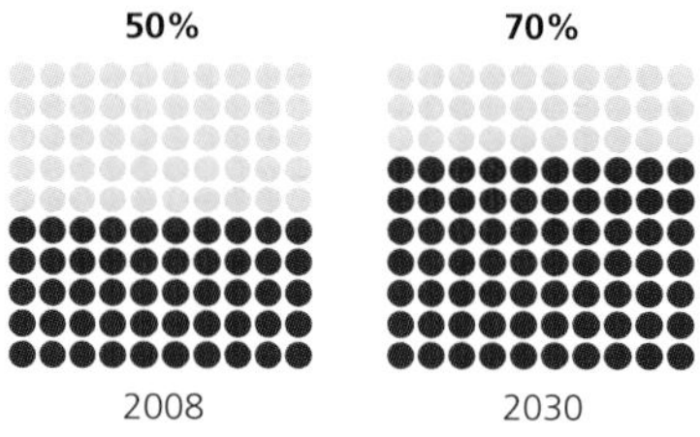

Lifestyle influences
30% of cancer cases are caused by five main attributes of life-style:

- obesity
- bad diet
- inactivity
- tobacco use
- alcohol use

◄ 94 Smoking

Commonest cancers
In each country
2008

- bladder
- breast
- cervix uteri
- colorectum
- Kaposi's sarcoma
- lip, mouth
- liver
- lung
- oesophagus
- prostate
- stomach
- thyroid
- no data

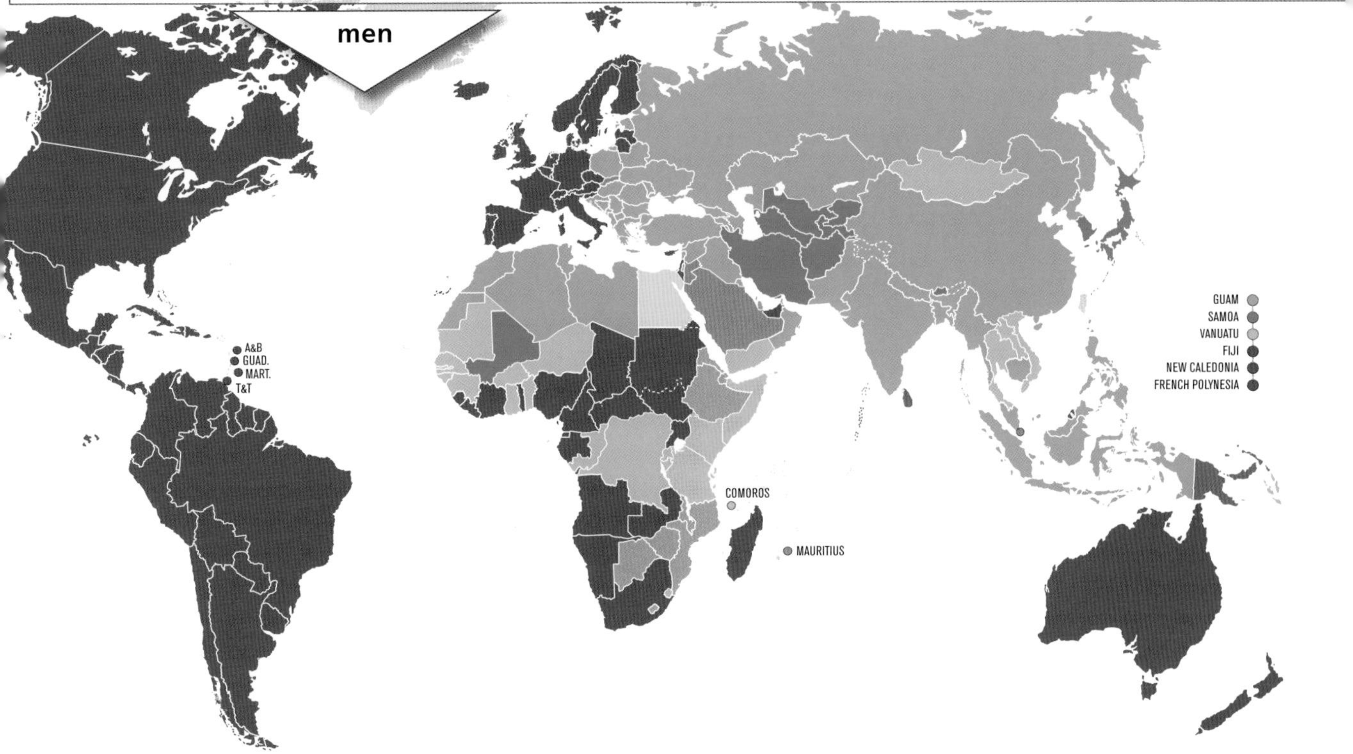

HIV/AIDS

HIV/AIDS has claimed more than 25 million lives over three decades. In 2010, there were approximately 34 million people living with HIV, 10 per cent of them children below the age of 15.

A cure for HIV infection has not been found, but effective treatment with anti-retroviral drugs allows patients to restrict the virus and enjoy healthy and productive lives. And with knowledge about how the virus is passed on through sexual contact and shared needles used for drugs, infection can be avoided.

Neither denying the problem nor trying to bar the door to people living with HIV/AIDS (as 49 countries still do) has worked as a preventive strategy. But, thanks to treatment and education, the numbers of new infections and deaths are declining. So, the epidemic can be stopped – but only if more resources are provided to fight it.

The impact of HIV/AIDS
Percentage of people aged 15–49 infected with HIV
2009
WHO regions

- 20.0% or more
- 10.0% – 19.9%
- 1.0% – 9.9%
- fewer than 1%
- no data

Number of children orphaned by AIDS

- 1 million or more
- 100,000 – 999,999

Living and dying with HIV/AIDS
Adults and children
1990–2010

- new HIV Infections
- AIDS-related deaths

Regional distribution
2010

- Africa
- Americas
- Eastern Mediterranean
- Europe
- South-East Asia
- Western Pacific

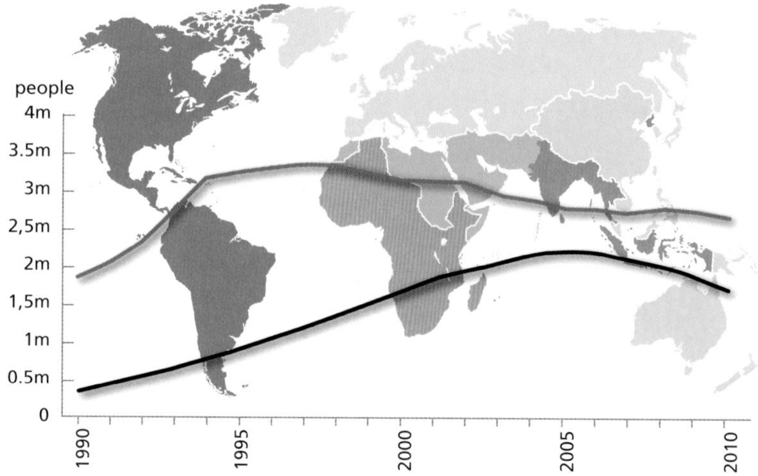

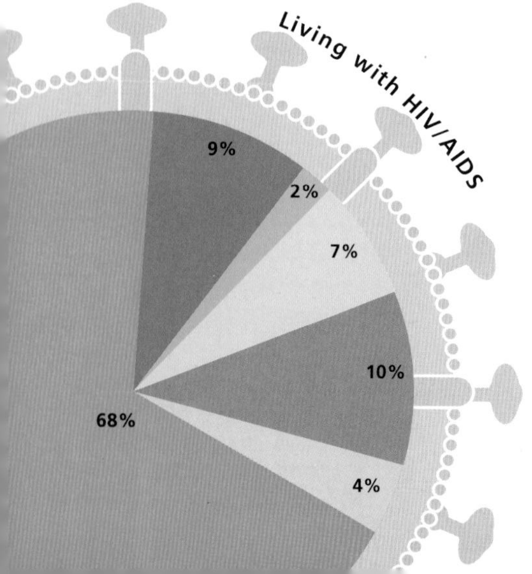

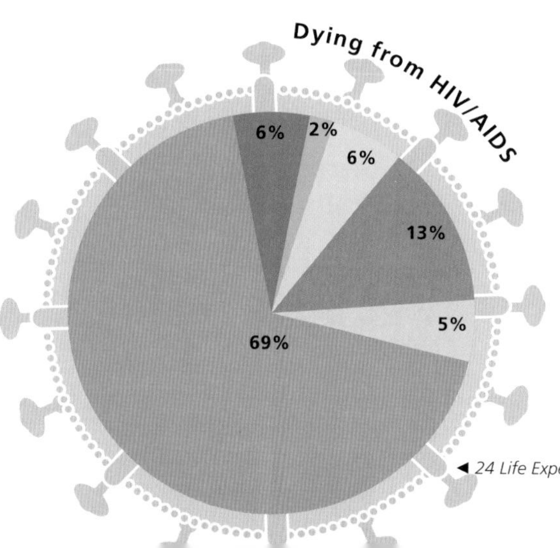

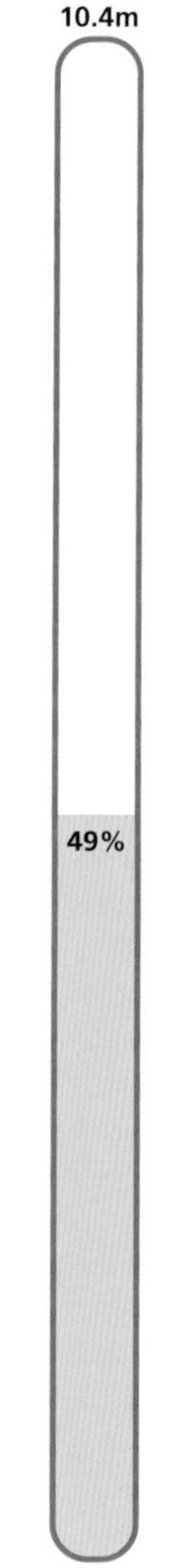

Sub-Saharan Africa

◄ 24 Life Expectancy; 54 Goals for Development

EST.
RUSSIA
UKRAINE
BAHAMAS
HAITI
JAMAICA
BARBADOS
TRINIDAD & TOBAGO
GUYANA
SURINAME
NIGERIA
CHAD
C.A.R
UGANDA
BURKINA FASO
GAMBIA
MALI
SUDAN
DJIBOUTI
KENYA
GUINEA-BISSAU
GUINEA
CÔTE D'IVOIRE
BENIN
SIERRA LEONE
LIBERIA
TOGO
South Sudan
THAILAND
BURUNDI
EQ. GUINEA
GABON
CONGO
GHANA
TANZANIA
CAMEROON
MAURITIUS
ZIMBABWE
FIJI
BOTSWANA
NAMIBIA
SWAZILAND
RWANDA
MALAWI
ANGOLA
MOZAMBIQUE
ZAMBIA
SOUTH AFRICA
LESOTHO

Barring the door

Countries imposing restrictions on entry, stay, or residence of people living with HIV
June 2011

RUSSIA
BELARUS
LITHUANIA
MONGOLIA
SLOVAKIA
MOLDOVA
TURKMENISTAN
UZBEKISTAN
ANDORRA
ARMENIA
NORTH KOREA
CYPRUS
SYRIA
IRAQ
TAJIKISTAN
LEBANON
KUWAIT
SOUTH KOREA
TURKS & CAICOS
ISRAEL
JORDAN
BAHRAIN
QATAR
TAIWAN
BELIZE
CUBA
EGYPT
SAUDI ARABIA
UAE
MARSHALL IS.
DOMINICAN REP.
SUDAN
OMAN
BRUNEI
ARUBA
YEMEN
MALAYSIA
NICARAGUA
SINGAPORE
SAMOA
COMOROS
PAPUA NEW GUINEA
PARAGUAY
MAURITIUS
SOLOMON IS.
AUSTRALIA
FIJI
TONGA
NEW ZEALAND

Anti-Retroviral Therapy (ART)

Number of people receiving ART as a percentage of those needing it
2010
UNAIDS regions

number needing ART

percentage receiving it

6m
6%
...ern & ...rn Africa

2.8m
30%
Western & Central Africa

2.3m
40%
East, South & South-East Asia

820,000
64%
Latin America & the Caribbean

570,000
23%
Europe & Central Asia

150,000
10%
North Africa & the Middle East

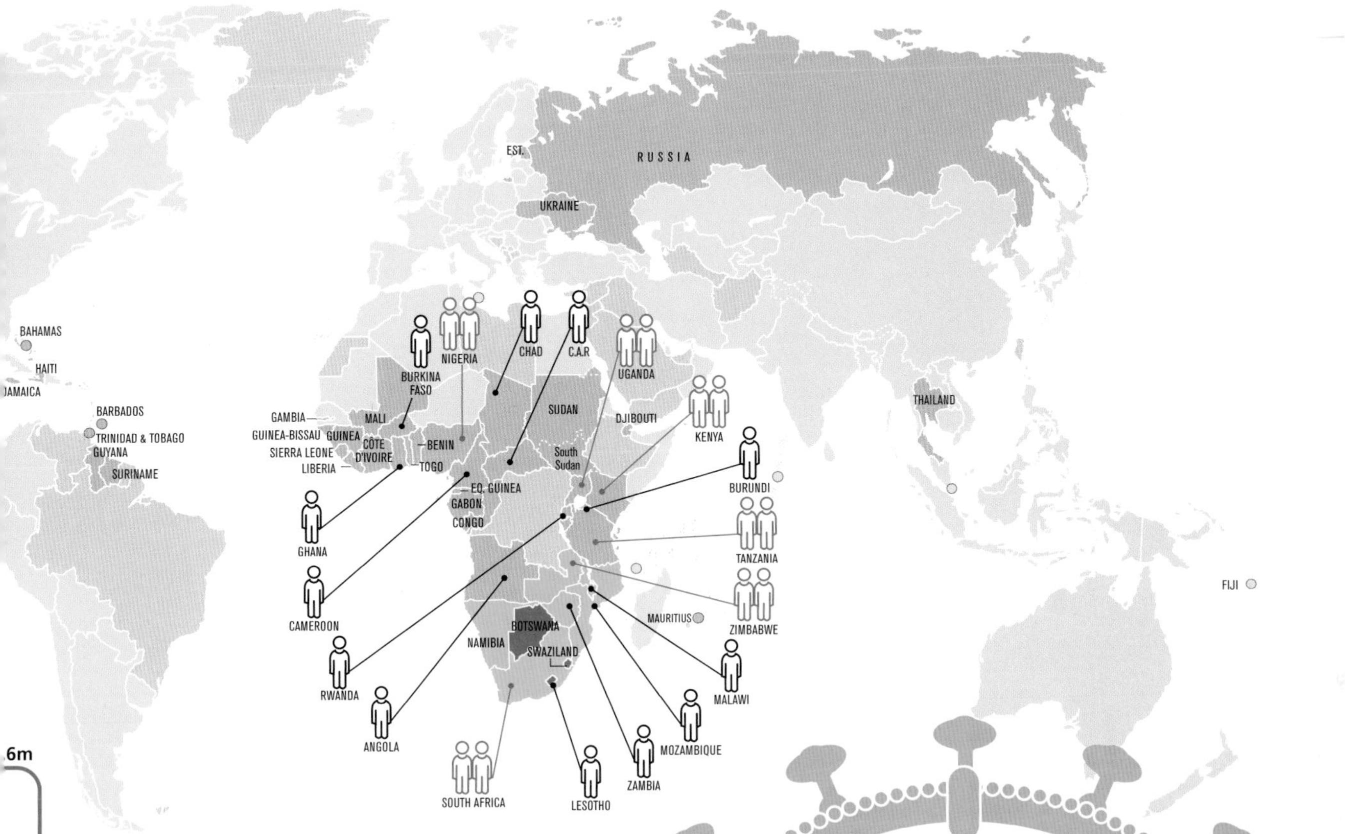

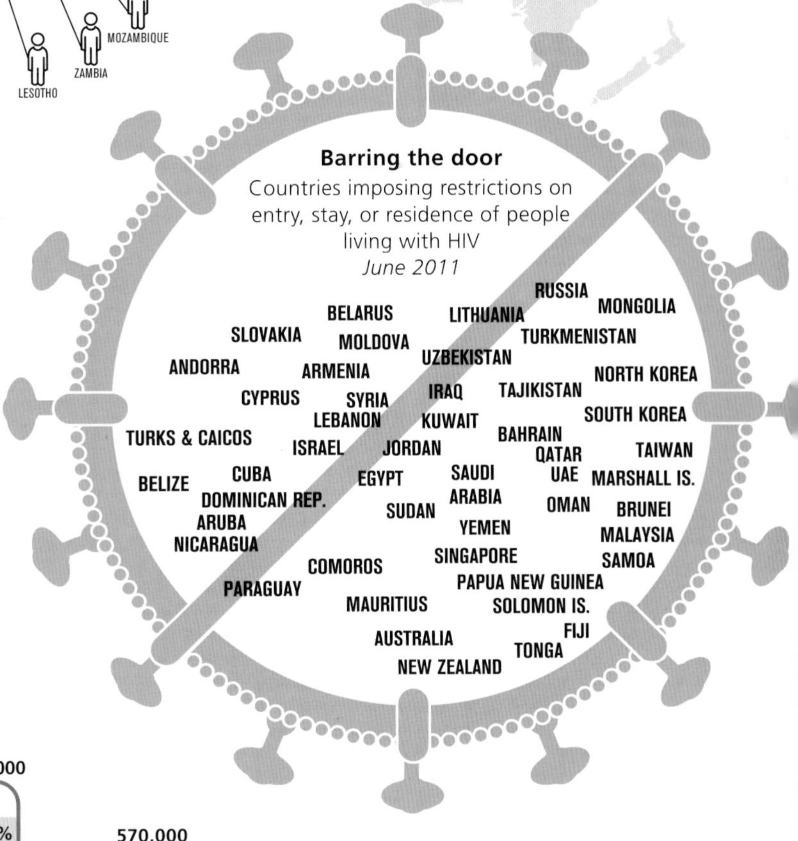

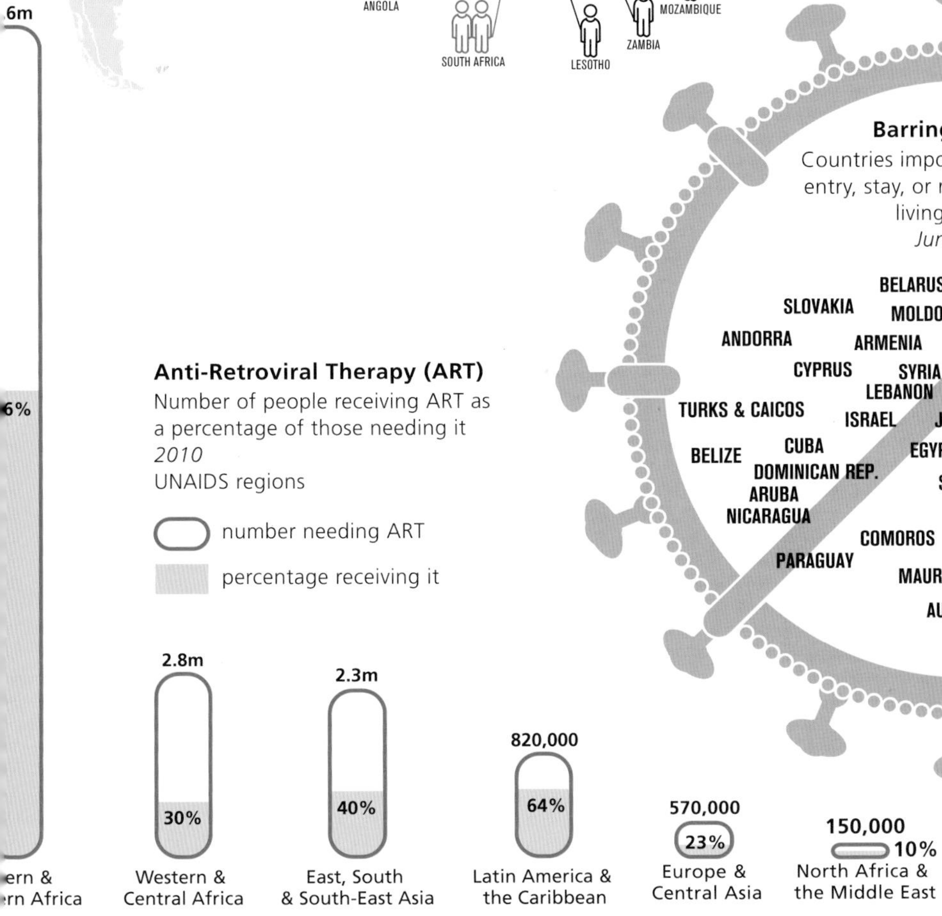

Mental Health

Worldwide about 450 million people suffer mental and behavioural disorders. Hundreds of millions more have psychological problems. Around 20 per cent of the world's children and adolescents have mental problems of some degree; about half of mental disorders begin before the age of 14. People with mental disorders are at greater risk of catching and passing on communicable diseases, and of committing suicide. About 800,000 people take their own lives each year and this is the third leading cause of death among young people.

In many countries, mental disorder is a taboo subject, more shaming to a family than other diseases and any other behaviour. As a result, the human rights of psychiatric patients are routinely abused in most countries – physical restraint, isolation, and the denial both of basic needs and of privacy. Alongside this, the stigma attached to mental disorder leads to this large and highly visible health issue being under-resourced. Average global spending on mental health is less than $2 per person per year, and in low-income countries the average is less than 25 cents per person – about one fifteenth of what is needed.

Over
50%
of people who commit suicide are aged
15–44
years

Mental-health resources
Median number of psychiatric beds in general hospitals per 1 million people
2011
WHO regions

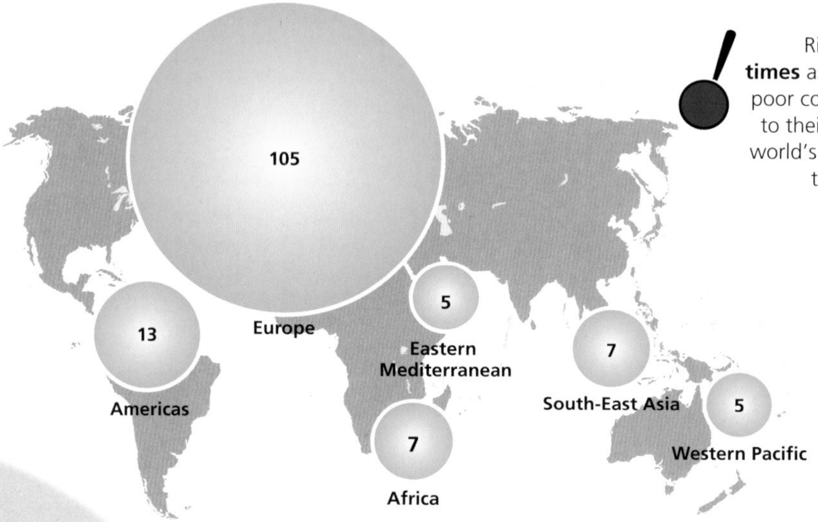

Rich countries have **170 times** as many psychiatrists as poor countries, proportionate to their population. **Half** the world's population has access to only one psychiatrist per **200,000** people.

Expenditure on medicines
For mental and behavioural disorders per 100,000 people by country income
2011

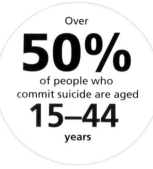

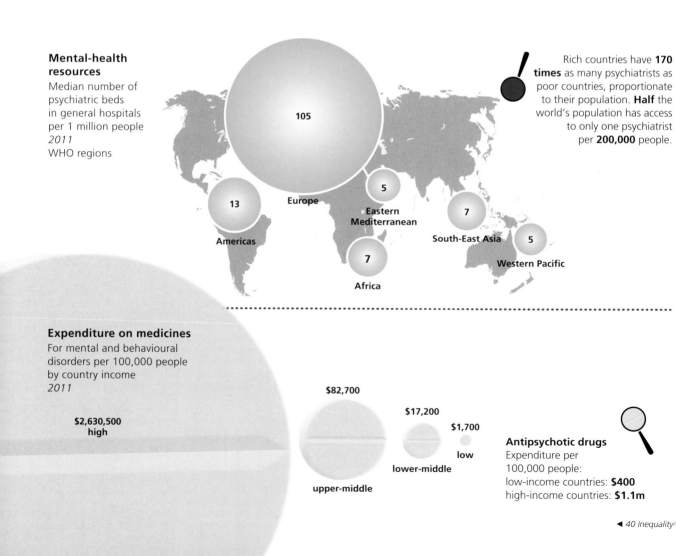

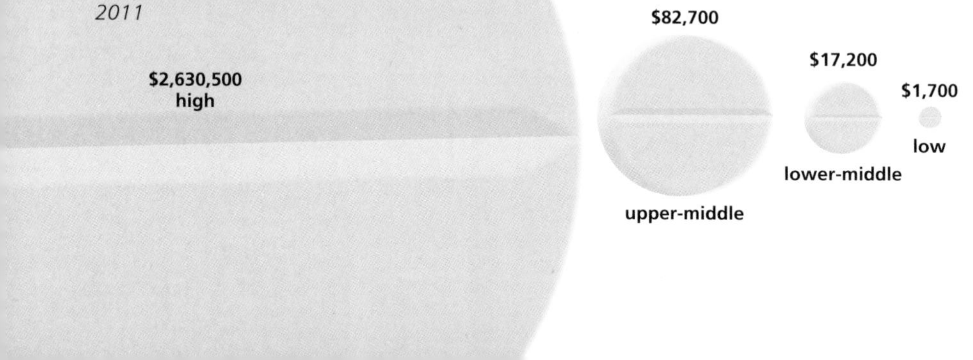

Antipsychotic drugs
Expenditure per 100,000 people:
low-income countries: **$400**
high-income countries: **$1.1m**

◄ 40 *Inequality*

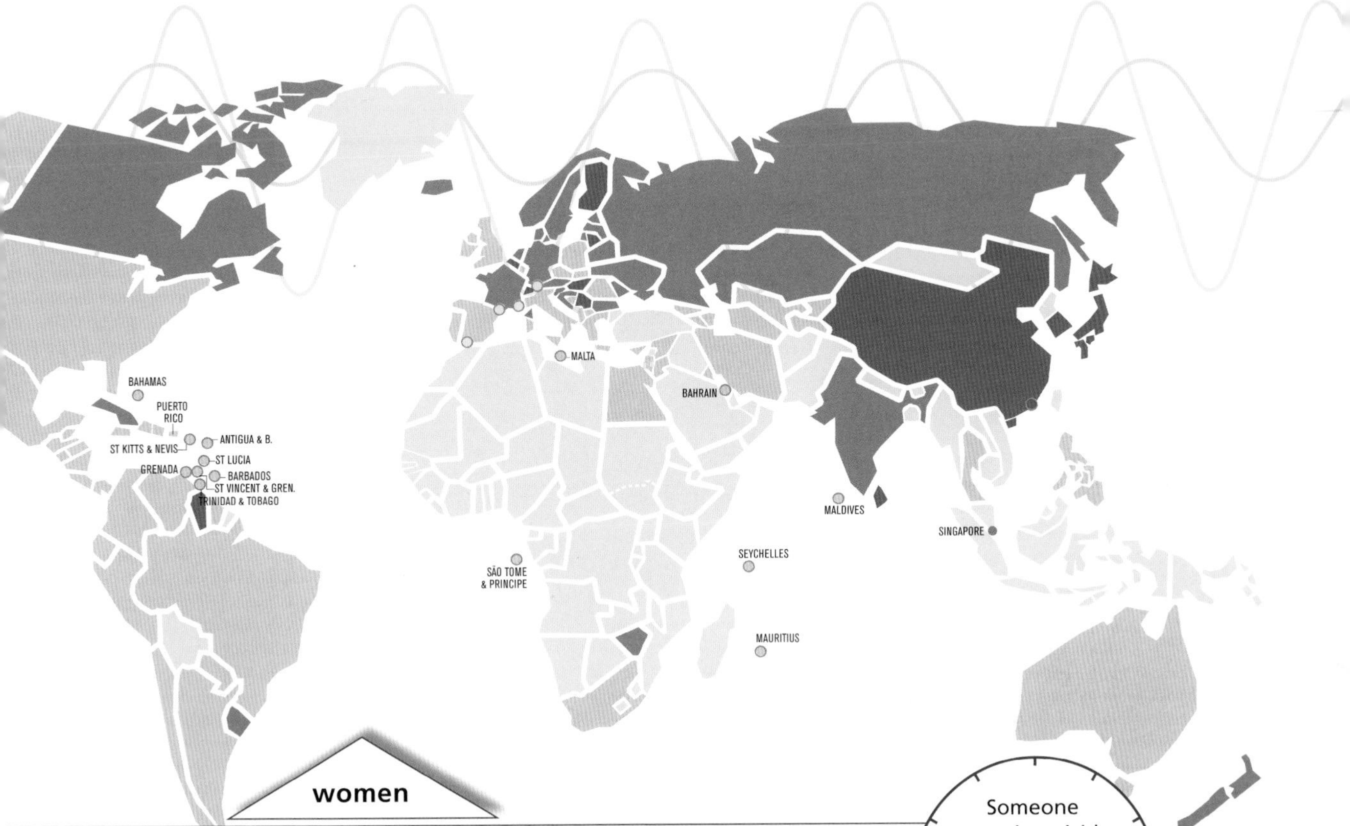

Suicide rates

Number of suicides per 100,000 people

2009 or latest available data

- 50 or more
- 25.0 – 49.9
- 10.0 – 24.9
- 5.0 – 9.9
- fewer than 5
- no data collected

Living with Disease

The burden of ill health on countries' populations is normally expressed in terms of the number of years of life lost compared to average life expectancy. But the burden of disease is greater than that: years are lost not only to premature death but also to disability and ill health. This century, the World Health Organization has adopted a new measure – the Disability Adjusted Life Year (or DALY) – to reflect this fuller sense of the disease burden. The DALY is calculated as the combined total of years of potential life lost to premature death plus years lived with disability. It is possible to compare all the countries for which there are data by breaking the DALY total down to reflect the rate per 100,000 people.

As a way of measuring the burden imposed by disease, it is limited to measuring time (rather than, for example, intensity of suffering while ill). But it is a fuller measure than the alternatives and is increasingly used.

A fraction over 50 per cent of the world's population lives in countries with a DALY of between 10,000 and 20,000 per 100,000 people. That can be thought of as the global norm. Two small, rich countries (Iceland and Kuwait) do better than that, and 83 other countries – some big and richly blessed with natural resources – do worse.

Cuba and the **USA**

have precisely the same disease burden

National disease burden

DALYs per 100,000 people

2004

A DALY (Disability Adjusted Life Year) measures the number of years lost due to ill-health, disability or early death.

- 9,800 – 14,999 *the rich country norm*
- 15,000 – 19,999 *the middle income norm*
- 20,000 – 39,999 *heavy disease burden*
- 40,000 – 59,999 *intense burden*
- 60,000 – 82,500 *extreme burden*
- no data

◀ 42 Quality of Life

Iceland
has the lightest disease burden

Sierra Leone
has the heaviest disease burden

Denmark
has the heaviest disease burden of the Scandinavian countries

Russia
has the heaviest disease burden of any country of the former Soviet Union

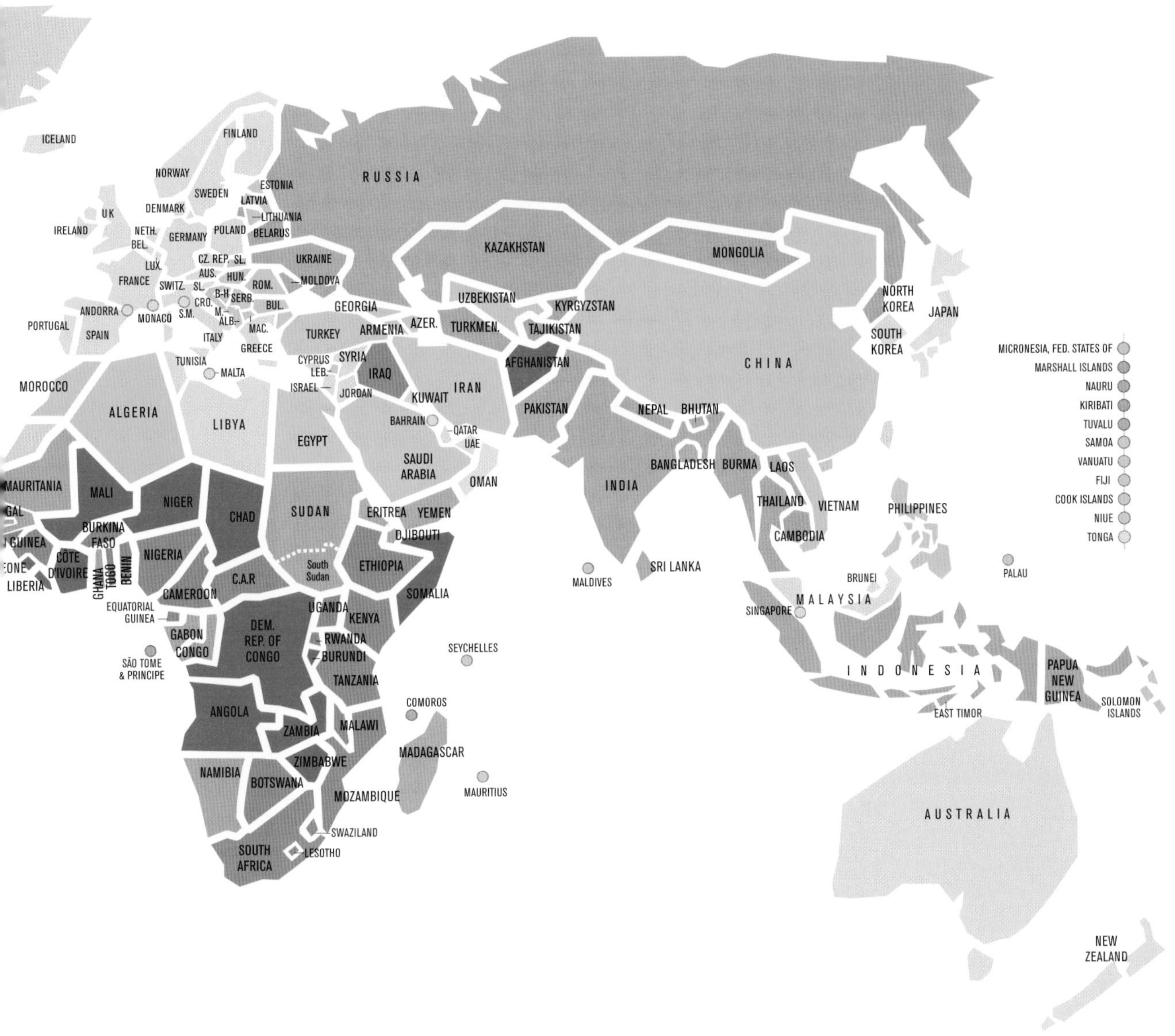

PART SIX

HEALTH OF THE PLANET

We know enough to understand the outlines of the deep global, environmental predicament we are in. We neither know nor understand all the details but we can see that the economic and industrial path we have been on for the last two centuries, along which we are not only still moving today but actually accelerating, is unsustainable in the long term.

Scientific knowledge may be imprecise on some of the key details but on the big issues there is no doubt. We are more people than ever before, using more water than ever before, and basic arithmetic shows that the majority of the world's population will face water scarcity before 2030. As our economic output has soared, we have pumped large amounts of carbon dioxide and other greenhouse gases into the atmosphere over the past 200 years and the laws of physics say the effect of that is to increase the global average temperature, which is happening. And at the same time, we have generated waste and thrown it away as garbage with abandon, and if we go to the right places we can see the consequences of that with our own eyes.

All these things we know. What we do not know is exactly how negative the consequences will be, how the different kinds of impact we have on the natural environment might interact with each other, and what the timescale is.

We can fill in some of the gaps in knowledge by taking note of the warning signs, and others by looking at projections whose assumptions are borne out by recent developments. It is not just in demography and resource use that this is a time of more and most and never before. There are increasing signs of human impact on the natural environment – on water supply, on plant and animal life, on land, and at sea.

Into the gaps in knowledge walk two contrary temptations: one is complacency – perhaps it will be all right; and the other is alarmism – we're doomed whatever we do. These two reactions are completely at odds with each other. Yet in another way they are mutually supportive because they both lead to inaction. If we are doomed and if we will probably be all right, the logic of both positions is to do nothing.

Not everybody is or should be a scientist and, while scientists could sometimes be of more help if they could only learn to express themselves in everyday language, nor does everybody even have to comprehend scientific arguments. People often come to intuitive understanding and that can be enough.

There is, fortunately, a growing awareness that action can and must be taken to slow the damage we are inflicting on the natural environment and steadily to change course. It is often said that this awareness has grown primarily in richer countries that can afford it but that is not really true. In India and in Kenya, among others, there are examples of important movements of environmental protection and care. Consciousness of the importance of the natural environment is by no means a rich-country luxury. There is at least one country in which the right of people to live in a supportive natural environment is inscribed in the constitution – the Philippines.

Action can be taken by individuals – in Europe and North America, for example, plenty of people sort their garbage so as much as possible can be recycled. Action can be taken by towns such as those that have introduced regulations including bans on the use of plastic bags. Action can be taken by property speculators, opting for carbon-neutral new buildings. By companies and government departments making their offices more energy efficient. By house owners putting solar panels on their roof for heating, and water butts in their back yards. By drivers opting for greener, smaller cars. Or for cycling or taking public transport whenever possible.

In the end, however, action has to be taken by governments, or little of any moment will move. They have the resources and the power to regulate and shape behaviour in ways that could at least slow the loss of biodiversity, limit waste, constrain energy use, and slow global warming. Some such actions have been taken; some forest cover is being regained, and many areas of land are protected from industrial use and urbanization.

Thus far, action has been limited. Many governments are aware that if they set out on that path, they will be committed to actions that are opposed by important lobby groups that carry economic weight and can exert political pressure. Equally, many citizens may find any consequent constraints on their behaviour to be an unreasonable imposition, which they too will oppose. A bold government might look at the example of smoking bans imposed by several countries in restaurants, cinemas, offices, pubs, and bars, and contemplate how angrily they were opposed at first, and how in most places where they have been implemented, they were accepted and tobacco consumption has fallen as a result.

But in general, political caution is at odds with caution on the environment. For on this decisive issue there is really no alternative in the end: to be cautious, we will have to be radical.

Warning Signs

The world faces a deep environmental crisis. Scientific precision about the risks is impossible, both because the study of this kind of risk is future-facing and because in some key respects (such as the number of species) the information we have is not complete. The frequency and scale of natural disasters seems to be increasing, but whether this is a limited fluctuation or a long-term trend is not yet clear.

The range of uncertainty in some projections and risk assessments is such that it is just possible, if in every case actuality turns out to be at the safer end, that overall, humanity will not be in too bad shape a century from now. But the mid-points in many of the projections combine to show a future that will not be like the past. We cannot assume the risks will be the same as we have previously faced.

Ordinary citizens find it even harder than scientists to get to grips with the scale of what may happen and the timescale on which it is unfolding. But there is evidence around us that things are changing in the natural world – and not many of the changes are to the good.

Shrinking Arctic ice: Sea-ice is shrinking in area and thickness. Mid-winter 2012, the volume of Arctic sea-ice was the lowest ever recorded for that time of year. Along the coast of Canada and Russia, a summer sea route has opened up, used by 32 cargo ships in 2011.

Polar bears threatened: As the ice shrinks this affects seals who breed on ice, and polar bears who hunt seals. The polar bear population is declining.

Losses from natural disasters in 2011:
$380 billion
– nearly double the previous record set in 2005

Melting permafrost in Alaska: A temperature increase of 3°–4°C since 1950 is causing roads and buildings to subside. The absence of summer sea-ice is leading to coastal erosion.

Glacial change in the Andes: The Quelccaya Glacier, Peru, is retreating 10 times more rapidly than it did in the 1970s and 1980s – by up to 60 metres a year.

Extinction: Current rates at which plant and animal species are becoming extinct are estimated to be 100 to 1,000 times faster than the average rate over the millennia of the planet's existence. Projections suggest up to 50% of known species are at risk of extinction by 2100.

Ocean dead zones: Industrial effluent has caused a surfeit of algae, which consume oxygen as they decay, producing 400 "dead zones" in the world's lakes and seas, covering a total of 245,000 square kilometres.

304 million people affected by natural disasters 2010
304,000 killed

Human impact of natural disasters

Affected people
- 1991–2000
- 2001–2010

Number recorded as killed
- 1991–2000
- 2001–2010

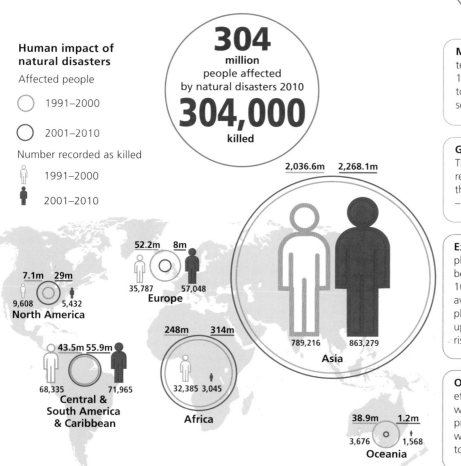

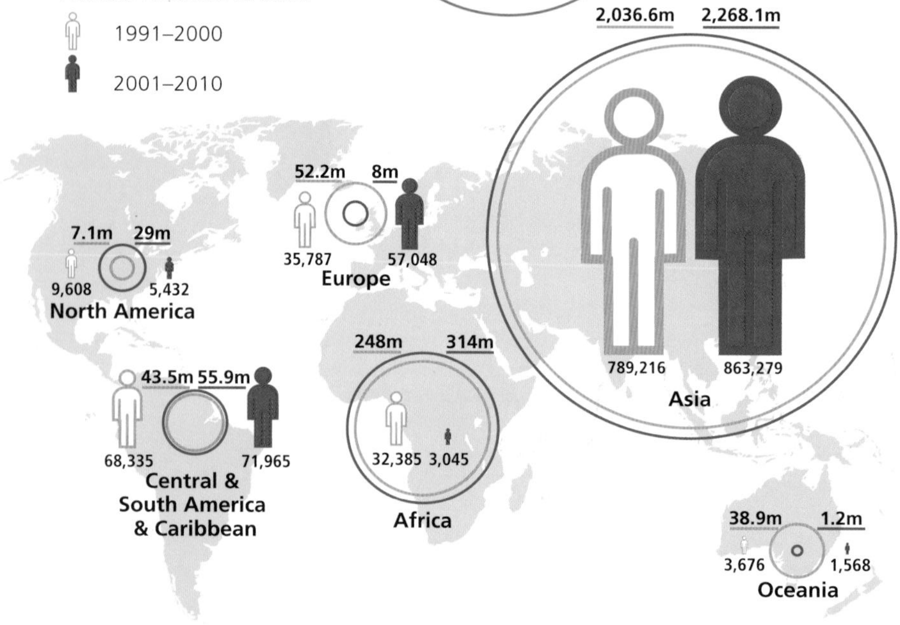

Changing ranges: Studies of the distribution of bird and butterfly species in North America and northern Europe over the past 35 years or so have revealed marked expansion northwards, with no southward expansion.

North Atlantic hurricanes: With annual fluctuations, the frequency and power of hurricanes trended down in the half century before the 1990s and has trended upwards since 1990.

Fires in Russia: Russia experienced forest fires in 2010 that killed 62 people and caused widespread destruction of crops to such an extent that world food prices rose. Fires in 2011 were more widespread, but fewer occurred in densely populated areas and farmland.

Floods in Pakistan: Monsoon flooding in Pakistan affected 18 million people, killing about 1,800, destroying almost 2 million homes. Monsoon floods in 2011 killed at least 300 people.

These days the water evaporates faster and the grass dries very quickly. Last March it rained, but very little. So now I try to cultivate. We have greatly changed our life but so far not much is going better.

A Maasai herder, Kenya, December 2011

Water mining in China: Urbanization, industrialization, increasing use of irrigation, and river pollution in northeast China are using up water from underground aquifers at an unsustainable rate.

Coral bleaching: When coral dies, it goes white – a natural process accelerated by warmer seas, pollution, increased exposure to UV radiation and chemical pollution, among other things. In 1998, the Great Barrier Reef had its most extensive coral bleaching for 700 years, followed in 2002 by an even more extensive bleaching.

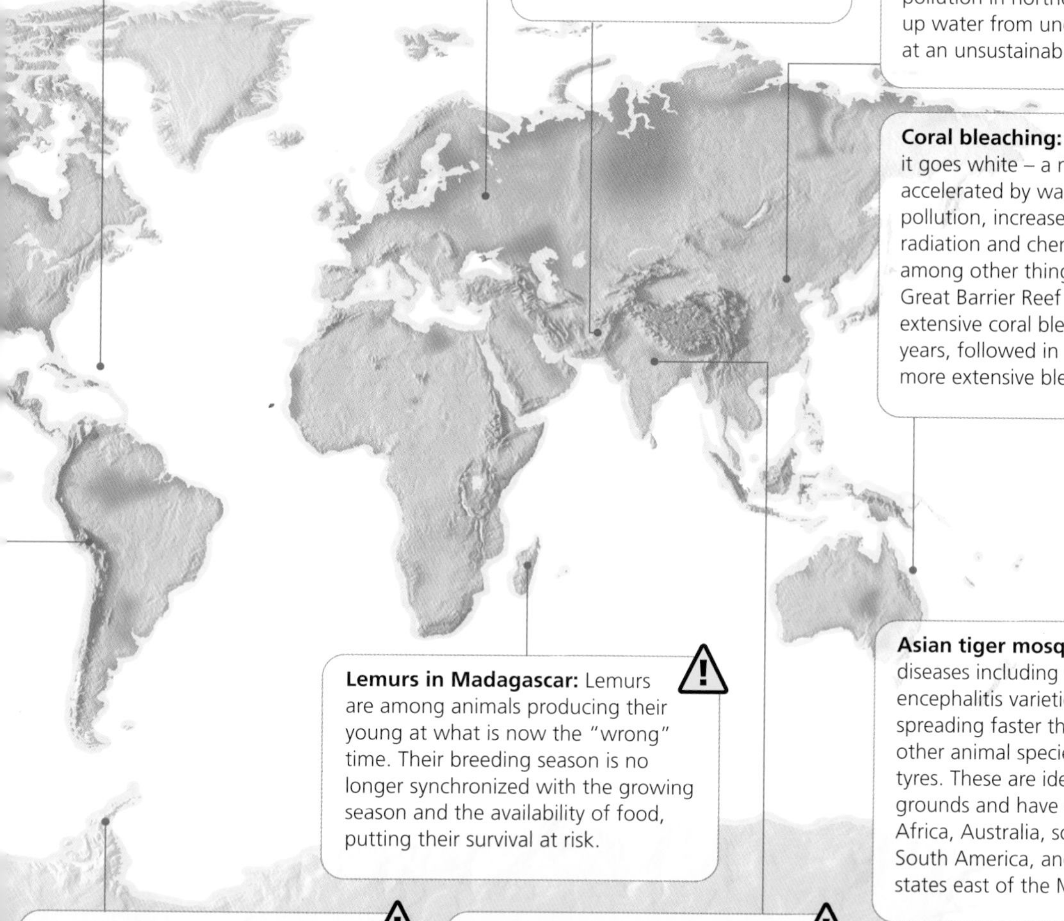

Lemurs in Madagascar: Lemurs are among animals producing their young at what is now the "wrong" time. Their breeding season is no longer synchronized with the growing season and the availability of food, putting their survival at risk.

Asian tiger mosquito: Carrying diseases including dengue and encephalitis varieties, this mosquito is spreading faster than almost any other animal species via the trade in tyres. These are ideal breeding grounds and have carried it into Africa, Australia, southern Europe, South America, and parts of the US states east of the Mississippi River.

Rapid rise in Antarctic: Temperatures in the Antarctic Peninsula have risen by 2.8°C over the last 50 years, leading to melting of ice shelves and increased glacier loss. Local flora and fauna are affected, including breeding colonies of Adélie penguins.

Vulture deaths in India: Three species of vulture have suffered a 97% decline in numbers. This has been traced to the widespread use of the drug diclofenac to prevent arthritis in cattle. The vultures' vital clean-up role has been taken over by feral dogs, leading to a rise in rabies.

Ocean acidification: An increasing concentration of carbon dioxide in the atmosphere has raised the acidity of the oceans by 27% over the past 200 years, which is affecting the shell growth of tiny organisms at the base of the food chain.

116 Climate Change; 118 Planetary Boundaries ▶

Biodiversity

The world is steadily losing species of plants and animals. In some species the rate of loss is accelerating. Efforts to stop or just slow the rate of loss have so far proven ineffectual, although among some of the states that are custodians of the world's forests, efforts to prevent further forest loss are starting to prove successful. While the world lost 3 per cent of forest cover from 1990 to 2010, among the ten biggest holders of forests, accounting for 65 per cent of the world total, the rate of loss was just 1 per cent. But the lost forest was largely rainforest, which has the richest biodiversity of any natural environment.

Threatened species

Species assessed as threatened as percentage of those evaluated by International Union for Conservation of Nature

2011

*representative sample assessed

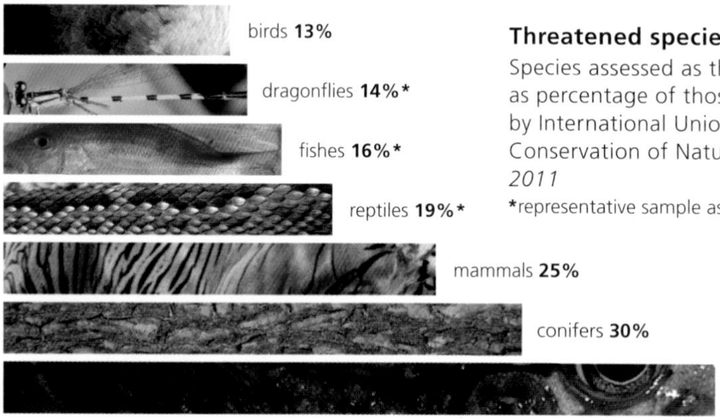

Protected areas

Percentage of a country's land recorded as nationally protected on World Database of Protected Areas

2010

25% or more

10% – 24%

less than 10%

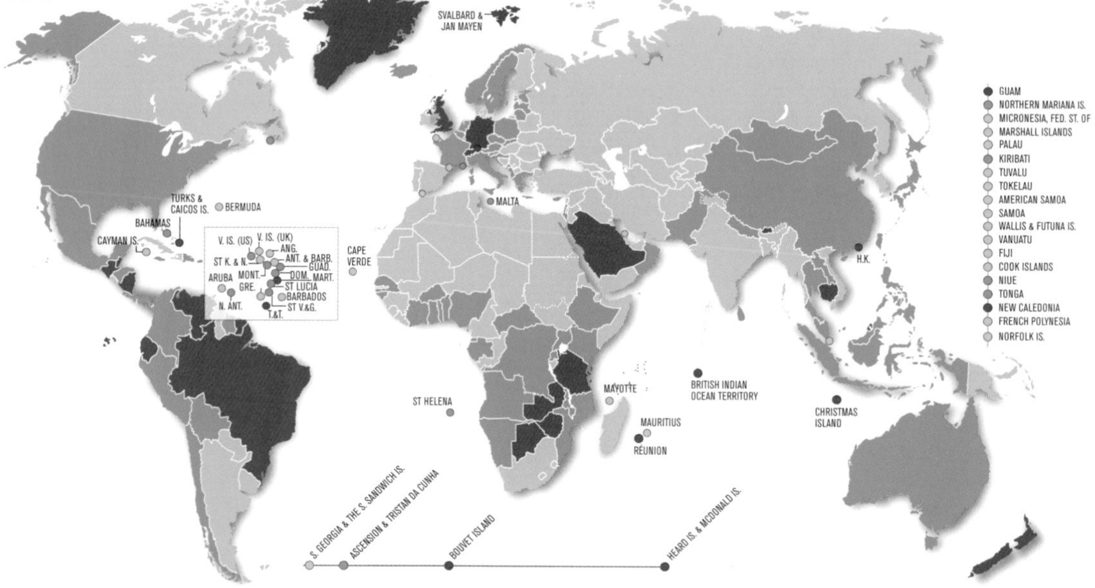

◀ 54 Goals for Development

Threatened mammals and birds
Number of species threatened
2012
100 or more
50 – 99
25 – 49
10 – 24
fewer than 10
no data
50 or more bird species threatened
RUSSIA
KAZAKHSTAN
MONGOLIA
CHINA
INDIA
JAPAN
NORTH KOREA
SOUTH KOREA
INDONESIA
MALAYSIA
AUSTRALIA
NEW ZEALAND
PAPUA NEW GUINEA
PHILIPPINES
SUDAN
ALGERIA
LIBYA
EGYPT
NIGERIA
ETHIOPIA
D.R. CONGO
MADAGASCAR
SOUTH AFRICA
Forest lost and gained
In top ten most forested countries
1990–2010
Forest lost 1990–2010:
square kilometres
1990 area
forest lost as percentage of 1990 area
Forest gained 1990–2010:
square kilometres
1990 area
forest gained as percentage of 1990 area
Brazil
10%
–553,170
Indonesia
20%
–241,130
Sudan (incl S. Sudan)
8%
–64,320
D.R. Congo
4%
–62,280
Peru
3%
–22,070
Canada
0
Russia
+1%
1,400
India
+7%
45,040
USA
+3%
76,870
China
+32%
497,451

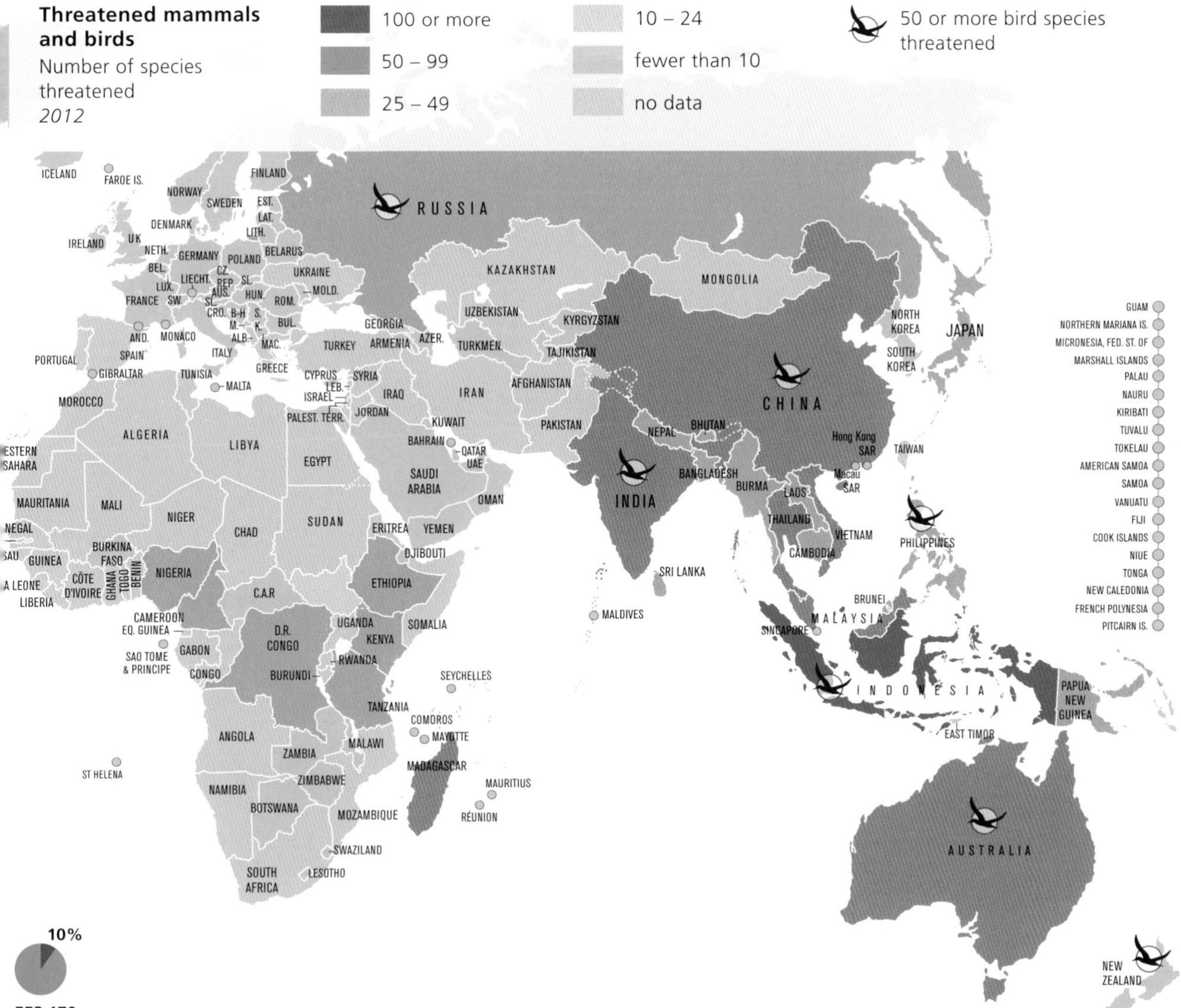

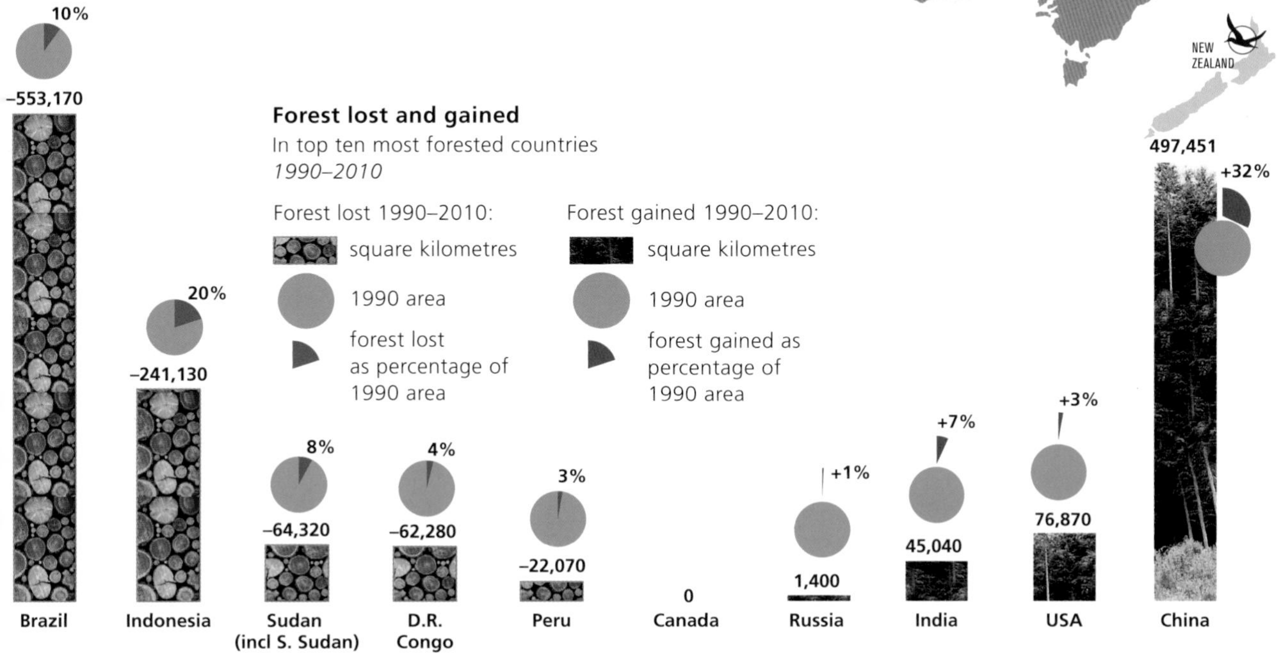

Water Resources

The world as a whole has plenty of water, but like every natural resource, nature distributes it unevenly and people's access to it is determined not only by nature but also by how the country is governed, its wealth, and how much of that wealth is devoted to meeting the needs of ordinary people.

There are two kinds of water scarcity. One results from over-withdrawal – taking more water out of the ground than is naturally restored by rainfall. The other is a social and economic issue – when there is no adequate infrastructure for delivering clean water to all. Unless these issues are addressed, estimates suggest that by 2025 two-thirds of the world's population will experience shortages of a clean water supply.

Large parts of both India and China face water problems. To hedge against the potential problems this could pose for their food supply, they and other governments have purchased large tracts of water-rich, arable land in Sub-Saharan Africa.

Total annual water withdrawal
1900–2000, 2025 projected
cubic kilometres

◄ 42 Quality of Life

Total consumption
Per capita per year
latest available data 2000–10
cubic metres

- 1,000 – 5,500
- 500 – 999
- 100 – 499
- less than 100
- no data

Water withdrawals
Water withdrawn as a percentage of renewable resources
latest available 2002–10

- 40% or more under severe strain
- 20% – 39% approaching strain

Lack of a safe supply
Percentage of people without access to an improved water source
2010

- 50% or more
- 30% – 49%

Improved water source: includes household connections, public standpipes, boreholes, protected dug wells, protected springs, rainwater collection.

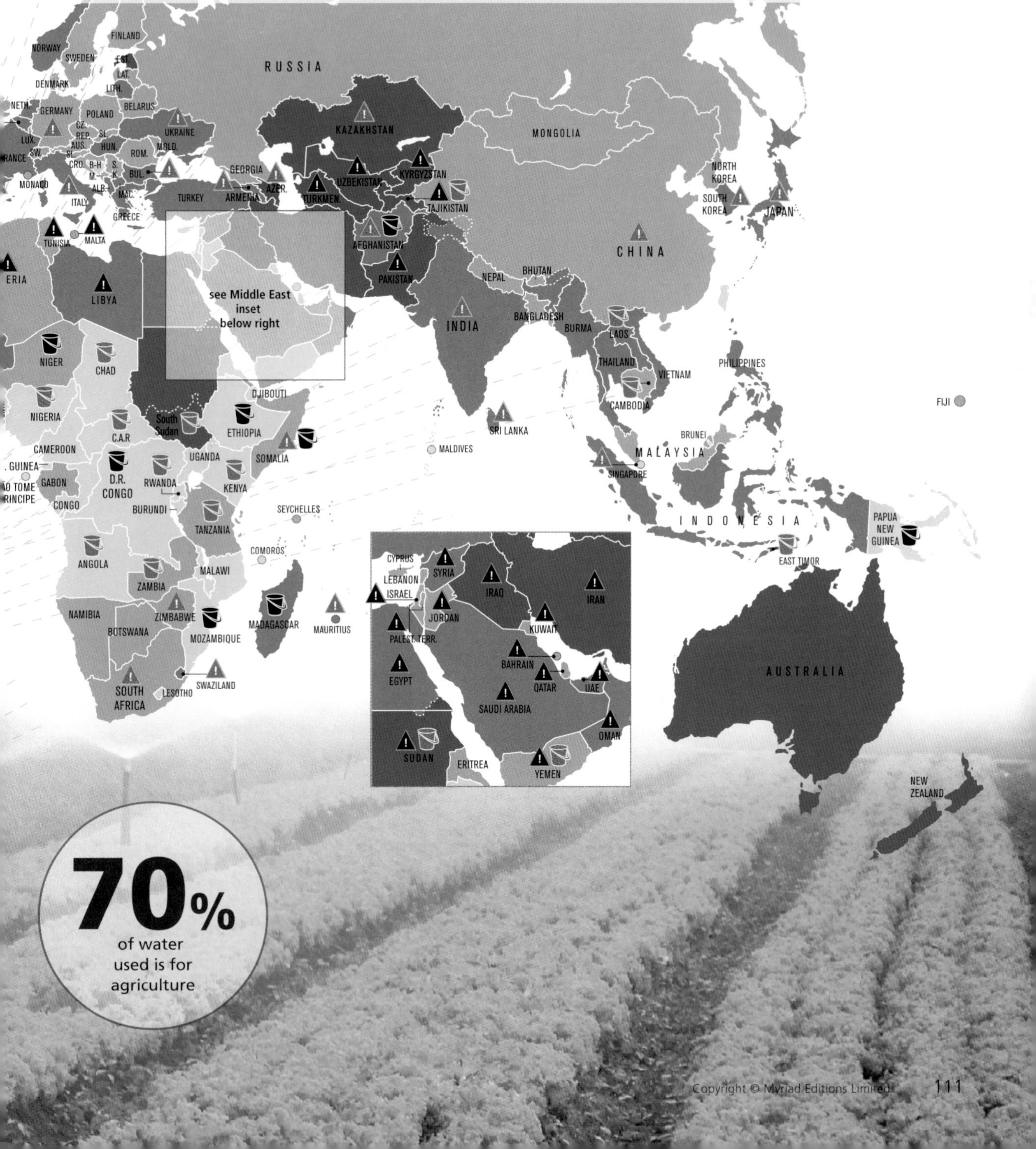

70% of water used is for agriculture

Waste

There is slowly growing recognition in a handful of countries that waste is a serious global problem. Most of what we use, we throw away, much of it thoughtlessly and some of that becomes a hazard to life and to nature. There are countries and local authorities that have passed laws to regulate the use of plastic bags and these seem to be having an effect.

Access to improved sanitation facilities has increased in most countries since 1990 and this not only improves public health but is also a part of waste management; a few countries, however, have moved in the wrong direction.

China: Banned flimsy plastic bags in 2008, and after 3 years it was claimed to have reduced annual use by 24 billion plastic bags, and saved the equivalent of 3.6m tonnes of oil.

Mumbai: The municipal corporation banned bags thinner than 50 microns after they blocked drains and contributed to major flooding in 2005.

South Australia: Since a plastic bag ban was imposed in 2009, household rubbish has been reduced by half.

Sanitation

Percentage of population with access to improved sanitation facilities
2010

- less than 25%
- 25% – 49%
- 50% – 74%
- 75% – 99%
- 100%
- no data
- access has increased by 25 percentage points or more *1990–2010*
- access has declined *1990–2010*

Tonnes of disposable nappies
3,266,000
in USA
690,000
in UK

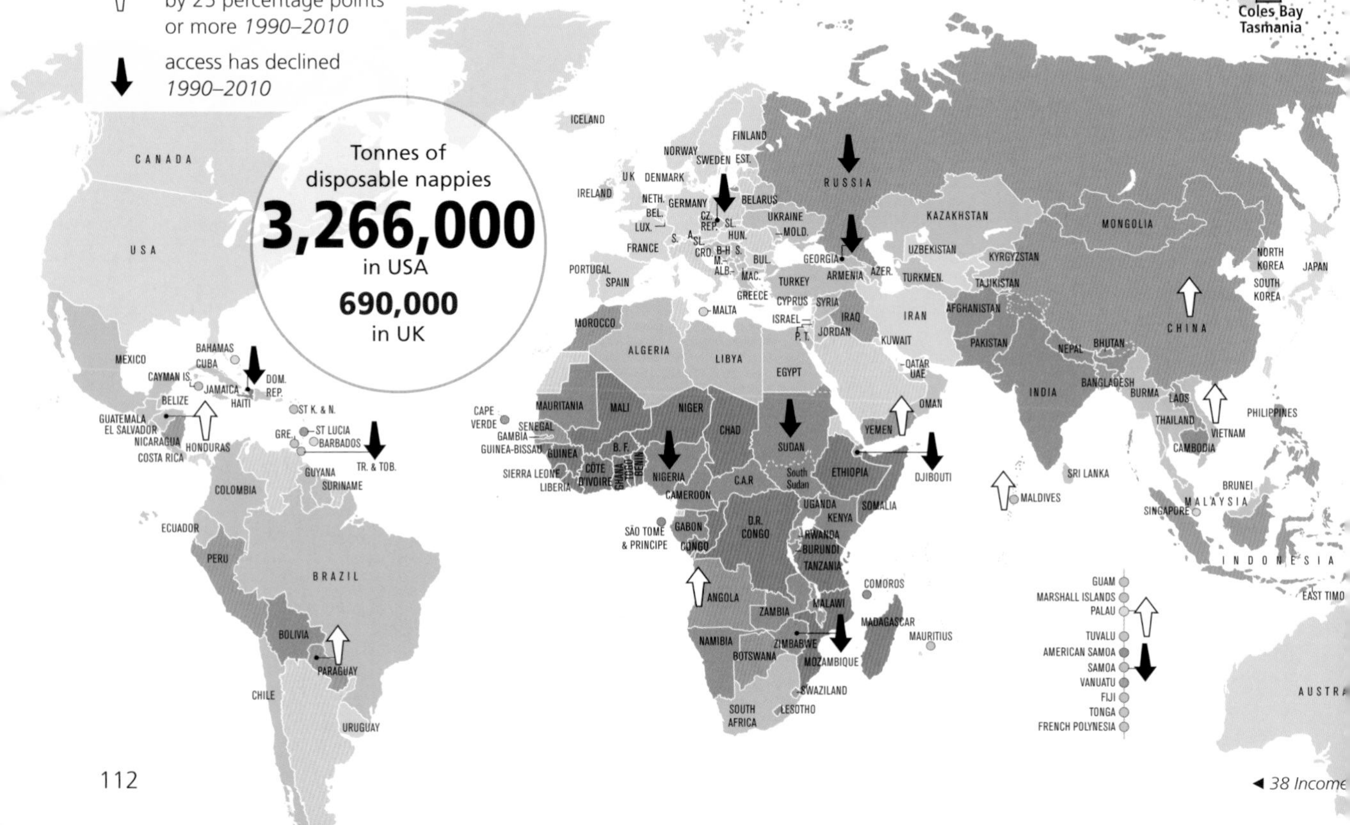

◄ 38 Income

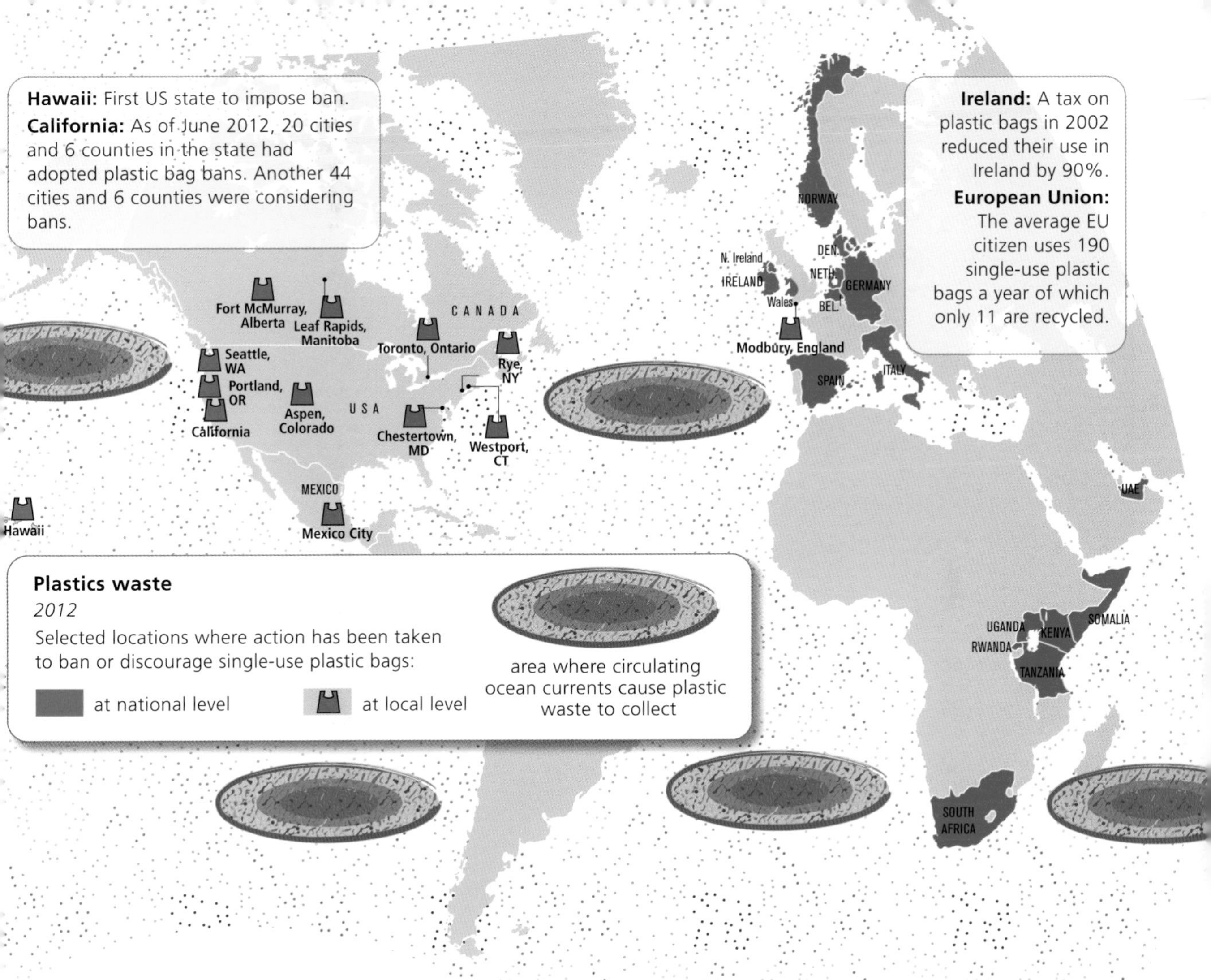

Hawaii: First US state to impose ban.

California: As of June 2012, 20 cities and 6 counties in the state had adopted plastic bag bans. Another 44 cities and 6 counties were considering bans.

Ireland: A tax on plastic bags in 2002 reduced their use in Ireland by 90%.

European Union: The average EU citizen uses 190 single-use plastic bags a year of which only 11 are recycled.

Plastics waste

2012

Selected locations where action has been taken to ban or discourage single-use plastic bags:

at national level

at local level

area where circulating ocean currents cause plastic waste to collect

Beach trash

Most common items of debris picked up on over 6,000 beaches in 108 countries as part of Ocean Conservancy clean up

2009

Plastic world

Global plastics production

1950–2010

tonnes

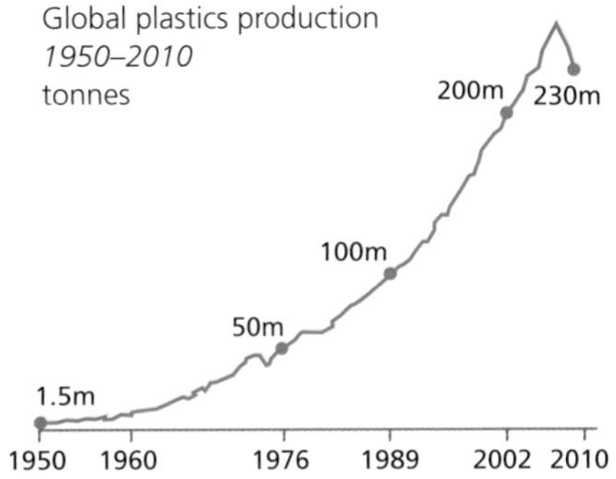

Energy Use

Everything that runs, runs on energy. As countries get richer they use more energy until a point comes when their economic base shifts from natural resources and industry to information and the service sectors. Most energy comes from oil, gas, coal, and uranium, whose extraction and use carry risks of pollution, sometimes with catastrophic effect.

The climate-change risks of continuing to emit so much carbon by using oil, gas, and coal have led to interest in alternatives. Because each has benefits and drawbacks, the lobbies for and against each one have cogent arguments. Nuclear power can look good from a climate perspective, less so when viewed through the lens of hazardous waste. Biofuels seem environmentally responsible, but producing them takes so much energy it is not clear how big the gain is, and they also take land out of food production. The wind, waves, tide, and sun are all sources of unending energy, but it has not so far been feasible to harness them on the necessary scale.

Whatever differences these energy sources make, the key alternative in the end may well turn out to be simply using less.

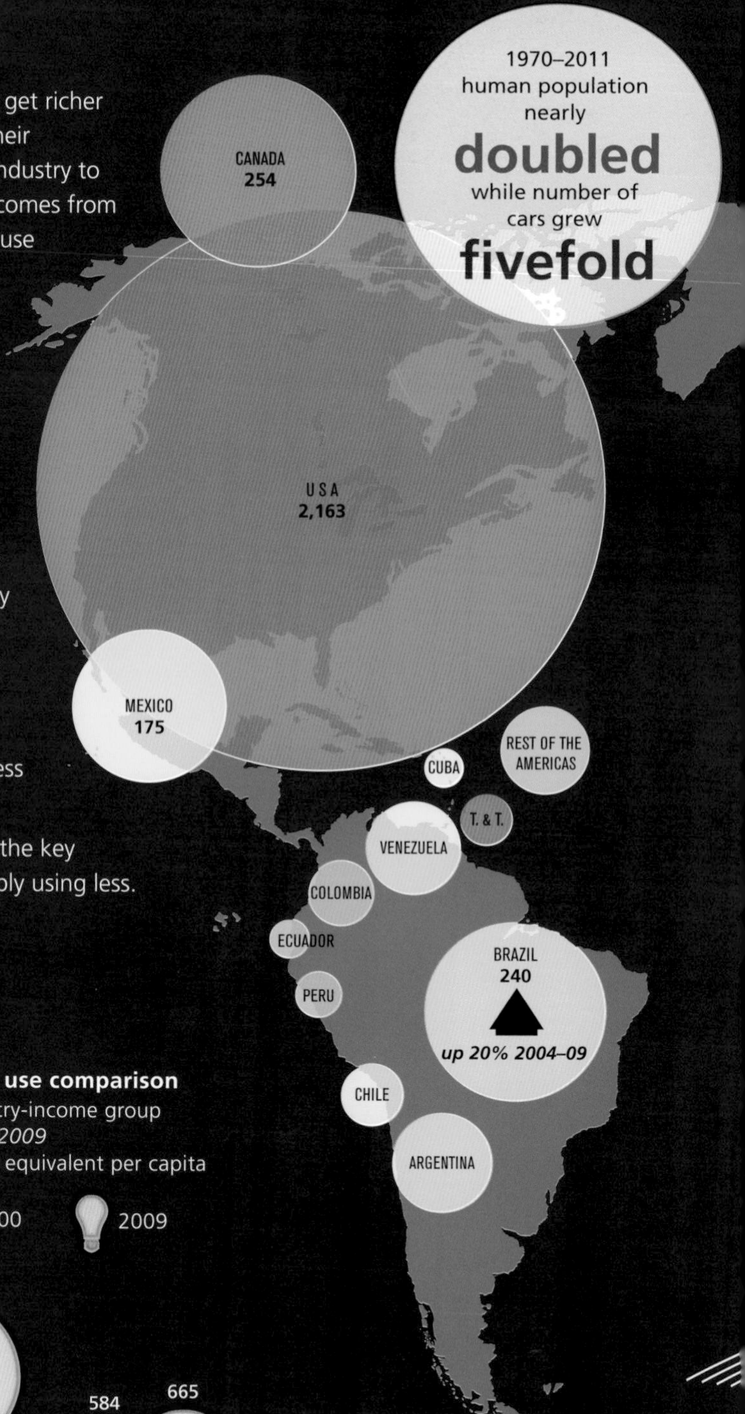

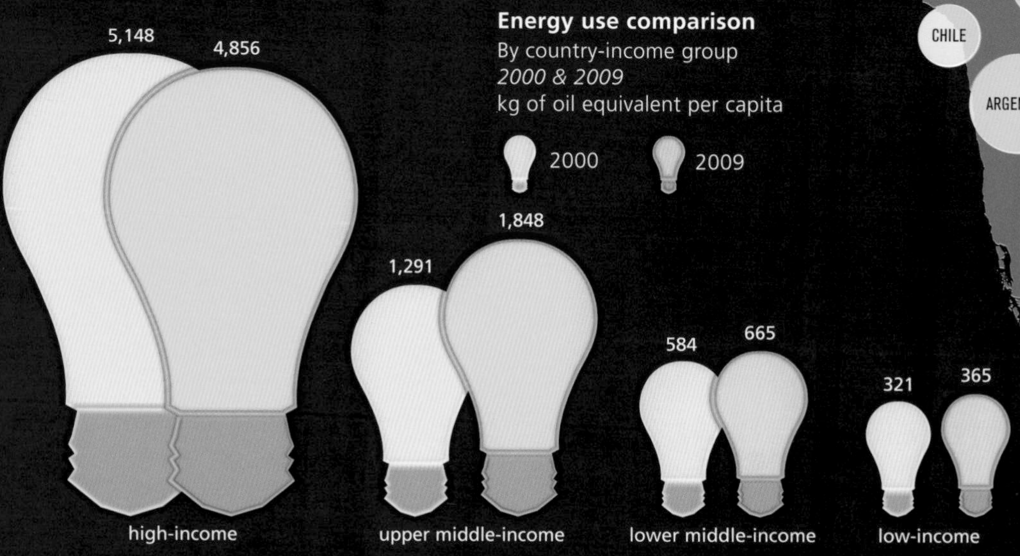

Total energy use
Amount used per year
2009
○ = 10 million tonnes of oil equivalent

Energy used per capita
2009
kg of oil equivalent
5,000 or more
3,000 – 4,999
1,000 – 2,999
fewer than 1,000

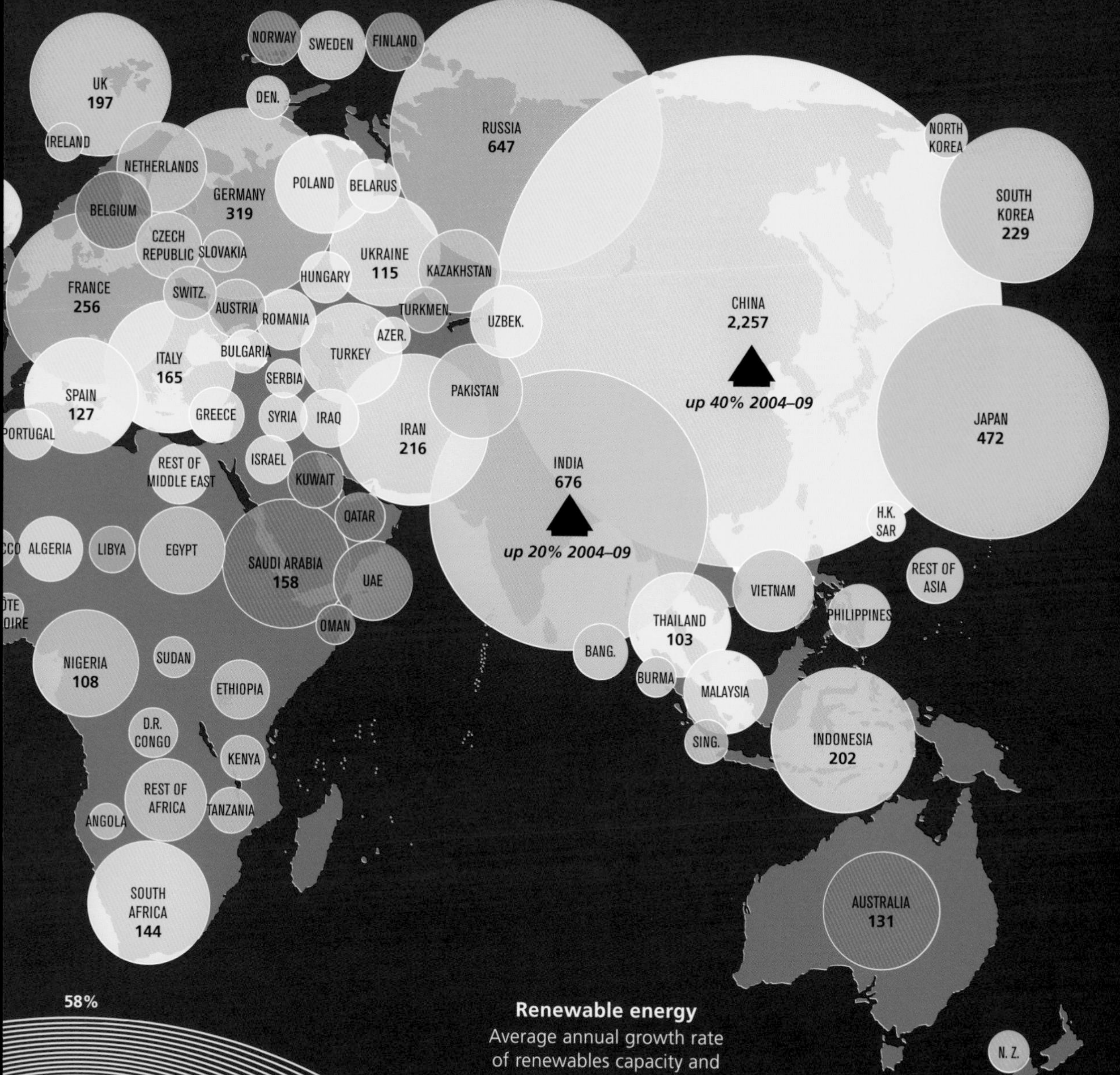

Renewable energy
Average annual growth rate of renewables capacity and biofuels production
2006–11

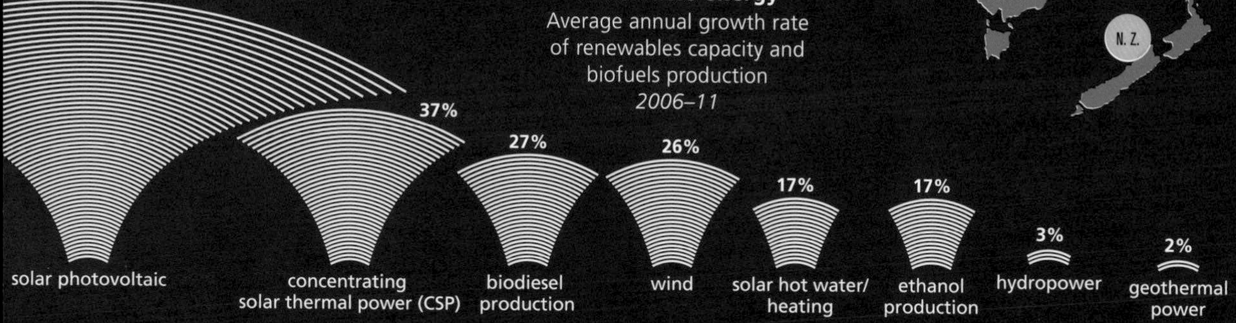

116 Climate Change ▶

Climate Change

The basic science of global warming and climate change is well established and is in doubt barely anywhere. The earth is habitable because of the effect of the so-called 'greenhouse gases' that prevent too much warmth escaping from the planet. Among the key greenhouse gases are carbon and methane. Any buildup of these gases intensifies the greenhouse effect and causes the planet to get warmer. This much has been understood since the mid-19th century.

In the past 200 years, about half a trillion tonnes of carbon dioxide (CO_2) have entered the atmosphere, mainly through use of coal and oil. Then there is methane, produced by raising livestock and a variety of industries as well as landfill sites. Less has been emitted but it is 20 times as effective a greenhouse gas as CO_2. Nitrous oxide (emitted mainly from agriculture) is 300 times as effective.

International climate change talks aim at controlling emissions to a maximum of 450 parts per million (ppm) of CO_2 equivalent in the atmosphere. This has been calculated as giving a 50:50 chance of restricting average global temperature increase to 2°C above pre-industrial era levels. This small-sounding increase will have a major impact on many regions' climate, and most of the expected effects are harmful – more floods, more droughts, shorter growing seasons.

While 450 ppm may give an even chance of staying within the 2° limit, there is also an even chance of further warming. Many scientists argue that to be sure of staying below 2°, the atmospheric concentration needed to be kept to 350 ppm – a level already exceeded.

Greenland ice sheet

As the ice melts, the height of surface ice decreases and is exposed to warmer temperatures at lower altitudes. This could accelerate melting and lead to the ice-sheets breaking up, with consequent sea-level rise over the coming three centuries.

1°C–2°C

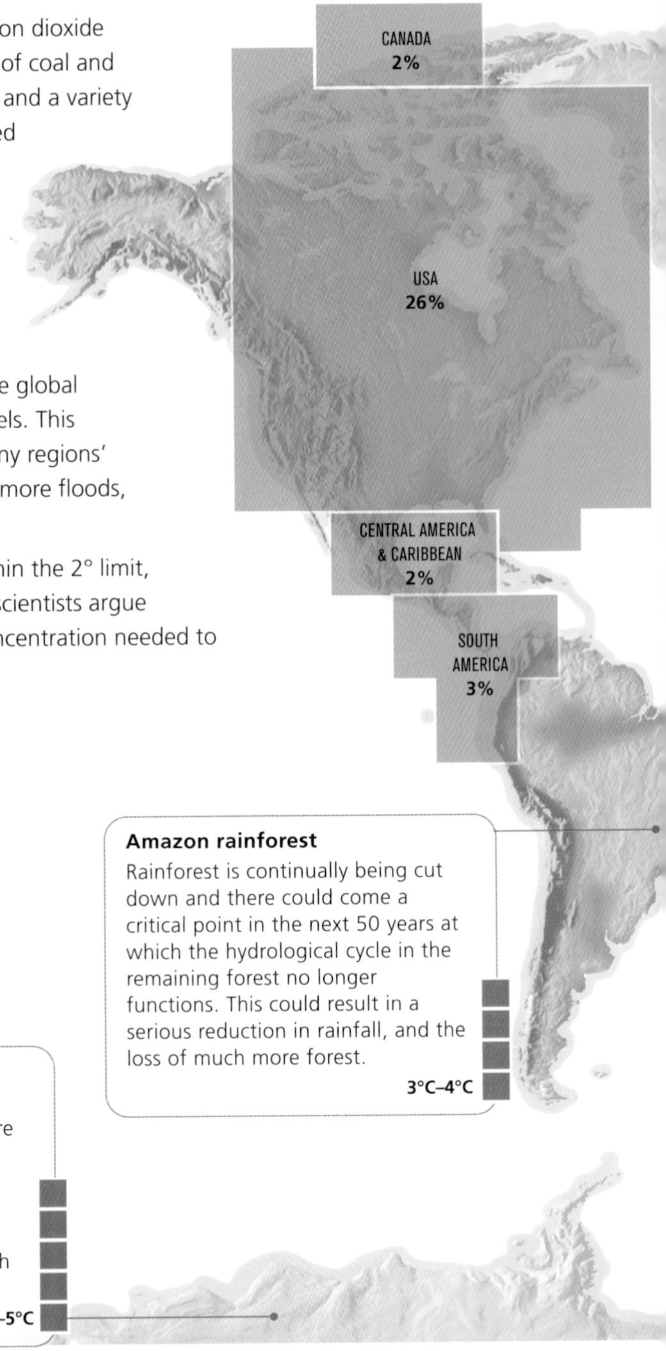

Amazon rainforest

Rainforest is continually being cut down and there could come a critical point in the next 50 years at which the hydrological cycle in the remaining forest no longer functions. This could result in a serious reduction in rainfall, and the loss of much more forest.

3°C–4°C

West Antarctic ice sheet

The ice-sheets are frozen into submarine mountains, the structure of which could be weakened by a warming ocean. The subsequent melting of the ice now above sea level could lead to a sea-level rise over the next 300 years of as much as 5 metres.

3°C–5°C

◀ 106 Warning Signs; 114 Energy Us

Saharan and West African monsoon

Small changes to the monsoon have triggered abrupt wetting and drying of the Sahara in the past. Drier conditions would produce additional dust across the Sahara, which affects distant rainfall too.

3°C–5°C

Sea-level rise

A widely accepted projection is for the sea level to rise by 18–59 cms by 2100. At present, actually observed sea-level rise is tracking the upper end of that range. Small island states and low-lying coastal cities face severe risks.

Past emissions and future consequences

share of total CO_2 emissions from fossil fuels and cement *1950–2007*

1% = 9,310 million tonnes CO_2

temperature increase at which transition could be triggered

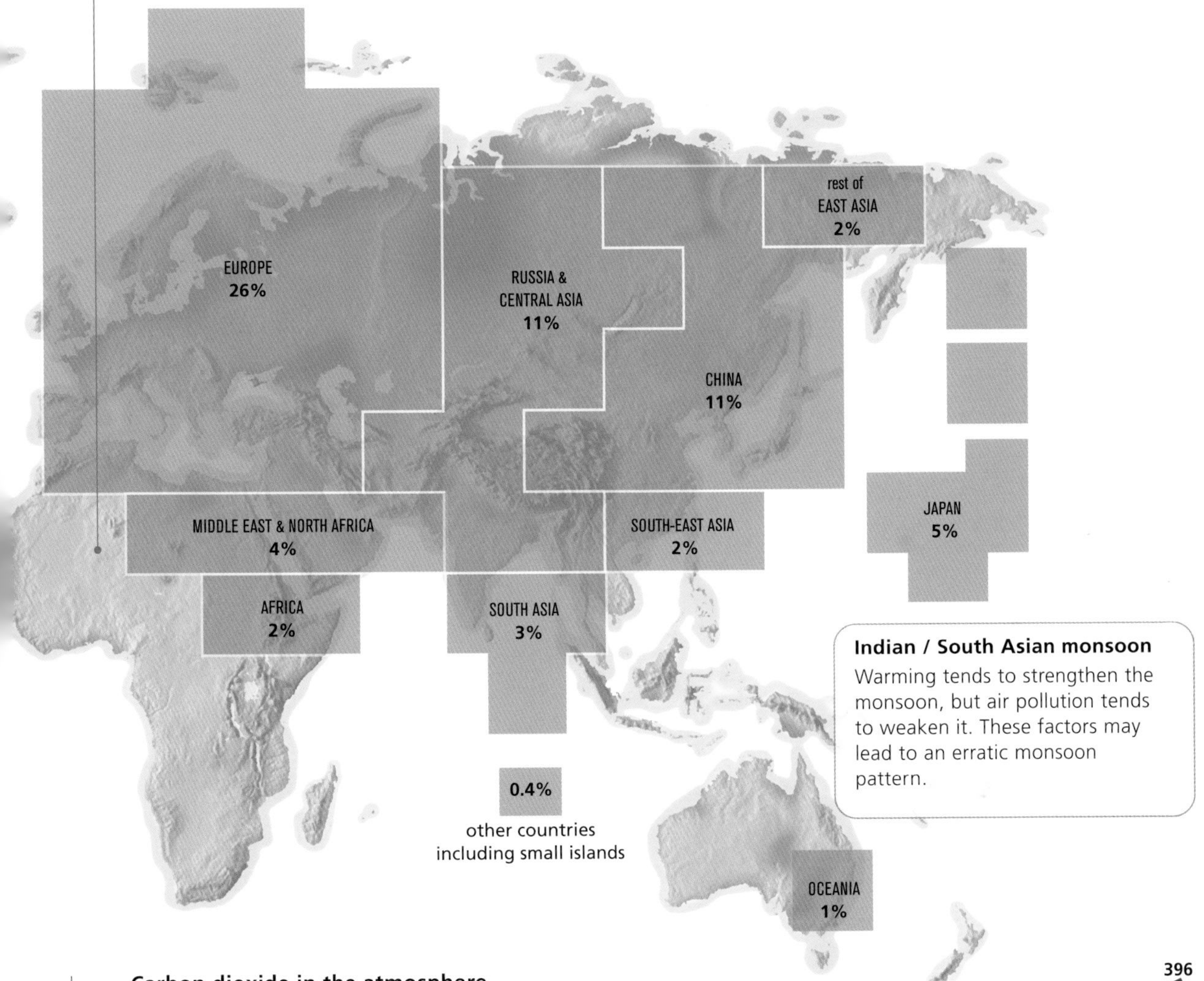

Indian / South Asian monsoon

Warming tends to strengthen the monsoon, but air pollution tends to weaken it. These factors may lead to an erratic monsoon pattern.

Carbon dioxide in the atmosphere

Global tropospheric concentration
1750–2012
parts per million

ice-core measurements

atmospheric readings

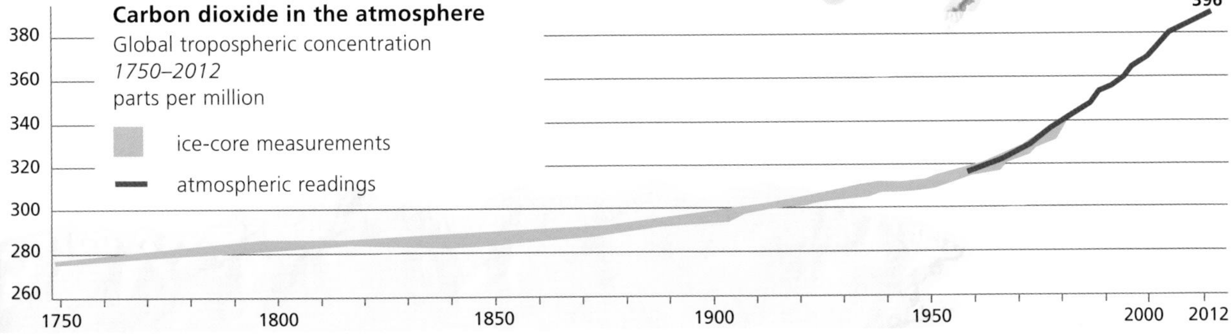

118 Planetary Boundaries ▶

Planetary Boundaries

Humanity's impact on the natural environment increases as population grows and industrial and agricultural production grow with it. We have never been here before – there has never been so much activity, never such a large population – so many of the consequences of our environmental impact are unknown. We don't really know how far we can go before the consequences get very serious. And compared to how much is already known about climate change, biodiversity loss and other issues, not much at all is known about the interaction between the impacts.

The concept of planetary boundaries, generated by a multinational group of 29 scientists brought together by the Stockholm Resilience Centre, is an attempt to deal with both these gaps in our knowledge. The idea looks likely to be an important part of the debate about environmental impact and policy in the coming decade.

Not every scientist agrees with the way in which the boundaries are defined and calculated. Some think they are too tight, some find them too loose. Some think a couple more boundaries should be brought into the picture.

Contested as it is, the concept of planetary boundaries brings the key issues into sharp relief. Inside the boundaries (wherever they precisely lie) we are operating more or less safely. If we transgress them, we don't know what will then unfold. According to one group of scientists, we have crossed three; there is time to ensure we do not cross more.

Planetary Boundaries
Assessment of the extent to which safe operating levels have been reached or transgressed
2012

boundary (limit of safe operating level)

estimated current level

	Measured by:	Boundary calculated as:
Climate change	Carbon dioxide in atmosphere	Increase to not more than 350 parts per million
Ocean acidification	Aragonite depletion in ocean	Reduction to not less than 80% of pre-industrial level
Ozone depletion	Concentration of ozone in stratosphere	No more than 5% reduction from pre-industrial level
Phosphorus cycle	Phosphorus in oceans	11 million tonnes per year
Nitrogen cycle	Nitrogen removed from atmosphere	35 million tonnes per year
Fresh water	Human consumption	4,000 cubic kilometres per year
Land use	Land used for crops	15% of land surface
Aerosols	Particles in the atmosphere	Not calculated
Chemical pollution	Concentration of toxic substances in environment	Not calculated
Biodiversity	Loss of species	10 species extinct per million per year

◄ *106 Warning Signs; 116 Climate Change*

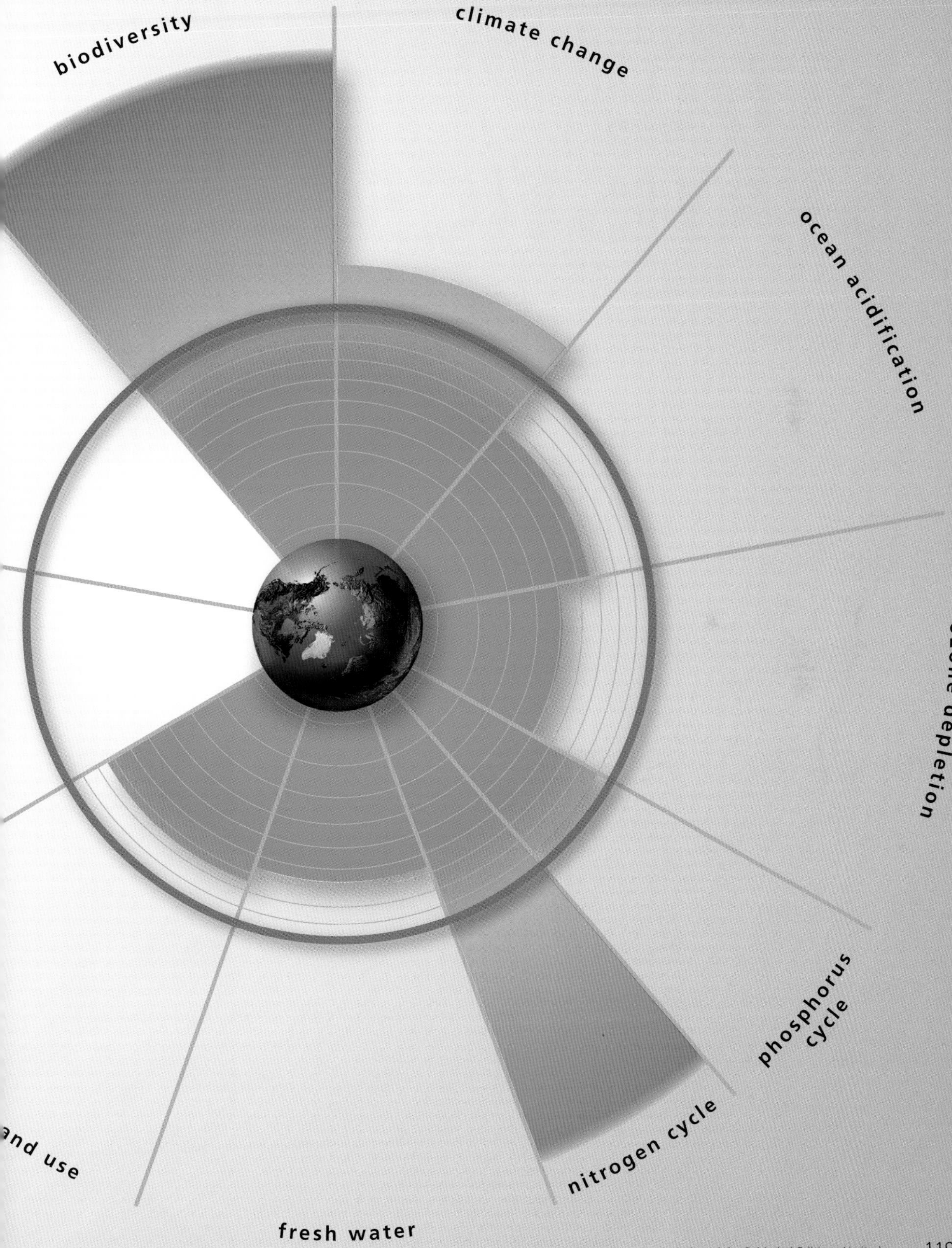
biodiversity
climate change
ocean acidification
ozone depletion
phosphorus cycle
nitrogen cycle
fresh water
and use

PART SEVEN

VITAL STATISTICS

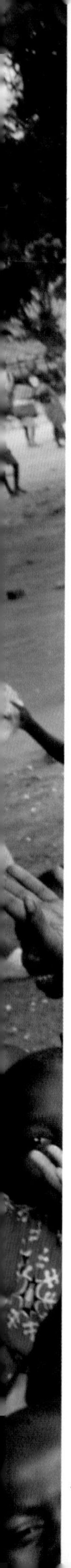

U.S.A

Indicators of Wellbeing

	Official capital	Land area	Population		Migrants	Life expectancy	Literat adult
		1,000 hectares *2008*	1,000s *2010*	rate of change *2005–10*	(excluding refugees) as % of total *2000*	at birth *2009*	as % of a populati *2010 c latest*
Afghanistan	Kabul	65,209	31,412	2.6%	0.3%	48	–
Albania	Tirane	2,740	3,204	0.4%	2.8%	73	96%
Algeria	Algiers	238,174	35,468	1.5%	0.7%	72	73%
Angola	Luanda	124,670	19,082	2.9%	0.3%	52	70%
Antigua and Barbuda	Saint John's	44	89	1.1%	23.6%	74	99%
Argentina	Buenos Aires	273,669	40,412	0.9%	3.6%	75	98%
Armenia	Yerevan	2,820	3,092	0.2%	10.5%	70	100%
Australia	Canberra	768,230	22,268	1.7%	21.9%	82	–
Austria	Vienna	8,245	8,394	0.4%	15.6%	80	–
Azerbaijan	Baku	8,266	9,188	1.4%	3.0%	68	100%
Bahamas	Nassau	1,001	343	1.4%	9.7%	76	–
Bahrain	Al-Manámah	71	1,262	11.1%	39.1%	74	91%
Bangladesh	Dhaka	13,017	148,692	1.1%	0.7%	65	56%
Barbados	Bridgetown	43	273	0.2%	10.9%	76	–
Belarus	Mensk	20,748	9,595	-0.5%	11.4%	70	100%
Belgium	Brussels	3,023	10,712	0.6%	9.1%	80	–
Belize	Belmopan	2,281	312	2.1%	15.0%	73	–
Benin	Porto-Novo	11,062	8,850	3.0%	2.5%	57	42%
Bhutan	Thimphu	4,700	726	1.9%	5.7%	63	53%
Bolivia	La Paz	108,438	9,930	1.6%	1.5%	68	91%
Bosnia and Herzegovina	Sarajevo	5,120	3,760	-0.1%	0.7%	76	98%
Botswana	Gaborone	56,673	2,007	1.4%	5.8%	61	84%
Brazil	Brasilia	845,942	194,946	0.9%	0.4%	73	90%
Brunei	Bandar Seri Begawan	527	399	1.9%	36.4%	77	95%
Bulgaria	Sofia	10,864	7,494	-0.6%	1.4%	74	98%
Burkina Faso	Ouagadougou	27,360	16,469	3.0%	6.4%	52	29%
Burma	Nay Pyi Taw	65,755	47,963	0.7%	0.2%	64	92%
Burundi	Bujumbura	2,568	8,383	2.9%	0.7%	50	67%
Cambodia	Phnom Penh	17,652	14,138	1.1%	2.2%	61	78%
Cameroon	Yaoundé	46,540	19,599	2.2%	1.0%	51	71%
Canada	Ottawa	909,351	34,017	1.0%	21.3%	81	–
Cape Verde	Praia	403	496	1.0%	2.4%	71	85%
Central African Republic	Bangui	62,300	4,401	1.8%	1.8%	48	55%
Chad	N'Djamena	125,920	11,227	2.7%	3.4%	48	34%
Chile	Santiago	74,880	17,114	1.0%	1.9%	79	99%
China	Beijing	932,749	1,341,335	0.5%	0.1%	74	94%
Colombia	Santafé de Bogotá	110,950	46,295	1.5%	0.2%	76	93%
Comoros	Moroni	186	735	2.7%	2.0%	60	74%
Congo	Brazzaville	34,150	4,043	2.7%	3.8%	55	–
Congo, Dem. Rep.	Kinshasa	226,705	65,966	2.8%	0.7%	49	67%
Costa Rica	San José	5,106	4,659	1.6%	10.5%	79	96%
Côte d'Ivoire	Yamoussoukro	31,800	19,738	1.8%	11.2%	50	55%
Croatia	Zagreb	5,592	4,403	-0.2%	15.9%	76	99%
Cuba	Havana	10,982	11,258	0.0%	0.1%	78	100%
Cyprus	Lefkosia (Nicosia)	924	1,104	1.3%	17.5%	81	98%
Czech Republic	Prague	7,726	10,493	0.5%	4.4%	77	–
Denmark	Copenhagen	4,243	5,550	0.5%	8.8%	79	–

Education primary enrolment *2010 or latest*	Undernourished as % of population *2007*	Overweight adults as % of population *2008*	Improved facilities % with access to water source *2010*	Improved facilities % with access to sanitation *2010*	DALYs years lost to ill-health, disability or early death per 100,000 people *2004*	
–	–	12%	50%	37%	76,578	Afghanistan
85	–	54%	95%	94%	15,921	Albania
94	–	48%	83%	95%	16,114	Algeria
–	41%	26%	51%	58%	79,754	Angola
88	21%	59%	–	–	16,049	Antigua and Barbuda
99	–	64%	–	–	15,599	Argentina
84	21%	55%	98%	90%	18,841	Armenia
97	–	61%	100%	100%	11,070	Australia
–	–	50%	100%	100%	12,069	Austria
85	–	57%	80%	82%	18,945	Azerbaijan
91	6%	69%	–	100%	18,626	Bahamas
97	–	70%	–	–	12,015	Bahrain
86	26%	8%	81%	56%	26,569	Bangladesh
–	–	68%	100%	100%	16,401	Barbados
94	–	56%	100%	93%	22,076	Belarus
99	–	52%	100%	100%	12,948	Belgium
97	–	71%	98%	90%	20,042	Belize
92	12%	26%	75%	13%	42,929	Benin
87	–	24%	96%	44%	23,916	Bhutan
94	27%	50%	88%	27%	25,544	Bolivia
87	–	58%	99%	95%	16,079	Bosnia and Herzegovina
87	25%	36%	96%	62%	49,246	Botswana
95	6%	53%	98%	79%	19,475	Brazil
93	–	31%	–	–	11,351	Brunei
97	–	54%	100%	100%	18,296	Bulgaria
63	8%	13%	79%	17%	54,802	Burkina Faso
–	–	19%	83%	76%	28,825	Burma
99	62%	15%	72%	46%	60,637	Burundi
95	25%	13%	64%	31%	36,464	Cambodia
92	22%	38%	77%	49%	45,774	Cameroon
99	–	61%	100%	100%	11,531	Canada
83	11%	38%	88%	61%	17,197	Cape Verde
69	40%	17%	67%	34%	55,133	Central African Republic
61	39%	16%	51%	13%	60,031	Chad
95	–	65%	96%	96%	12,995	Chile
–	10%	25%	91%	64%	15,279	China
90	9%	50%	92%	77%	19,142	Colombia
87	47%	20%	95%	36%	24,949	Comoros
59	13%	22%	71%	18%	36,740	Congo
–	–	11%	45%	24%	65,555	Congo, Dem. Rep.
–	–	60%	97%	95%	12,519	Costa Rica
57	14%	27%	80%	24%	60,795	Côte d'Ivoire
89	–	53%	99%	99%	15,369	Croatia
99	–	53%	94%	91%	13,937	Cuba
99	–	56%	100%	100%	12,010	Cyprus
–	–	62%	100%	98%	14,326	Czech Republic
95	–	48%	100%	100%	13,447	Denmark

Indicators of Wellbeing

	Official capital	Land area	Population		Migrants (excluding refugees) as % of total	Life expectancy	Literate adults as % of adult population
		1,000 hectares *2008*	1,000s *2010*	rate of change *2005–10*	*2000*	at birth *2009*	*2010 or latest*
Djibouti	Djibouti	2,318	889	1.9%	13.0%	60	–
Dominica	Roseau	75	68	-0.3%	8.3%	74	–
Dominican Republic	Santo Domingo	4,838	9,927	1.4%	4.2%	71	88%
East Timor	Dili	1,487	1,124	2.1%	1.2%	67	51%
Ecuador	Quito	27,684	14,465	1.5%	2.9%	75	84%
Egypt	Cairo	99,545	81,121	1.8%	0.3%	71	66%
El Salvador	San Salvador	2,072	6,193	0.5%	0.7%	72	84%
Equatorial Guinea	Malabo	2,805	700	2.8%	1.1%	53	93%
Eritrea	Asmara	10,100	5,254	3.2%	0.3%	66	67%
Estonia	Tallinn	4,239	1,341	-0.1%	13.6%	75	100%
Ethiopia	Addis Ababa	100,000	82,950	2.2%	0.6%	54	30%
Fiji	Suva	1,827	861	0.9%	2.2%	69	–
Finland	Helsinki	30,459	5,365	0.5%	4.2%	80	–
France	Paris	55,010	62,787	0.6%	10.7%	81	–
Gabon	Libreville	25,767	1,505	1.9%	18.9%	62	88%
Gambia	Banjul	1,000	1,728	2.8%	16.6%	60	46%
Georgia	Tbilisi	6,949	4,352	-0.6%	4.0%	71	100%
Germany	Berlin	34,877	82,302	-0.1%	13.1%	80	–
Ghana	Accra	22,754	24,392	2.4%	7.6%	60	67%
Greece	Athens	12,890	11,359	0.3%	10.1%	80	97%
Grenada	St George's	34	104	0.3%	12.1%	73	96%
Guatemala	Guatemala City	10,843	14,389	2.5%	0.4%	69	74%
Guinea	Conakry	24,572	9,982	2.0%	3.8%	52	39%
Guinea-Bissau	Bissau	2,812	1,515	2.0%	1.2%	49	52%
Guyana	Georgetown	19,685	754	0.2%	1.5%	67	–
Haiti	Port-au-Prince	2,756	9,993	1.3%	0.3%	62	49%
Honduras	Tegucigalpa	11,189	7,601	2.0%	0.3%	69	84%
Hungary	Budapest	8,961	9,984	-0.2%	3.7%	74	99%
Iceland	Reykjavik	10,025	320	1.5%	11.3%	82	–
India	New Delhi	297,319	1,224,614	1.4%	0.4%	65	63%
Indonesia	Jakarta	181,157	239,871	1.1%	0.1%	68	92%
Iran	Tehran	162,855	73,974	1.2%	2.8%	73	85%
Iraq	Baghdad	43,737	31,672	2.9%	0.3%	66	78%
Ireland	Dublin	6,889	4,470	1.4%	19.6%	80	–
Israel	Jerusalem	2,164	7,418	2.3%	40.4%	82	–
Italy	Rome	29,411	60,551	0.6%	7.4%	82	99%
Jamaica	Kingston	1,083	2,741	0.4%	1.1%	71	86%
Japan	Tokyo	36,450	126,536	0.0%	1.7%	83	–
Jordan	Amman	8,824	6,187	2.9%	45.9%	71	92%
Kazakhstan	Astana	269,970	16,026	1.1%	19.5%	64	100%
Kenya	Nairobi	56,914	40,513	2.6%	2.0%	60	87%
Kiribati	Tarawa	81	100	1.6%	2.0%	68	–
Korea, North	Pyongyang	12,041	24,346	0.5%	0.2%	70	100%
Korea, South	Seoul	9,873	48,184	0.5%	1.1%	80	–
Kuwait	Kuwait City	1,782	2,737	3.8%	68.8%	78	94%
Kyrgyzstan	Bishkek	19,180	5,334	1.1%	4.0%	66	99%
Laos	Vientiane	23,080	6,201	1.5%	0.3%	63	73%

ducation primary nrolment *2010 or latest*	Under-nourished as % of population *2007*	Over-weight adults as % of population *2008*	Improved facilities % with access to water source *2010*	sanitation *2010*	DALYs years lost to ill-health, disability or early death per 100,000 people *2004*	
44	26%	34%	88%	50%	35,428	Djibouti
93	–	57%	–	–	16,038	Dominica
80	24%	55%	86%	83%	21,303	Dominican Republic
82	31%	13%	69%	47%	28,090	East Timor
95	15%	56%	94%	92%	17,713	Ecuador
93	–	70%	99%	95%	18,613	Egypt
94	9%	63%	88%	87%	18,867	El Salvador
54	–	36%	–	–	56,480	Equatorial Guinea
36	65%	11%	–	–	27,457	Eritrea
94	–	51%	98%	95%	18,900	Estonia
83	41%	8%	44%	21%	47,529	Ethiopia
89	–	67%	98%	83%	17,753	Fiji
96	–	53%	100%	100%	13,205	Finland
98	–	46%	100%	100%	12,262	France
80	–	44%	87%	33%	31,510	Gabon
67	19%	28%	89%	68%	36,037	Gambia
100	6%	53%	98%	95%	15,715	Georgia
97	–	55%	100%	100%	12,536	Germany
76	–	30%	86%	14%	34,141	Ghana
99	–	49%	100%	98%	11,826	Greece
93	21%	56%	–	97%	18,911	Grenada
95	22%	54%	92%	78%	22,026	Guatemala
73	16%	22%	74%	18%	44,488	Guinea
52	22%	21%	64%	20%	59,745	Guinea-Bissau
95	8%	45%	94%	84%	27,666	Guyana
–	57%	32%	69%	17%	36,911	Haiti
97	12%	52%	87%	77%	20,009	Honduras
91	–	58%	100%	100%	17,941	Hungary
98	–	56%	100%	100%	9,803	Iceland
91	19%	11%	92%	34%	27,316	India
95	13%	21%	82%	54%	23,854	Indonesia
99	–	55%	96%	100%	17,517	Iran
88	–	65%	79%	73%	53,044	Iraq
96	–	61%	100%	99%	11,692	Ireland
97	–	60%	100%	100%	10,031	Israel
98	–	49%	100%	–	11,245	Italy
80	5%	56%	93%	80%	16,314	Jamaica
100	–	22%	100%	100%	10,170	Japan
89	–	69%	97%	98%	14,935	Jordan
89	–	57%	95%	97%	27,583	Kazakhstan
82	33%	21%	59%	32%	42,452	Kenya
97	–	81%	–	–	24,065	Kiribati
–	35%	17%	98%	80%	21,749	Korea, North
99	–	31%	98%	100%	12,928	Korea, South
88	–	79%	99%	100%	9,829	Kuwait
84	11%	47%	90%	93%	23,066	Kyrgyzstan
93	22%	15%	67%	63%	29,205	Laos

Indicators of Wellbeing

	Official capital	Land area	Population		Migrants	Life expectancy	Literate adults
		1,000 hectares *2008*	1,000s *2010*	rate of change *2005–10*	(excluding refugees) as % of total *2000*	at birth *2009*	as % of a populati *2010 o latest*
Latvia	Riga	6,229	2,252	-0.5%	15.0%	72	100%
Lebanon	Beirut	1,023	4,228	0.8%	17.8%	74	90%
Lesotho	Maseru	3,035	2,171	1.0%	0.3%	48	90%
Liberia	Monrovia	9,632	3,994	4.5%	2.3%	56	59%
Libya	Tripoli	175,954	6,355	1.9%	10.4%	72	89%
Lithuania	Vilnius	6,268	3,324	-0.5%	4.0%	73	100%
Luxembourg	Luxembourg	259	507	2.1%	35.2%	81	–
Macedonia	Skopje	2,543	2,061	0.2%	6.3%	74	97%
Madagascar	Antananarivo	58,154	20,714	2.9%	0.2%	65	64%
Malawi	Lilongwe	9,408	14,901	3.0%	1.8%	47	74%
Malaysia	Kuala Lumpur	32,855	28,401	1.7%	8.4%	73	92%
Maldives	Malé	30	316	1.4%	1.0%	75	98%
Mali	Bamako	122,019	15,370	3.1%	1.2%	53	26%
Malta	Valletta	32	417	0.4%	3.8%	80	92%
Marshall Islands	Majuro	18	54	0.8%	2.7%	59	–
Mauritania	Nouakchott	103,070	3,460	2.5%	2.9%	58	57%
Mauritius	Port Louis	203	1,299	0.7%	3.3%	73	88%
Mexico	Mexico City	194,395	113,423	1.3%	0.7%	76	93%
Micronesia, Fed. Sts.	Palikir	70	111	0.3%	2.4%	69	–
Moldova	Chisinau	3,287	3,573	-1.1%	11.4%	69	98%
Mongolia	Ulaan Baatar	156,650	2,756	1.6%	0.4%	69	97%
Montenegro	Podgorica	1,381	631	0.2%	6.8%	75	–
Morocco	Rabat	44,630	31,951	1.0%	0.2%	73	56%
Mozambique	Maputo	78,638	23,391	2.4%	1.9%	49	55%
Namibia	Windhoek	82,329	2,283	1.9%	6.3%	57	89%
Nepal	Kathmandu	14,300	29,959	1.9%	3.2%	67	59%
Netherlands	Amsterdam	3,388	16,613	0.4%	10.5%	81	–
New Zealand	Wellington	26,771	4,368	1.1%	22.4%	81	–
Nicaragua	Managua	12,140	5,788	1.3%	0.7%	74	78%
Niger	Niamey	126,670	15,512	3.5%	1.3%	57	29%
Nigeria	Abuja	91,077	158,423	2.5%	0.7%	54	61%
Norway	Oslo	30,428	4,883	1.1%	10.0%	81	–
Oman	Muscat	30,950	2,782	2.7%	28.4%	74	87%
Pakistan	Islamabad	77,088	173,593	1.8%	2.3%	63	56%
Palestinien Territories	–	602	4,039	2.6%	43.6%	–	95%
Panama	Panama City	7,443	3,517	1.7%	3.4%	77	94%
Papua New Guinea	Port Moresby	45,286	6,858	2.4%	0.4%	63	60%
Paraguay	Asunción	39,730	6,455	1.8%	2.5%	74	95%
Peru	Lima	128,000	29,077	1.1%	0.1%	76	90%
Philippines	Manila	29,817	93,261	1.7%	0.5%	70	95%
Poland	Warsaw	30,633	38,277	0.1%	2.2%	76	100%
Portugal	Lisbon	9,150	10,676	0.2%	8.6%	79	95%
Puerto Rico	San Juan	887	3,749	-0.2%	8.1%	–	90%
Qatar	Doha	1,100	1,759	15.2%	86.5%	78	95%
Romania	Bucharest	22,998	21,486	-0.3%	0.6%	73	98%
Russia	Moscow	1,638,139	142,958	-0.1%	8.7%	68	100%
Rwanda	Kigali	2,467	10,624	2.9%	4.5%	59	71%

ducation primary enrolment *2010 or latest*	Under-nourished as % of population *2007*	Over-weight adults as % of population *2008*	Improved facilities % with access to water source *2010*	sanitation *2010*	DALYs years lost to ill-health, disability or early death per 100,000 people *2004*	
93	–	54%	99%	–	19,615	Latvia
90	–	63%	100%	–	18,161	Lebanon
73	14%	41%	78%	26%	41,163	Lesotho
75	32%	23%	73%	18%	70,241	Liberia
–	–	65%	–	97%	14,414	Libya
94	–	57%	–	–	18,401	Lithuania
96	–	57%	100%	100%	12,341	Luxembourg
87	–	53%	100%	88%	16,777	Macedonia
98	25%	11%	46%	15%	35,656	Madagascar
91	27%	21%	83%	51%	58,748	Malawi
94	–	45%	100%	96%	14,616	Malaysia
96	10%	41%	98%	97%	19,952	Maldives
75	12%	21%	64%	22%	62,726	Mali
91	–	62%	100%	100%	11,141	Malta
80	–	80%	94%	75%	24,578	Marshall Islands
76	8%	39%	50%	26%	35,732	Mauritania
94	–	49%	99%	89%	16,801	Mauritius
98	–	69%	96%	85%	14,702	Mexico
–	–	77%	–	–	15,051	Micronesia, Fed. Sts.
88	–	49%	96%	85%	20,892	Moldova
90	27%	47%	82%	51%	20,343	Mongolia
83	–	55%	98%	90%	16,802	Montenegro
90	–	49%	83%	70%	16,684	Morocco
92	38%	23%	47%	18%	48,090	Mozambique
89	18%	35%	93%	32%	30,131	Namibia
–	17%	9%	89%	31%	29,514	Nepal
99	–	48%	100%	100%	11,486	Netherlands
99	–	64%	100%	–	11,612	New Zealand
92	19%	58%	85%	52%	17,453	Nicaragua
57	16%	14%	49%	9%	78,040	Niger
61	6%	29%	58%	31%	56,297	Nigeria
99	–	55%	100%	100%	11,790	Norway
77	–	58%	89%	99%	11,892	Oman
66	25%	24%	92%	48%	26,112	Pakistan
75	21%	–	85%	92%	–	Palestinien Territories
97	15%	61%	–	–	14,694	Panama
–	–	48%	40%	45%	28,634	Papua New Guinea
85	10%	51%	86%	71%	16,826	Paraguay
94	16%	48%	85%	71%	17,672	Peru
92	13%	27%	92%	74%	19,525	Philippines
96	–	56%	–	–	14,911	Poland
99	–	55%	99%	100%	13,615	Portugal
–	–	–	–	–	–	Puerto Rico
93	–	72%	100%	100%	10,301	Qatar
90	–	49%	–	–	17,685	Romania
92	–	58%	97%	70%	27,885	Russia
96	32%	20%	65%	55%	59,702	Rwanda

Indicators of Wellbeing

	Official capital	Land area	Population		Migrants	Life expectancy	Literat adults
		1,000 hectares 2008	1,000s 2010	rate of change 2005–10	(excluding refugees) as % of total 2000	at birth 2009	as % of ac populatic 2010 or latest
Samoa	Apia	283	183	0.3%	5.0%	70	99%
São Tomé and Principe	São Tomé	96	165	1.6%	3.2%	68	89%
Saudi Arabia	Riyadh	214,969	27,448	2.7%	27.8%	72	86%
Senegal	Dakar	19,253	12,434	2.7%	1.6%	62	50%
Serbia	Belgrade	7,747	9,856	0.0%	5.3%	74	–
Seychelles	Victoria	46	87	0.7%	12.8%	73	92%
Sierra Leone	Freetown	7,162	5,868	2.6%	1.8%	49	41%
Singapore	Singapore	69	5,086	3.5%	40.7%	82	95%
Slovakia	Bratislava	4,810	5,462	0.2%	2.4%	75	–
Slovenia	Ljubljana	2,014	2,030	0.3%	8.1%	79	100%
Solomon Islands	Honiara	2,799	538	2.7%	1.3%	71	–
Somalia	Mogadishu	62,734	9,331	2.2%	0.2%	51	–
South Africa	Pretoria	121,447	50,133	1.0%	3.7%	54	89%
South Sudan	Juba	64,433	10 625	–	–	n/a	27%
Spain	Madrid	49,919	46,077	1.2%	14.1%	82	98%
Sri Lanka	Colombo	6,463	20,860	1.0%	1.7%	71	91%
St. Lucia	Castries	–	174	1.1%	5.9%	74	–
St. Vincent and Grenadines	Kingstown	–	109	0.1%	7.9%	73	–
Sudan	Khartoum	186,148	43,552	2.5%	1.7%	59	70%
Suriname	Paramaribo	15,600	525	1.0%	7.5%	72	95%
Swaziland	Mbabane	1,720	1,186	1.4%	3.4%	49	87%
Sweden	Stockholm	41,033	9,380	0.8%	14.1%	81	–
Switzerland	Bern	4,000	7,664	0.7%	23.2%	82	–
Syria	Damascus	18,378	20,411	2.0%	9.8%	74	84%
Taiwan	Taipei	3,226	23 113	1.3%	–	78	96%
Tajikistan	Dushanbe	13,996	6,879	2.9%	4.0%	68	100%
Tanzania	Dar es Salaam	88,580	44,841	0.7%	1.5%	55	73%
Thailand	Bangkok	51,089	69,122	2.2%	1.7%	70	94%
Togo	Lomé	5,439	6,028	-1.3%	2.7%	59	57%
Tonga	Nuku'alofa	72	104	0.6%	0.8%	71	99%
Trinidad and Tobago	Port-of-Spain	513	1,341	0.4%	2.6%	70	99%
Tunisia	Tunis	15,536	10,481	1.1%	0.3%	75	78%
Turkey	Ankara	76,963	72,752	1.3%	1.9%	75	91%
Turkmenistan	Ashgabat	46,993	5,042	1.2%	4.0%	63	100%
Uganda	Kampala	19,710	33,425	3.2%	1.9%	52	73%
Ukraine	Kyiv	57,938	45,448	-0.6%	11.6%	68	100%
United Arab Emirates	Abu Dhabi	8,360	7,512	12.3%	70.0%	78	90%
United Kingdom	London	24,193	62,036	0.6%	10.4%	80	–
United States	Washington D.C.	916,192	310,384	0.9%	13.5%	79	–
Uruguay	Montevideo	17,502	3,369	0.3%	2.4%	76	98%
Uzbekistan	Tashkent	42,540	27,445	1.1%	4.2%	69	99%
Vanuatu	Port-Vila	1,219	240	2.5%	0.3%	71	82%
Venezuela	Caracas	88,205	28,980	1.7%	3.5%	75	95%
Vietnam	Hanoi	31,007	87,848	1.1%	0.1%	72	93%
Yemen	Sanaá	52,797	24,053	3.1%	2.1%	65	62%
Zambia	Lusaka	74,339	13,089	2.7%	1.8%	48	71%
Zimbabwe	Harare	38,685	12,571	0.0%	2.9%	49	92%

ucation primary nrolment 2010 or latest	Under-nourished as % of population 2007	Over-weight adults as % of population 2008	Improved facilities % with access to water source 2010	sanitation 2010	DALYs years lost to ill-health, disability or early death per 100,000 people 2004	
90	–	86%	96%	98%	16,836	Samoa
98	–	37%	89%	26%	33,751	São Tomé and Principe
86	–	71%	–	–	15,453	Saudi Arabia
73	19%	28%	72%	52%	39,066	Senegal
94	–	56%	99%	92%	16,802	Serbia
94	8%	58%	–	–	16,297	Seychelles
–	35%	28%	55%	13%	82,444	Sierra Leone
–	–	28%	100%	100%	10,542	Singapore
–	–	58%	100%	100%	15,340	Slovakia
97	–	61%	99%	100%	14,002	Slovenia
81	11%	68%	–	–	19,257	Solomon Islands
–	–	22%	29%	23%	68,800	Somalia
85	–	68%	91%	79%	44,148	South Africa
–	–	–	55%	–	–	South Sudan
100	–	58%	100%	100%	11,352	Spain
95	20%	22%	91%	92%	24,521	Sri Lanka
91	8%	54%	96%	65%	15,586	St. Lucia
95	–	58%	–	–	18,743	St. Vincent and Grenadines
39	22%	25%	58%	26%	38,779	Sudan
90	15%	58%	92%	83%	21,237	Suriname
83	19%	50%	71%	57%	50,860	Swaziland
96	–	50%	100%	100%	11,478	Sweden
94	–	44%	100%	100%	10,745	Switzerland
95	–	66%	90%	95%	13,660	Syria
–	–	–	–	–	–	Taiwan
97	26%	34%	64%	94%	25,000	Tajikistan
96	34%	24%	53%	10%	48,494	Tanzania
90	16%	31%	96%	96%	20,525	Thailand
93	30%	21%	61%	13%	41,837	Togo
99	–	88%	100%	96%	–	Tonga
93	11%	65%	94%	92%	19,721	Trinidad and Tobago
98	–	56%	–	–	14,653	Tunisia
95	–	64%	100%	90%	15,246	Turkey
–	7%	44%	–	98%	26,320	Turkmenistan
92	22%	21%	72%	34%	50,471	Uganda
89	–	52%	98%	94%	23,689	Ukraine
90	–	72%	100%	98%	10,036	United Arab Emirates
100	–	62%	100%	100%	12,871	United Kingdom
91	–	69%	99%	100%	13,937	United States
99	–	57%	100%	100%	16,245	Uruguay
87	11%	48%	87%	100%	19,669	Uzbekistan
97	–	65%	90%	57%	17,783	Vanuatu
92	7%	68%	–	–	16,061	Venezuela
94	11%	10%	95%	76%	15,327	Vietnam
73	30%	46%	55%	53%	35,531	Yemen
91	44%	18%	61%	48%	62,500	Zambia
–	30%	29%	80%	40%	67,959	Zimbabwe

Economy & Environment

	GNI PPP$		Human Development Index	Gini Index	Gender Inequality Index	Government gross debt	Corruption Perception Index
	total millions *2010 or latest*	per capita *2010 or latest*	*2011*	*2009 or latest*	score *2011*	as % of GDP *2010*	score *2010*
Afghanistan	36,503	860	0.398	29.40	0.71	–	1.
Albania	27,294	8,740	0.739	34.51	0.27	60%	3.
Algeria	287,203	8,120	0.698	–	0.41	–	2.
Angola	104,266	5,400	0.486	–	–	31%	2.
Antigua and Barbuda	1,795	15,350	0.764	–	–	93%	
Argentina	629,310	15,250	0.797	45.84	0.37	48%	3.
Armenia	17,503	5,450	0.716	30.86	0.34	39%	2.
Australia	823,018	38,380	0.929	–	0.14	18%	8.
Austria	333,875	39,390	0.885	–	0.13	70%	7.
Azerbaijan	83,936	9,050	0.700	33.71	0.31	11%	2.
Bahamas	10,502	24,580	0.771	–	0.33	47%	7.
Bahrain	–	24,710	0.806	–	0.29	32%	5.
Bangladesh	269,657	1,800	0.500	31.02	0.55	–	2.
Barbados	5,183	18,830	0.793	–	0.36	114%	7.
Belarus	128,961	14,250	0.756	27.22	–	18%	2.
Belgium	417,252	37,800	0.886	–	0.11	97%	7.
Belize	2,139	5,970	0.699	–	0.49	82%	
Benin	14,048	1,580	0.427	–	0.63	31%	3.
Bhutan	3,622	4,950	0.522	–	0.49	–	5.
Bolivia	46,041	4,610	0.663	57.26	0.48	37%	2.
Bosnia and Herzegovina	33,520	8,970	0.733	36.21	–	37%	3.
Botswana	27,492	13,710	0.633	–	0.51	13%	6.
Brazil	2,144,886	10,920	0.718	53.90	0.45	66%	3.
Brunei	19,661	49,730	0.838	–	–	0%	5.
Bulgaria	101,238	13,250	0.771	45.32	0.25	18%	3.
Burkina Faso	20,658	1,250	0.331	–	0.60	28%	3.
Burma	93,539	–	0.483	–	0.49	43%	1.
Burundi	3,379	400	0.316	33.27	0.48	48%	1.
Cambodia	29,424	2,040	0.523	44.37	0.50	30%	2.
Cameroon	44,507	2,230	0.482	38.91	0.64	13%	2.
Canada	1,309,483	37,280	0.908	–	0.14	84%	8.
Cape Verde	1,841	3,790	0.568	–	–	80%	5.
Central African Republic	3,465	780	0.343	56.30	0.67	33%	2.
Chad	13,653	1,210	0.328	–	0.74	36%	2.
Chile	250,480	13,900	0.805	52.33	0.37	9%	7.
China	10,221,684	7,570	0.687	41.53	0.21	18%	3.
Colombia	419,515	9,000	0.710	58.49	0.48	37%	3.
Comoros	802	1,080	0.433	–	–	52%	2.
Congo	12,899	3,050	0.533	47.32	0.63	17%	2.
Congo, Dem. Rep.	21,354	320	0.286	44.43	0.71	30%	2.
Costa Rica	52,491	10,840	0.744	50.31	0.36	39%	4.
Côte d'Ivoire	35,756	1,800	0.400	41.50	0.66	67%	2.
Croatia	82,527	18,730	0.796	33.65	0.17	40%	4.
Cuba	–	–	0.776	–	0.34	62%	4.
Cyprus	24,831	30,180	0.840	–	0.14	–	6.
Czech Republic	241,005	23,640	0.865	–	0.14	40%	4.
Denmark	227,982	40,290	0.895	–	0.06	44%	9.

…dow …omy	Military expenditure	Energy Use		CO_2 emissions	Water withdrawals		
…% of …mal …omy …-2007	as % of GDP *2009*	million tonnes oil equiv. *2009*	kg oil equiv. per capita *2009*	tonnes per capita *2008*	cubic metres per capita *2010 or latest*	as % of total renewable resources *2008 or latest*	
–	1.8%	–	–	0	938	36%	Afghanistan
34%	2.0%	2	538	1.3	595	4%	Albania
33%	3.8%	40	1,138	3.2	196	53%	Algeria
47%	4.2%	12	641	1.4	43	0%	Angola
–	0.7%	–	–	5.1	78	3%	Antigua and Barbuda
25%	0.8%	74	1,853	4.8	865	4%	Argentina
44%	4.7%	3	843	1.8	920	36%	Armenia
14%	2.0%	131	5,971	18.6	1,152	5%	Australia
10%	0.7%	32	3,784	8.1	452	5%	Austria
58%	3.5%	12	1,338	5.4	1,384	35%	Azerbaijan
27%	1.4%	–	–	6.5	–	–	Bahamas
18%	3.6%	9	8,096	21.4	386	206%	Bahrain
35%	1.1%	30	201	0.3	241	3%	Bangladesh
–	1.0%	–	–	5.0	226	76%	Barbados
46%	1.8%	27	2,815	6.5	435	7%	Belarus
22%	1.3%	57	5,300	9.8	590	34%	Belgium
43%	1.0%	–	–	1.3	570	1%	Belize
50%	1.5%	3	404	0.5	19	0%	Benin
29%	–	–	–	1.0	466	0%	Bhutan
66%	1.7%	6	638	1.3	234	0%	Bolivia
34%	1.4%	6	1,580	8.3	90	1%	Bosnia and Herzegovina
33%	3.2%	2	1,034	2.5	107	2%	Botswana
39%	1.6%	240	1,243	2.1	306	1%	Brazil
31%	3.2%	3	7,971	27.5	302	1%	Brunei
35%	1.9%	17	2,305	6.6	817	29%	Bulgaria
41%	1.3%	–	–	0.1	76	8%	Burkina Faso
–	–	15	316	0.3	729	3%	Burma
40%	3.2%	–	–	0	43	2%	Burundi
49%	2.5%	5	371	0.3	160	0%	Cambodia
32%	1.6%	7	361	0.3	58	0%	Cameroon
16%	1.5%	254	7,534	16.3	1,470	2%	Canada
35%	0.6%	–	–	0.6	49	7%	Cape Verde
45%	1.8%	–	–	0.1	17	0%	Central African Republic
44%	6.4%	–	–	0	42	1%	Chad
19%	3.1%	29	1,698	4.4	718	1%	Chile
13%	1.5%	2,257	1,695	5.3	410	20%	China
37%	4.1%	32	697	1.5	308	1%	Colombia
39%	–	–	–	0.2	17	1%	Comoros
46%	1.4%	1	356	0.5	14	0%	Congo
47%	1.1%	23	357	0	12	0%	Congo, Dem. Rep.
26%	0.7%	5	1,067	1.8	656	2%	Costa Rica
45%	1.4%	10	535	0.4	82	2%	Côte d'Ivoire
32%	1.6%	9	1,965	5.3	143	1%	Croatia
–	3.1%	12	1,022	2.8	676	20%	Cuba
28%	2.0%	3	2,298	7.9	167	18%	Cyprus
18%	1.6%	42	4,004	11.2	165	13%	Czech Republic
18%	1.4%	19	3,369	8.4	119	11%	Denmark

Economy & Environment

	GNI PPP$		Human Development Index	Gini Index	Gender Inequality Index	Government gross debt	Corrupti Percepti Index
	total millions *2010 or latest*	per capita *2010 or latest*	*2011*	*2009 or latest*	score *2011*	as % of GDP *2010*	score *2010*
Djibouti	2,149	2,440	0.430	–	–	58%	3
Dominica	812	9,370	0.724	–	–	86%	5
Dominican Republic	89,600	8,960	0.689	48.44	0.48	29%	2
East Timor	4,046	3,570	0.495	31.93	–	–	2
Ecuador	114,008	8,830	0.720	48.99	0.47	18%	2
Egypt	491,329	6,160	0.644	32.14	–	74%	2
El Salvador	40,552	6,390	0.674	46.57	0.49	51%	3
Equatorial Guinea	16,635	23,570	0.537	–	–	8%	1
Eritrea	2,841	540	0.349	–	–	145%	2
Estonia	26,541	19,510	0.835	–	0.19	7%	6
Ethiopia	86,087	1,030	0.363	29.76	–	37%	2
Fiji	3,880	4,450	0.688	–	–	56%	
Finland	198,866	37,180	0.882	–	0.07	48%	9
France	2,254,888	34,440	0.884	–	0.11	84%	7
Gabon	19,655	13,150	0.674	41.45	0.51	18%	3
Gambia	2,246	1,290	0.420	–	0.61	57%	3
Georgia	22,235	4,960	0.733	41.34	0.42	39%	4
Germany	3,115,390	38,140	0.905	–	0.09	80%	8
Ghana	39,439	1,600	0.541	42.76	0.60	41%	3
Greece	312,704	27,380	0.861	–	0.16	142%	3
Grenada	1,033	7,550	0.748	–	–	115%	
Guatemala	66,844	4,600	0.574	53.69	0.54	18%	2
Guinea	10,211	1,020	0.344	39.35	–	89%	2
Guinea-Bissau	1,795	1,180	0.353	–	–	48%	2
Guyana	2,606	3,560	0.633	–	0.51	61%	2
Haiti	11,619	1,110	0.454	–	0.60	16%	1
Honduras	28,648	3,740	0.625	57.70	0.51	26%	2
Hungary	195,457	19,270	0.816	31.18	0.24	80%	4
Iceland	8,991	28,720	0.898	–	0.10	97%	8
India	4,159,721	3,560	0.547	36.80	0.62	69%	3
Indonesia	1,008,241	4,170	0.617	36.76	0.50	27%	3
Iran	839,981	11,380	0.707	38.28	0.48	12%	2
Iraq	108,103	3,350	0.573	30.86	0.58	112%	1
Ireland	150,094	32,520	0.908	–	0.20	96%	7
Israel	210,846	27,630	0.888	–	0.14	78%	5
Italy	1,923,684	31,130	0.874	–	0.12	119%	3
Jamaica	19,747	7,450	0.727	–	0.45	140%	3
Japan	4,411,692	34,780	0.901	–	0.12	220%	8
Jordan	35,077	5,810	0.698	37.72	0.46	61%	4
Kazakhstan	175,727	10,610	0.745	30.88	0.33	11%	2
Kenya	66,568	1,630	0.509	47.68	0.63	51%	2
Kiribati	352	3,510	0.624	–	–	–	3
Korea, North	–	–	..	–	–	31%	1
Korea, South	1,422,703	29,010	0.897	–	0.11	–	5
Kuwait	–	58,350	0.760	–	0.23	11%	4
Kyrgyzstan	11,291	2,180	0.615	33.43	0.37	63%	2
Laos	15,129	2,390	0.524	36.74	0.51	61%	2

dow nomy % of mal nomy –2007	Military expenditure as % of GDP *2009*	Energy Use million tonnes oil equiv. *2009*	Energy Use kg oil equiv. per capita *2009*	CO_2 emissions tonnes per capita *2008*	Water withdrawals cubic metres per capita *2010 or latest*	Water withdrawals as % of total renewable resources *2008 or latest*	
–	3.5%	–	–	0.6	25	6%	Djibouti
–	–	–	–	1.9	244	–	Dominica
32%	0.6%	8	826	2.2	393	17%	Dominican Republic
–	–	–	–	0.2	1,105	14%	East Timor
32%	3.5%	11	796	1.9	1,194	4%	Ecuador
35%	2.2%	72	903	2.7	973	95%	Egypt
45%	0.6%	5	828	1.0	230	5%	El Salvador
31%	0.1%	–	–	7.3	31	0%	Equatorial Guinea
40%	4.2%	1	142	0.1	121	9%	Eritrea
31%	1.8%	5	3,543	13.6	1,337	14%	Estonia
39%	1.4%	33	402	0.1	81	5%	Ethiopia
32%	1.9%	–	–	1.5	100	0%	Fiji
18%	1.6%	33	6,213	10.6	309	1%	Finland
15%	2.1%	256	3,970	5.9	512	15%	France
48%	1.2%	2	1,214	1.7	101	0%	Gabon
44%	0.7%	–	–	0.3	52	1%	Gambia
66%	5.6%	3	723	1.2	411	3%	Georgia
16%	1.4%	319	3,889	9.6	391	21%	Germany
41%	0.7%	9	388	0.4	49	2%	Ghana
28%	3.0%	29	2,609	8.7	841	13%	Greece
–	–	–	–	2.4	97	–	Grenada
51%	0.4%	10	701	0.9	249	3%	Guatemala
39%	1.6%	–	–	0.1	188	1%	Guinea
41%	1.6%	–	–	0.2	136	1%	Guinea-Bissau
34%	1.0%	–	–	2.0	2,222	1%	Guyana
56%	0.2%	3	263	0.3	134	9%	Haiti
48%	0.8%	4	592	1.2	184	1%	Honduras
24%	1.1%	25	2,480	5.4	557	5%	Hungary
16%	–	5	16,405	7.0	539	0%	Iceland
22%	3.1%	676	560	1.5	621	34%	India
19%	0.9%	202	851	1.7	517	6%	Indonesia
18%	2.6%	216	2,951	7.4	1,306	68%	Iran
–	6.3%	32	1,035	3.4	2,616	87%	Iraq
16%	0.6%	14	3,216	9.9	227	2%	Ireland
22%	6.9%	22	2,878	5.2	282	102%	Israel
27%	1.4%	165	2,735	7.4	790	24%	Italy
35%	0.5%	3	1,208	4.5	223	6%	Jamaica
11%	1.0%	472	3,700	9.5	714	21%	Japan
19%	5.5%	7	1,260	3.7	166	90%	Jordan
41%	1.3%	66	4,091	15.1	2,218	29%	Kazakhstan
33%	1.8%	19	474	0.3	73	9%	Kenya
–	–	–	–	0.3	–	–	Kiribati
–	–	19	795	3.2	361	11%	Korea, North
27%	2.7%	229	4,701	10.4	549	37%	Korea, South
19%	4.3%	30	11,402	30.1	441	2075%	Kuwait
40%	0.8%	3	559	1.2	2,015	44%	Kyrgyzstan
30%	0.3%	–	–	0.3	718	1%	Laos

Economy & Environment

	GNI PPP$		Human Development Index	Gini Index	Gender Inequality Index	Government gross debt	Corruption Perception Index
	total millions *2010 or latest*	per capita *2010 or latest*	*2011*	*2009 or latest*	score *2011*	as % of GDP *2010*	score *2010*
Latvia	36,538	16,350	0.805	–	0.22	40%	4.
Lebanon	59,540	14,260	0.739	–	0.44	137%	2.
Lesotho	4,275	1,840	0.450	–	0.53	38%	3.
Liberia	1,365	340	0.329	38.16	0.67	119%	3.
Libya	105,745	16,740	0.760	–	0.31	0%	2
Lithuania	58,634	17,870	0.810	37.57	0.19	39%	4
Luxembourg	31,050	63,950	0.867	–	0.17	17%	8.
Macedonia	22,798	10,830	0.728	44.20	0.15	18%	3.
Madagascar	19,851	950	0.480	47.24	–	35%	3.
Malawi	12,816	850	0.400	–	0.59	43%	3.
Malaysia	403,891	14,110	0.761	46.21	0.29	54%	4.
Maldives	2,563	5,450	0.661	–	0.32	65%	2.
Mali	15,758	1,020	0.359	38.99	0.71	28%	2.
Malta	10,325	23,160	0.832	–	0.27	67%	5.
Marshall Islands	–	–	..	–	–	–	
Mauritania	8,338	1,950	0.453	–	0.61	86%	2.
Mauritius	17,914	13,670	0.728	–	0.35	51%	5.
Mexico	1,632,957	14,360	0.770	51.74	0.45	43%	3.
Micronesia, Fed. Sts.	388	3,420	0.636	–	–	–	
Moldova	11,976	3,340	0.649	38.03	0.30	30%	2.
Mongolia	10,118	3,630	0.653	33.03	0.41	–	2.
Montenegro	8,073	12,590	0.771	29.99	–	44%	4.
Morocco	149,302	4,620	0.582	40.88	0.51	50%	3.
Mozambique	21,654	920	0.322	45.66	0.60	32%	2.
Namibia	14,668	6,380	0.625	–	0.47	18%	4.
Nepal	36,196	1,200	0.458	–	0.56	36%	2.
Netherlands	694,664	42,610	0.910	–	0.05	64%	8.
New Zealand	121,277	28,050	0.908	–	0.20	32%	9.
Nicaragua	16,148	2,630	0.589	52.33	0.51	82%	2.
Niger	11,178	720	0.295	34.04	0.72	18%	2.
Nigeria	354,946	2,160	0.459	–	–	16%	2.
Norway	286,347	57,100	0.943	–	0.08	54%	9.
Oman	68,305	24,960	0.705	–	0.31	6%	4.
Pakistan	484,362	2,780	0.504	32.74	0.57	57%	2.
Palestinien Territories	–	2,710	0.641	–	–	–	
Panama	44,896	12,910	0.768	52.34	0.49	41%	3.
Papua New Guinea	16,564	2,400	0.466	–	0.67	–	2.
Paraguay	32,767	5,440	0.665	51.95	0.48	15%	2.
Peru	259,567	9,070	0.725	47.96	0.42	18%	3.
Philippines	370,748	3,950	0.644	44.04	0.43	47%	2.
Poland	731,509	19,010	0.813	34.21	0.16	56%	5.
Portugal	261,578	24,710	0.809	–	0.14	83%	6.
Puerto Rico	–	–	–	–	–	–	5.
Qatar	–	–	0.831	41.10	0.55	18%	7.
Romania	306,370	14,060	0.781	31.15	0.33	35%	3.
Russia	2,726,810	19,190	0.755	42.27	0.34	10%	2.
Rwanda	12,259	1,150	0.429	53.08	0.45	18%	5.

…dow …nomy	Military expenditure	Energy Use		CO2 emissions	Water withdrawals		
% of …rmal …nomy …–2007	as % of GDP 2009	million tonnes oil equiv. 2009	kg oil equiv. per capita 2009	tonnes per capita 2008	cubic metres per capita 2010 or latest	as % of total renewable resources 2008 or latest	
29%	1.2%	4	1,871	3.3	176	1%	Latvia
33%	4.1%	7	1,580	4.1	317	19%	Lebanon
31%	3.3%	–	–	–	25	2%	Lesotho
44%	0.9%	–	–	0.2	60	0%	Liberia
34%	2.8%	20	3,258	9.5	796	711%	Libya
32%	1.1%	8	2,512	4.5	704	10%	Lithuania
10%	0.5%	4	7,934	21.5	136	2%	Luxembourg
38%	1.7%	3	1,352	5.8	502	16%	Macedonia
41%	1.1%	–	–	0.1	899	4%	Madagascar
42%	1.1%	–	–	0.1	82	6%	Malawi
31%	2.0%	67	2,391	7.6	488	2%	Malaysia
30%	4.0%	–	–	3.0	19	16%	Maldives
41%	2.0%	–	–	0	545	7%	Mali
27%	0.7%	1	1,931	6.2	134	71%	Malta
–	–	–	–	1.9	–	–	Marshall Islands
–	3.8%	–	–	0.6	572	14%	Mauritania
23%	0.2%	–	–	3.1	568	26%	Mauritius
30%	0.5%	175	1,559	4.3	704	17%	Mexico
–	–	–	–	0.6	–	–	Micronesia, Fed. Sts.
–	0.4%	2	687	1.3	483	16%	Moldova
18%	0.9%	3	1,194	4.1	195	1%	Mongolia
–	1.4%	–	–	3.1	255	–	Montenegro
35%	3.3%	15	477	1.5	428	43%	Morocco
–	0.9%	10	427	0.1	39	0%	Mozambique
30%	3.3%	2	764	1.8	152	2%	Namibia
37%	1.4%	10	338	0.1	345	5%	Nepal
13%	1.5%	78	4,729	10.6	639	12%	Netherlands
12%	1.2%	17	4,032	7.8	1,200	1%	New Zealand
45%	0.7%	3	540	0.8	247	1%	Nicaragua
–	1.0%	–	–	0.1	202	7%	Niger
–	0.9%	108	701	0.6	79	4%	Nigeria
19%	1.6%	28	5,849	10.5	622	1%	Norway
18%	8.7%	15	5,554	17.3	516	84%	Oman
36%	2.4%	86	502	1.0	1,057	74%	Pakistan
–	–	–	–	0.5	112	50%	Palestinien Territories
–	1.1%	3	896	2.0	147	0%	Panama
37%	0.5%	–	–	0.3	61	0%	Papua New Guinea
39%	0.9%	5	749	0.7	88	0%	Paraguay
58%	1.2%	16	550	1.4	728	1%	Peru
42%	0.9%	39	424	0.9	875	17%	Philippines
27%	1.7%	94	2,464	8.3	313	19%	Poland
23%	1.6%	24	2,266	5.3	812	12%	Portugal
–	–	–	–	–	264	14%	Puerto Rico
19%	2.5%	24	14,911	49.1	377	381%	Qatar
33%	1.4%	34	1,602	4.4	320	3%	Romania
44%	3.1%	647	4,561	12.0	455	1%	Russia
–	2.2%	–	–	0.1	17	2%	Rwanda

Economy & Environment

	GNI PPP$		Human Development Index	Gini Index	Gender Inequality Index	Government gross debt	Corruption Perception Index
	total millions *2010 or latest*	per capita *2010 or latest*	*2011*	*2009 or latest*	score *2011*	as % of GDP *2010*	score *2010*
Samoa	782	4,200	0.688	–	–	–	3.9
São Tomé and Principe	318	1,910	0.509	–	–	78%	3.0
Saudi Arabia	609,782	22,540	0.770	–	0.65	11%	4.4
Senegal	23,810	1,910	0.459	39.19	0.57	38%	2.9
Serbia	80,826	11,230	0.766	28.16	–	44%	3.3
Seychelles	1,835	21,050	0.773	65.77	–	83%	4.8
Sierra Leone	4,851	820	0.336	–	0.66	57%	2.5
Singapore	283,254	55,380	0.866	–	0.09	97%	9.2
Slovakia	124,807	23,120	0.834	–	0.19	42%	4.0
Slovenia	54,356	27,140	0.884	–	0.18	37%	5.9
Solomon Islands	1,192	2,200	0.510	–	–	26%	2.7
Somalia	–	–	..	–	–	–	1.0
South Africa	517,673	10,280	0.619	67.40	0.49	36%	4.1
South Sudan	–	–	–	–	–	–	–
Spain	1,465,197	31,640	0.878	–	0.12	60%	6.2
Sri Lanka	104,568	4,980	0.691	40.26	0.42	–	3.3
St. Lucia	1,830	8,520	0.723	–	–	77%	7.0
St. Vincent and Grenadines	1,184	8,260	0.717	–	–	82%	5.8
Sudan	88,573	2,020	0.408	–	0.61	68%	1.6
Suriname	3,991	7,610	0.680	–	–	18%	3.0
Swaziland	5,910	4,950	0.522	–	0.55	18%	3.1
Sweden	372,623	39,660	0.904	–	0.05	40%	9.3
Switzerland	391,004	48,960	0.903	–	0.07	55%	8.8
Syria	104,626	5,150	0.632	–	0.47	27%	2.6
Taiwan	758,600	–	–	32.60	–	40%	6.1
Tajikistan	14,692	2,120	0.607	–	0.35	37%	2.3
Tanzania	62,999	1,420	0.466	37.58	0.59	44%	3.0
Thailand	565,806	8,120	0.682	–	0.38	44%	3.4
Togo	5,391	890	0.435	34.41	0.60	28%	2.4
Tonga	477	4,640	0.704	–	–	–	3.1
Trinidad and Tobago	32,255	24,040	0.760	–	0.33	40%	3.2
Tunisia	95,577	8,130	0.698	–	0.29	40%	3.8
Turkey	1,129,893	15,180	0.699	43.23	0.44	42%	4.2
Turkmenistan	37,765	7,350	0.686	–	–	7%	1.6
Uganda	41,804	1,240	0.446	44.30	0.58	18%	2.4
Ukraine	303,807	6,560	0.729	27.51	0.34	40%	2.3
United Arab Emirates	350,971	49,050	0.846	–	0.23	18%	6.8
United Kingdom	2,230,578	36,590	0.863	–	0.21	77%	7.8
United States	14,635,600	47,120	0.910	–	0.30	92%	7.1
Uruguay	45,719	13,890	0.783	42.42	0.35	55%	7.0
Uzbekistan	87,747	3,090	0.641	–	–	10%	1.6
Vanuatu	1,035	4,450	0.617	–	–	–	3.5
Venezuela	350,192	11,950	0.735	43.50	0.45	39%	1.9
Vietnam	267,048	2,960	0.593	37.57	0.31	53%	2.9
Yemen	60,117	2,350	0.462	37.69	0.77	41%	2.1
Zambia	17,831	1,370	0.430	–	0.63	27%	3.2
Zimbabwe	–	–	0.376	–	0.58	56%	2.2

dow omy	Military expenditure	Energy Use		CO_2 emissions	Water withdrawals		
% of mal omy -2007	as % of GDP *2009*	million tonnes oil equiv. *2009*	kg oil equiv. per capita *2009*	tonnes per capita *2008*	cubic metres per capita *2010 or latest*	as % of total renewable resources *2008 or latest*	
–	–	–	–	0.9	–	–	Samoa
–	–	–	–	0.8	53	0%	São Tomé and Principe
18%	11.0%	158	5,888	16.6	928	936%	Saudi Arabia
44%	1.7%	3	243	0.4	222	6%	Senegal
–	2.2%	14	1,974	6.8	418	3%	Serbia
–	0.8%	–	–	7.8	161	–	Seychelles
46%	0.6%	–	–	0.2	110	0%	Sierra Leone
13%	4.3%	18	3,704	6.7	82	32%	Singapore
18%	1.5%	17	3,086	6.9	127	1%	Slovakia
26%	1.6%	7	3,417	8.5	464	3%	Slovenia
34%	–	–	–	0.4	–	–	Solomon Islands
–	–	–	–	0.1	378	22%	Somalia
27%	1.5%	144	2,921	8.9	272	25%	South Africa
–	–	–	–	–	–	58%	South Sudan
23%	1.2%	127	2,756	7.2	705	29%	Spain
44%	3.5%	9	449	0.6	639	25%	Sri Lanka
–	–	–	–	2.3	98	–	St. Lucia
–	–	–	–	1.8	93	–	St. Vincent and Grenadines
–	1.3%	16	372	0.3	1,037	58%	Sudan
38%	1.1%	–	–	4.7	1,396	1%	Suriname
–	–	–	–	1.1	962	23%	Swaziland
19%	1.3%	45	4,883	5.3	286	2%	Sweden
9%	0.8%	27	3,480	5.3	360	5%	Switzerland
19%	4.2%	23	1,123	3.6	867	86%	Syria
25%	2.5%	–	–	–	–	–	Taiwan
42%	1.0%	2	342	0.5	1,903	75%	Tajikistan
56%	1.2%	20	451	0.2	145	5%	Tanzania
51%	1.8%	103	1,504	4.2	845	13%	Thailand
–	1.6%	3	445	0.2	33	1%	Togo
–	–	–	–	1.7	–	–	Tonga
33%	0.5%	20	15,158	37.4	178	6%	Trinidad and Tobago
37%	1.2%	9	881	2.4	296	61%	Tunisia
31%	1.8%	98	1,359	4.0	573	18%	Turkey
–	–	20	3,933	9.7	5,415	101%	Turkmenistan
42%	2.0%	–	–	0.1	12	0%	Uganda
50%	1.2%	115	2,507	7.0	801	28%	Ukraine
26%	3.6%	60	8,588	25.0	740	1867%	United Arab Emirates
13%	2.7%	197	3,183	8.5	213	9%	United Kingdom
9%	4.7%	2,163	7,051	18.0	1,583	16%	United States
51%	1.1%	4	1,224	2.5	1,101	3%	Uruguay
–	–	49	1,758	4.6	2,358	118%	Uzbekistan
–	–	–	–	0.4	–	–	Vanuatu
34%	1.0%	67	2,357	6.1	359	1%	Venezuela
15%	2.2%	64	745	1.5	965	9%	Vietnam
27%	3.5%	8	324	1.0	162	169%	Yemen
47%	1.7%	8	617	0.2	163	2%	Zambia
62%	–	10	763	0.7	334	21%	Zimbabwe

Notes & Sources

For sources available on the internet, in most cases only the root address has been given. To view the source, it is recommended that the reader types the title of the page or document into a search engine.

Part One: Who We Are

Evans NJ. Indirect passage from Europe: Transmigration via the UK, 1836–1914. *Journal for Maritime Research* 3(1) (2001): 70–84.

Seabright P. *The Company of Strangers*. Princeton, NJ: Princeton University Press, 2006, p. 205.

20 The States of the World

Sovereignty won; State formation

Turner B (editor). *The Statesman's Yearbook 2008: The politics, cultures and economies of the world*. Hampshire: Palgrave Macmillan, 2008.

The World Factbook. www.cia.gov [Accessed 13 April 2012].

22 Population

UNFPA. *State of World Population 2011. People and possibilities in a world of 7 billion*. www.unfpa.org

United Nations Department of Economic and Social Affairs: Population Division, Population Estimates and Projections Section, and World Fertility Policies 2011. esa.un.org

The World Bank. World Development Indicators online. data.worldbank.org

The World Factbook. www.cia.gov

People in the world

UN Population Division. World Population Prospects. The 2010 Revision. esa.un.org

Changing population

esa.un.org

24 Life Expectancy

UNAIDS www.unaids.org

Life expectancy; Gender difference

WHO. *World Health Statistics 2011*. Part II. Global health indicator tables and footnotes. www.who.int

The World Factbook. www.cia.gov

Growing older

Riley J. Estimates of regional and global life expectancy, 1800–2001. *Population and Development Review* 31(3) (2005); 537-43. Table 1. www.jstor.org

WHO 2011. op.cit.

26 Ethnicity & Diversity

Ethnic, national, and racial minorities; The language of government

The World Factbook. www.cia.gov

BBC News country profiles. news.bbc.co.uk

Ethnologue: Languages of the World. www.ethnologue.com

Minority Rights Group. *World Directory of Minorities and Indigenous Peoples*. www.minorityrights.org

Federal Research Division, US Library of Congress. Library of Congress Country Studies. lcweb2.loc.gov

Migrants

UN Population Division Dept. of Economic and Social Affairs. International Migration 2009. www.un.org/esa

28 Religious Beliefs

O'Brien J, Palmer M. *The Atlas of Religion*. London: Earthscan, 2007.

The World Factbook. www.cia.gov

Mapping the global Muslim population. The Pew Research Center / Pew Forum on Religious and Public Life, Washington, DC, Oct 2009. www.pewforum.org

A report on the size and distribution of the world's Christian population. Dec 2011. www.pewforum.org

30 Literacy & Education

Provost, C. Global teacher shortage threatens progress on education. 7 Oct 2011. www.guardian.co.uk

Adult illiteracy; Enrolment in education

The World Bank. World Development Indicators online. data.worldbank.org

The World Factbook. www.cia.gov

20% of adults…

UNESCO Institute for Statistics. Adult and youth literacy: Global trends in gender parity. UIS Factsheet, Sept 2010, no.3. www.uis.unesco.org

32 Urbanization

UN Habitat. *State of the World's Cities 2010/2011*. www.unhabitat.org

Pavgi K. The 7 fastest-growing cities in the world. 26 Oct 2011. www.foreignpolicy.com

Urban population; City scale

The World Bank. World Development Indicators online. data.worldbank.org

Ten largest cities; There were 1.2 billion…

UN Dept. of Economic and Social Affairs: Population Division, World Urbanization Prospects, 2009 Revision. File 11a. esa.un.org

34 Diversity of Cities

Cities around the world

The largest cities in the world by land area, population and density. Largest cities and their mayors in 2011. www.citymayors.com

10 biggest metro areas. www.dimensionsguide.com

Individual city entries on en.wikipedia.org

McFarlane, C. Sanitation in Mumbai's informal settlements: Governance, infrastructure and cost recovery, 2008. www.irmgard-coninx-stiftung.de

Iraq smog 'kills 3,600 in month'. BBC News, 9 Jan 2007. news.bbc.co.uk

Gatored Community. 12 July 2009. www.snopes.com

Emergy D. Alligators in the sewers. urbanlegends.about.com

Comparative wealth of city dwellers

The richest cities in the world. 22 Aug 2009. www.citymayors.com

Part Two: Wealth & Poverty

38 Income

Gross National Income; Growth spurt; Economic output increased…

The World Bank. World Development Indicators online. data.worldbank.org

The World Factbook. www.cia.gov

Who crashed in the 2008 crash?

Gallup. Chinese struggling less than Americans to afford basics. www.gallup.com

40 Inequality

Distribution of wealth; World poverty; 16% of global economic…

The World Bank. World Development Indicators online. data.worldbank.org

The hands of a few

The world's billionaires 2008, 2009, 2011. www.forbes.com

42 Quality of Life

Relative human development

UNDP. *Human Development Report 2011*. Table 1. hdr.undp.org

The happiness league; Daily experience of life

High wellbeing eludes the masses in most countries worldwide. 19 April 2011. www.gallup.com.

The alternative view

Colwell J. North Korean 'Global Happiness Index' ranks China no. 1, USA dead last. 31 May 2011. www.shanghaiist.com

North Korea: One of the happiest places on Earth? 1 June 2011. www.newsfeed.time.com

Quality carbon

The World Bank. World Development Indicators online. data.worldbank.org

44 Transnationals

UN Population Division. World Population Prospects. The 2010 Revision. esa.un.org

Corporate wealth

The World Bank. World Development Indicators online. data.worldbank.org

The World Factbook. www.cia.gov

Global 500 money.cnn.com

Business Pundit: Scary (but true) facts about Walmart. www.businesspundit.com

McDonalds. www.aboutmcdonalds.com

Kraft. en.wikipedia.org

Nestle. en.wikipedia.org

Wheel of Fortune; Profitability

Global 500. money.cnn.com

The World Bank op.cit.

46 Banks

Bank wealth; Weighed in the balance…

The World Bank. World Development Indicators online. data.worldbank.org

Fortune Global 500 2011. money.cnn.com

Comparative wealth; World annual output...
World's 50 biggest banks 2011. 7 Sept 2011. www.gfmag.com
The World Bank. World Development Indicators online. data.worldbank.org
Cap in hand; Peaks and troughs of the banking crisis
Iceland ex-PM Geir Haarde found guilty of banking crash failure. 23 April 2012. www.worldfinancialpost.com
Bank bail-outs cost taxpayers £4,473bn. 28 Oct2008. www.telegraph.co.uk
The true cost of the bank bailout. Bloomberg analysts, quoted by PBS, 9 March 2010. www.pbs.org
A national sex strike! 27 March 2012. www.dailymail.co.uk
From excessive levels...
Duncan H. Something went very wrong with UK banking and we need to put it right. 30 June 2012. www.dailymail.co.uk

48 Corruption
Level of corruption
Transparency International. Corruption Perceptions Index 2011. cpi.transparency.org
The shadow economy
Schneider F, Buehn A, Montenegro CE. Shadow economies all over the world. The World Bank, 2010. Table 3.6.6. www-wds.worldbank.org
Estimate of assets...
Revealed: global super-rich has at least $21tn hidden in secret tax havens. 22 July 2012. www.taxjustice.net
Stewart H. £13tn hoard hidden from taxman by global elite. 21 July 2012. www.guardian.co.uk
The World Bank. World Development Indicators online. data.worldbank.org
Riley T. Time to tackle tax havens. 28 Nov 2011. www.newint.org

50 Debt
Government gross debt
General government gross debt. www.imf.org
Current account balance
The World Factbook. www.cia.gov
Net debt
The Global Debt Clock. www.economist.com
CIA World Factbook. www.cia.gov
UN Population Division. World Population Prospects. The 2010 Revision. esa.un.org

52 Tourism
Economic significance of tourism; Departures; Arrivals
The World Bank. World Development Indicators online. data.worldbank.org
Projected change tourist trips
International tourists to hit 1.8 billion by 2030. 11 Oct 2011. PR11079. www.media.unwto.org

54 Goals for Development
The Millennium Development Goals Report 2011. New York: United Nations, 2011. www.un.org
The World Development Report 2011. Washington DC: World Bank, 2011. wdr2011.worldbank.org
Millennium Development Goals
Millennium Development Goals: 2011 Progress Chart. www.un.org
Overseas aid
The World Bank. World Development Indicators. data.worldbank.org
OECD Development Co-operation Directorate (DCD-DAC). www.oecd.org
Zimmerman F, Smith K. More Actors, more money, more ideas for international development co-operation. *Journal for International Development.* (2011) 23: 722-738.

Part Three: War & Peace
Pinker S. *The Better Angels of our Nature.* London: Penguin, 2011.
Bell C. *On the Law of Peace.* Oxford: Oxford University Press, 2008.
World Development Report 2011: Conflict, security and development. Washington DC: World Bank, 2011.

58 War in the 21st Century
At war; Beyond national borders; Two decades of growing peace
Uppsala University. Uppsala Conflict Data Programme. www.pcr.uu.se. Updated from press reports up to May 2012.

60 Warlords, Ganglords, and Militias
Non-state armed forces
Uppsala University, Uppsala Conflict Data Programme. www.pcr.uu.se. Updated from press reports up to May 2012.
Child soldiers
Child Soldiers Global Report 2008. London: Coalition to Stop the Use of Child Soldiers, 2008. www.childsoldiersglobalreport.org

62 Military Muscle
Military spending; Armed forces top ten
IISS. *The Military Balance 2011.* Oxon: Routledge, 2011. pp. 471-477.
Top military spenders; Nuclear weapons; Nuclear warhead stockpiles
Stockholm International Peace Research Institute. SIPRI Yearbooks 1989, 2001 & 2011. Oxford: Oxford University Press.

64 The New Front Line
Drones
Drones team. Obama 2012 Pakistan strikes. 11 Jan 2012. www.thebureauinvestigates.com
Meikle J. Jimmy Carter savages US foreign policy over drone strikes. 25 Jun 2012 www.guardian.co.uk
Reprieve. Drone strikes. www.reprieve.org.uk
Woods C. Drones: Barack Obama's secret war. 13 Jun 2012. www.newstatesman.com
Special forces
Ansari U. Sino-Pakistani Special Forces exercise begins. 14 Nov 2011. www.defensenews.com
Graham-Harrison E. British and US special forces rescue kidnapped aid workers in Afghanistan. 2 Jun 2012. www.guardian.co.uk
Urban M. Inside story of the UK's secret mission to beat Gaddafi. BBC News Magazine. 19 Jan 2012. www.bbc.co.uk
US special forces 'parachuted into North Korea'. The Telegraph. 29 May 2012. www.telegraph.co.uk
Zhe Z. China's new special forces marching into view. 08 Sep 2009. www.chinadaily.com.cn
Cyber
Arthur C. Cyber attacks widespread, says report. 28 Jan 2010. www.guardian.co.uk
Associated Press. China victim of 500,000 cyber-attacks in 2010, says security agency. 9 Aug 2011. www.guardian.co.uk
Beaumont P. US appoints first cyber warfare general. 23 May 2010. www.guardian.co.uk
Beaumont P. Stuxnet worm heralds new era of global cyberwar. 30 Sep 2010. www.guardian.co.uk
Hopkins N. US and China engage in cyber war games. 16 April 2012. www.guardian.co.uk
Marching off to cyberwar. The internet. 4 Dec 2008. www.economist.com
Reuters. Biggest series of cyber-attacks in history uncovered. 3 Aug 2011. www.guardian.co.uk
Silverstein R, Sahimi M. Obama's virus wars: mutually assured cyber-destruction. 8 June 2012. www.guardian.co.uk
Whitehead T. Cyber crime a global threat, MI5 head warns. 26 Jun 2012. www.telegraph.co.uk
Terrorism
Carter S, Cox A. One 9/11 tally: $3.3 trillion. 8 Sept 2011. www.nytimes.com
New York & Washington DC, Bali, Madrid, Beslan, London, Karachi & Rawalpindi. BBC world news. news.bbc.co.uk
Pidd H. Mumbai terror attacks suspect arrested by Indian police. 26 June 2012. www.guardian.co.uk
Ugandans jailed for Kampala World Cup bombing. 16 Sep 2011. www.bbc.co.uk
Wikipedia. Terrorism in the People's Republic of China. en.wikipedia.org
World Bank, 2011: *World Development Report 2011: Conflict security and Development.* p5. worldbank.org

66 Casualties of War
The 21st-century toll; Death toll
Uppsala University, Department of Peace and Conflict Research. www.pcr.uu.se
Iraq Body Count. Iraqi deaths from violence 2003-11. www.iraqbodycount.org
BBC. Iraq war in figures. www.bbc.co.uk
Cave D. Mexico updates death toll in drug war to 47,515, but critics dispute the data. 11 Jan 2012. www.nytimes.com
Ratnayake R et al. The many victims of war: Indirect conflict deaths. Complex Emergency Database. Sept 2008. www.cedat.be
The World Bank World Development Report 2011: Conflict, security and development. wdr2011.worldbank.org

68 Refugees
Flight; Displaced; Stateless
United Nations High Commissioner for Refugees. *UNHCR Statistical Yearbook 2010*. Tables 1&2. www.unhcr.org
Major refugee populations; Over 85% of refugees...
UNHCR 2010, Table 5.
United Nations Relief and Works Agency for Palestinian Refugees. Where UNRWA works. www.unrwa.org

70 Peacekeeping
The UN Secretary-General's High Level Panel on Threats, Challenges and Change. *A More Secure World: Our shared responsibility.* United Nations, 2004. www.un.org
Forces for peace; Locations of missions; South Asian contributions
As of 29 Feb 2012. www.un.org
2,997 UN peacekeepers died...; There have been 66...
Peacekeeping Fact Sheet as of 7 June 2012. www.un.org
Non-UN operations
Center of International Cooperation. *Annual Review of Global Peace Operations 2012*. Table 5.10. London: Lynne Rienner, 2011.

72 Global Peacefulness
Institute for Economics & Peace. Global Peace Index. www.visionofhumanity.org

Part Four: Rights & Respects
76 Political Systems
Political systems
The World Factbook. www.cia.gov
BBC News Country Profiles. news.bbc.co.uk
Ethnologue: Languages of the World. www.ethnologue.com
Minority Rights Group, World Directory of Minorities and Indigenous Peoples. www.minorityrights.org
Amnesty International Report 2012. www.amnesty.org
Freedom in the World 2012 and 2011. www.freedomhouse.org
Federal Research Division, US Library of Congress, Library of Congress Country Studies. lcweb2.loc.gov
Living politics
Turner B (editor). *The Statesman's Yearbook 2008*. Hampshire: Palgrave Macmillan, 2008.
The World Factbook. www.cia.gov [Accessed 13 April 2012].

78 Religious Rights
O'Brien J, Palmer M. *The Atlas of Religion*. London: Earthscan, 2007.
The World Factbook. www.cia.gov
US State Department reports on religious freedom by country. www.state.gov
International Coalition for Religious Freedom country reports. www.religiousfreedom.com

80 Human Rights
Extreme abuse of human rights; Slavery in the fishing fleet
Amnesty International. *Amnesty International Report 2012*. Amnesty International: London. 2012. files.amnesty.org
Judicial killings
Amnesty International. Death sentences and executions 2011. Amnesty International: London. 2012. www.amnesty.org
Death Penalty Information Center. www.deathpenaltyinfo.org
Sex trafficking
US State Department. *Trafficking in Persons Report, 2011*. www.state.gov

82 Children's Rights
UNICEF. Childinfo: Monitoring the situation of children and women. www.childinfo.org
USA and Somalia
United Nations Treaty Collection. Chapter IV Human Rights: 11. Convention on the Right of the Child. treaties.un.org
Where children are working; Children at risk
Diallo Y et al. *Global Child Labour Developments: Measuring trends from 2004–2008*.Table 2. ILO: 2010.
Children not in school
The World Bank. World Development Indicators online. data.worldbank.org
Birth registration
UNICEF Statistics. Birth Registration. www.childinfo.org

Children & schools in conflict
EFA Global Monitoring Report. The hidden crisis: Armed conflict and education. UNESCO, 2011. unesdoc.unesco.org

84 Women's Rights
Global 500: Our annual ranking of the world's largest corporations. Top companies: biggest employers. money.cnn.com
Allen, K. Women look away now: You are working for free. 4 Nov 2011. www.guardian.co.uk
Progress of the World's Women 2011-2012. progress.unwomen.org
Equal Rights; Women in parliament
Human Development Report 2011. Table 4. UNDP, 2011. hdr.undp.org
Seager J. *The Atlas of Women in the World*. London: Earthscan, 2009.
Inter-Parliamentary Union. Women in National parliaments, Situation as of 30 Nov 2011. ww.ipu.org
Women as head of government
Based on list of elected or appointed female heads of government, Wikipedia [Accessed 20 Feb 2012]. en.wikipedia.org
Excludes: ceremonial heads of state, short-term acting prime ministers. Includes: appointed prime ministers in a democratic presidential system, heads of governments attempting the transition to democracy (Bolivia 1979–80, Lithuania 1990–91, Liberia 1996–97, Kyrgyzstan 2010–11).

86 Gay Rights
The right to serve
Countries that disallow homosexuals from serving in the military. en.wikipedia.org
Legal status of same-sex acts and relationships
Jones B, Itaborahy E & LP. *State-sponsored Homophobia: A world survey of laws criminalising same-sex sexual acts between consenting adults*. IGLA, 2011. old.ilga.org
Johnson R. Legal Gay Marriage: Gay marriage laws by state and country. gaylife.about.com

Part Five: Health of the People
Wilkinson R, Picket K. *The Spirit Level: Why equality is better for everyone*. London: Penguin, 2010.

90 Malnutrition
The simmering food crisis. International Institute of Strategic Studies (London) briefing. Nov 2008. www.iiss.org
Moulds J. Food price crisis feared as erratic weather wreaks havoc on crops. 22 July 2012. www.guardian.co.uk
Undernourished people; Trends in undernourishment
United Nations Statistics Division. Millennium Development Goals Indicators. mdgs.un.org
Food shortages
FAO. Crop prospects and food situation, No. 4, Dec 2011. www.fao.org
India
The World Bank. World Development Indicators online. data.worldbank.org
UN Population Division. World Population Prospects. The 2010 Revision. esa.un.org
Greece
Farr LD. Food aid takes off in Athens. 15 Feb 2012. www.huffingtonpost.com
Smith H. Greek homeless shelters take in casualties of debt crisis. 10 Feb 2012. www.guardian.co.uk
Food price rise
Center for International Policy (Tortuga, Mexico), Americas Program. The food crisis strikes again. 19 Oct 2011 www.cipamericas.org
Vitamin A deficiency
WHO Global Database on Vitamin A Deficiency. Global prevalence of vitamin A deficiency in populations at risk 1995-2005. whqlibdoc.who.int

92 Obesity
WHO. Media Centre. Fact sheet No. 311: Obesity and overweight. www.who.int
Overweight adults
WHO. Global Health Observatory Data Repository. Overweight (body mass index ≥25). apps.who.int
WHO. Global Strategy on Diet, Physical Activity and Health. www.who.int
Increased risk of disease
Global Health Risks: Mortality and burden of disease attributable to selected major risks. WHO, 2009. p.18. www.who.int

America growing obese
Centers for Disease Control and Prevention (CDC). Data and Statistics. Obesity rates among all children in the United States. www.cdc.gov
CDC. US Obesity Trends: Trends by State 1985-2010. www.cdc.gov
$100 billion...
Fast food facts from the Super Size Me website. www.vivavegie.org

94 Smoking
WHO Fact Sheet No. 339. Tobacco. July 2011. www.who.int
Where cigarettes are being smoked
The Tobacco Atlas. Cigarette consumption. Inset 2: World cigarette consumption, by region, 2007. www.tobaccoatlas.org
Deaths; Global cigarette consumption
Shafey O, Eriksen M, Ross H, Mackay J. *The Tobacco Atlas*, 3rd Edition. Atlanta, Georgia: American Cancer Society, 2009. www.tobaccoatlas.org
Spreading the word
WHO Report on the Global Tobacco Epidemic, 2011: Warning about the dangers of tobacco. Tables 2.3.1-2.3.6. whqlibdoc.who.int
Smoking
WHO, 2011. Appendix VII. www.who.int

96 Cancers
Quotation from James Watson
Mukherjee S. *The Emperor of All Maladies. A biography of cancer*. London: Harper Collins/Fourth Estate, 2011. p.393.
Unequal death rates; Increasing incidence; Cancer cases in poorer countries; Lifestyle influences
WHO World Cancer Report 2008, International Agency for Research on Cancer, 2008. www.iarc
Globocan Cancer Fact Sheets. www.globocan.iarc
Commonest cancers
Ferlay J et al. GLOBOCAN 2008 v1.2, Cancer incidence and mortality worldwide: IARC CancerBase No. 10 [Internet]. Lyon, France: International Agency for Research on Cancer, 2010. globocan.iarc.fr [Accessed 16 Mar 2012].

98 HIV/AIDS
WHO. HIV/AIDS. Fact sheet No.360. HIV/AIDS. Nov 2011. www.who.int
UNAIDS. World AIDS Day Report: 2011, p.7. www.unaids.org
The impact of HIV/AIDS
United Nations Statistics Division. Millennium Development Goals Indicators. mdgs.un.org
Number of children orphaned by AIDS
UNICEF. *Children and AIDS: Fifth stocktaking report, 2010*. Goal 4. Protecting and supporting children affected by HIV and AIDS. www.unicef.org
Living and dying with HIV/AIDS
WHO/UNAIDS/UNICEF. Global HIV/AIDS response: Epidemic update and health sector progress towards Universal Access. Progress Report 2011. Annex 8 HIV and AIDS statistics, by WHO and UNICEF regions, 2010, p.210. www.unaids.org
Anti-retroviral therapy (ART)
UNAIDS. Data tables 2011. p.5. www.unaids.org
Barring the door
Mapping of restrictions on the entry, stay and residence of people living with HIV. UNAIDS, May 2009. Updated for developments as of June 2011. www.unaids.org

100 Mental Health
Mental Health Atlas 2011. Geneva: World Health Organization, 2011. www.who.int
WHO Fact sheet No.220. Mental health: Strengthening our response. Sept 2010. www.who.int
Fact File: 10 facts on mental health. www.who.int
Over 50%...; Mental-health resources; Rich countries have...; Expenditure on medicines; Antipsychotic drugs...
WHO, 2011. op. cit.
Suicide rates; Someone commits suicide...
Suicide rates per 100,000 by country, year and sex (Table). www.who.int [Accessed 13 April 2012].

102 Living with Disease
WHO. Death and DALY estimates for 2004 by cause for WHO Member States: Persons, all ages. DALY rates. www.who.int [Accessed 13 April 2012].

Part Six: Health of the Planet
106 Warning Signs
Human impact of natural disasters
International Federation of Red Cross and Red Crescent Societies. *World Disasters Report, 2011*. Annex: Table 13 www.ifrc.org
Shrinking Arctic ice
Vidal J. Weird weather around the world sees in 2012. *The Guardian*. 12 Jan 2012. www.guardian.co.uk
Asian tiger mosquito
Global Invasive Species Database. Aedes albopictus. www.issg.org
Changing ranges
Brommer J. The range margins of northern birds shift polewards. *Ann. Zool. Fennici* 41 (2004): 391–397.
Hitch AT, Leberg PL. Breeding distributions of north American bird species moving north as a result of climate change. *Conserv. Biol.* 21 (2007): 534–539.
Climate change is driving poleward shifts in the distributions of species. Cited by BirdLife www.birdlife.org
La Sorte FA, Thompson FR. Poleward shifts in winter ranges of North American birds. *Ecology* 88 (2007): 1803–1812.
Parmesan C et al. Poleward shifts in geographical ranges of butterfly species associated with regional warming. *Nature*, 1999. 399: 579-83.
Thomas CD, Lennon JJ. Birds extend their ranges northwards. *Nature* 399 (1999): 213.
Coral bleaching
Brokaw, T. Global warming: Signs and sources. dsc.discovery.com
Extinction
Lawton JH, May RM. *Extinction rates*. Oxford: Oxford University Press. 2005.
Fires in Russia
Wildfires in Russia more rampant in 2011, spread over east. *RIA Novotsi*. 7 June 2011 en.rian.ru
Billette A. Russian forests burn for second successive year. *Guardian Weekly*. 9 Aug 2011. www.guardian.co.uk
Floods in Pakistan
Pakistan Floods progress report July 2010-July 2011. www.oxfam.org
Singapore Red Cross. Pakistan floods: The deluge of disaster. 15 Sept 2010. reliefweb.int
Guerin O. Pakistan floods. BBC News. www.bbc.co.uk
Glacial change in the Andes
Peru's Quelccaya glacier could disappear within 10 years, specialist says. Andean Air Mail & Peruvian Times. 6 Aug 2010, quoting Jose Machare, a climate change specialist at Peru's Geological Society. www.peruviantimes.com
Lemurs in Madagascar
Walker G, King D, *The Hot Topic* London: Bloomsbury, 2008.
Melting permafrost in Alaska
Romanovsky VE. How rapidly is permafrost changing and what are the impacts of these changes? www.arctic.noaa.gov
North Atlantic hurricanes
Geophysical Fluid Dynamics Laboratory/NOAA. Hurricane power dissipation index. www.gfdl.noaa.gov
Ocean acidification
Ocean acidification. www.antarctica.gov.au
Ocean dead zones
Faeth P, Methan T. Nutrient runoff creates dead zone. World Resources Institute, 2005 Jan. archive.wri.org
Diaz RJ, Rosenberg R. Spreading dead zones and consequences for marine ecosystems. *Science* 321 (2008): 926-929. www.sciencemag.org
Earth Observatory. Ocean dead zones. 17 July 2010. earthobservatory.nasa.gov
Rapid rise in Antarctic
Vaughan DG. Antarctic Peninsula: rapid warming. British Antarctic Survey, Natural Environment Research Council. www.antarctica.ac.uk
Ducklow HW et al. Marine pelagic ecosystems: The West Antarctic Peninsula. Philosophical Transactions of the Royal Society. *B-Biological Sciences* 362 (2007): 67-94.
Shrinking Arctic ice
Byers M, Canada can help Russia with northern sea route. *The Moscow Times*. 8 June 2012. www.themoscowtimes.com
These days the water evaporates...
Vidal J. From Cairo to the Cape, climate change begins to take hold of Africa. *The Guardian* 01 Dec 2011 www.guardian.co.uk

Vulture deaths in India
Vultures are under threat from the veterinary drug diclofenac. www.birdlife.org
Water mining in China
Economy EC. The great leap backward? Council on Foreign Relations. Foreign Affairs, 2007 Sept/Oct. www.foreignaffairs.org

108 Biodiversity
Threatened mammals and birds
The IUCN Red List of Threatened Species. Summary statistics version 2012.1. www.iucnredlist.org
Threatened species
Summary Statistics. Figure 2: The proportion of extant species on the IUCN Red List of Threatened Species version 2011.2. www.iucnredlist.org
Protected areas
World Database on Protected Areas (2011) National stats for 1990-2010 from the 2011 MDG analysis. www.wdpa.org/Statistics.aspx
Forest lost and gained
FAO (2010) Global Forest Resources Assessment 2010. Global Tables. www.fao.org

110 Water Resources
Hot issues: water scarcity. www.fao.org [Accessed 16 June 2012].
Maplecroft index identifies Bahrain, Qatar, Kuwait and Saudi Arabia as world's most water stressed countries. 26 May 2011. maplecroft.com
Diouf J. Agriculture, food security and water: Towards a blue revolution. OECD Observer no. 236, March 2003. www.oecdobserver.org
Total consumption; Water withdrawals; 70% of...
FAO. 2012. AQUASTAT database, Food and Agriculture Organization of the United Nations (FAO). www.fao.org. [Accessed 12 June 2012].
Lack of a safe supply
The World Bank. World Development Indicators online. data.worldbank.org
The World Factbook. www.cia.gov
Total annual water withdrawal
Shiklomanov I. World water resources at the beginning of the 21st century. The dynamics. Table 7. webworld.unesco.org

112 Waste
Plastics waste; Oceans
UNEP Year Book: Emerging issues in our global environment. United Nations Environment Programme 2011. www.unep.org
The next wave of plastic bag bans. 7 June 2012. oceana.org
Braiker B. Los Angeles votes to ban plastic bags. 24 May 2012. USNews Blog. www.guardian.co.uk
Plastic Bag Ban. plasticbagbanreport.com [Accessed 20 June 2012] .
Toronto plastic bag ban surprises Mayor Rob Ford. 7 June 2012. www.bbc.co.uk
Top 5 places with plastic bag bans. 7 June 2012. www.globaltvedmonton.com
Summers C. What should be done about plastic bags? 19 March 2012. www.bbc.co.uk
Fleury J. Mumbai aims at total ban of plastic bags. 16 June 2012. articles.timesofindia.indiatimes.com
Plastic bags banned in Karwar city limits. 9 Aug 2010. articles.timesofindia.indiatimes.com
Plastic bags banned in Tirumala. 11 Aug 2010. www.hindu.com
Plastic bags to be seized in Vasco from today. 19 Aug 2011. articles.timesofindia.indiatimes.com
Young T. Rajasthan bans use of plastic bags. 28 July 2010. www.businessgreen.com
Watts J. China plastic bag ban 'has saved 1.6m tonnes of oil'. 22 May 2009. www.guardian.co.uk
Plastic bags ban. 26 May 2011. www.clearchinese.com
Geganto R. Plastic bag ban fuels packaging wars. 16 June 2012. Philippine Daily Inquirer. opinion.inquirer.net
Plastic ban comes into effect. 2 Jan 2011. www.igeorgetownpenang.com
South Australia – feedback on result of 2009 ban. www.paperbagco.co.uk
Coles Bay, Tasmania. en.wikipedia.org
Phase-out of lightweight plastic bags. en.wikipedia.org
Beach trash
UNEP op. cit. p.31.
Plastic world
UNEP op. cit. p.22.
Sanitation
The World Bank. World Development Indicators online. data.worldbank.org

Tonnes of disposable nappies
Early Day Motion 1169, Disposable nappy waste. 9 Dec 2010. www.parliament.uk
Butler K, Gilson D. A brief history of the disposable diaper. May/June 2008. www.motherjones.com

114 Energy Use
Total energy use; Energy use per capita; Energy use comparison
IEA data downloaded from The World Bank. World Development Indicators online. data.worldbank.org
Renewable energy
Eric Martinot and REN21 Renewable Energy Policy Network for the 21st Century. Renewables 2012 Global Status Report. www.map.ren21.net
1970–2011 human population...
Number of cars. The Physics Factbook. hypertextbook.com citing: Stein, Jay. New cars for better future: Driving us crazy. Earthgreen, 1990
Tencer D. 24 Oct 2011. Number of cars worldwide surpasses 1 billion: Can the world handle this many wheels? www.huffingtonpost.ca

116 Climate Change
Past emissions
Climate Analysis Indicators Tool (CAIT) Version 7.0. Washington, DC: World Resources Institute, 2010.
Future consequences
Lenton TM et al.Tipping elements in the Earth's climate system. PNAS 105(6) (2008): 1786–1793.
Shellnhuber HJ. Tipping elements in the Earth system. PNAS 106 (49) (2009): 20561–20563.
IOM. Compendium of IOM's activities in migration, climate change and the environment. Geneva: International Organization for Migration. 2009.
Sea-level rise
Brokaw T. Global warming: Signs and sources. dsc.discovery.com
Carbon dioxide in the atmosphere
Earth System Research Laboratory. Global Monitoring Division. Recent Mauna Loa CO2. www.esrl.noaa.gov [Accessed 18 June 2012].
UNEP Vital Graphics, quoting David J Hofmann of the Office of Atmospheric Research at the National Oceanic and Atmospheric Administration, March 2006. www.grida.no/climate
Blasing TJ. Recent greenhouse gas concentrations. DOI: 10.3334/CDIAC/atg.032. Updated Dec. 2009. Carbon Dioxide Information Analysis Center. cdiac.ornl.gov [Accessed 2011 March 29].
Neftel A et al. Historical carbon dioxide record from the Siple Station ice core. In Boden TA et al, editors. Trends'93: A compendium of data on global change. ORNL/CDIAC-65. Carbon Dioxide Information Analysis Center. Oak Ridge National Laboratory; 1994.
Keeling CD, Whorf TP. Carbon Dioxide Research Group, Scripps Institution of Oceanography, University of California; 2001.

118 Planetary Boundaries
Rockström J et al. Planetary boundaries: Exploring the safe operating space for humanity. *Ecology and Society* 14 (2009): 2. www.ecologyandsociety.org
Pearce F. From ocean to ozone: Earth's nine life-support systems. *New Scientist* (Feb 2010) 2749. www.newscientist.com

Part Seven: Vital Statistics
Indicators of Wellbeing
Official capital: geography.about.com; infoplease.com; www.cia.gov. **Land area:** www.fao.org. **Population:** See source for p22. **Migrants:** Source for p26. **Life expectancy:** Source for p24. **Literate adults, Education:** Source for p.30. **Undernourished:** Source for p90. **Overweight:** Source for p92. **Access to improved water:** Source for p110. **Sanitation:** Source for p112. **DALYs:** Source for p102.

Economy & Environment
GNI: See source for p38. **Human Development Index:** Source for p42. **Gini Index:** Source for p40. **Government gross debt:** Source for p50. **Corruptions Perception Index, Shadow economy:** Source for p48. **Military expenditure:** Source for p62. **Energy Use:** Source for p114. **CO_2 emissions:** The World Development Indicators worldbank.org. **Water withdrawals:** Source for p110.

Index

Afghanistan
  attacks on schools 83
  drone attacks in 65
  refugees from 68
  war in 58
agriculture 110, 111, 118, 119
al-Qaeda 64, 65
Amazon rainforest 116
Antarctic 107, 116
Anti-Retroviral Therapy 99
Arctic 106, 107, 116
Argentina, Buenos Aires 32
armed conflicts 11, 56, 57, 58–59, 60–61
  casualties of 66–67
  over ethnic or national identity 26
  over religious differences 28
  non-state 60–61, 66
  over independence 20
armed forces 62–63
  child 60
  non-state 60–61
  peacekeeping 70–71
  special 64, 65
Australia, South, plastic bag ban 112

Bank of America 46, 47
banks 36, 46–47
  billionaires 40–41
biodiversity 106, 107, 108–09, 118, 119
Brazil
  billionaires in 40
  change in GNI 38
  overseas aid 54
  São Paulo 32, 34
Buddhism 28–29
Burma, parliament 77

Canada, billionaires in 40
cancer 13, 89, 93, 94, 96–97
carbon dioxide emissions 43, 104, 114, 116, 117, 118, 119
child mortality 55
children
  as soldiers 60
  birth registration of 83
  education of 30
  HIV/AIDS 98, 99
  cancer 96
  mental problems 100–01
  not in school 82
  obese 92
  rights of 82–83
  working 82
China
  billionaires in 41
  change in GNI 10, 38
  role in global development 54
  cyber space 65
  Global Happiness Index 42
  GNI compared to bank wealth 47
  lending 50
  military spending 63
  plastic bag ban 112
  poverty 38
  purchase of land overseas 110
  Shanghai 33, 34, 35
  special forces 65
  terrorist attacks in 65
  Tibet 79
  water shortage in 107, 110, 111
Christianity 28–29
cities 32–33, 34–35
climate change 72, 106, 107, 114, 116–17, 118, 119
Cold War 9, 21, 58, 62, 70, 76
Colombia 60, 68
Comoros, coups in 77
Congo, Democratic Republic of 58, 61, 68
coral bleaching 107
corruption 48–49
Cuba 42, 102
current account balance 50
cyber attacks 64, 65
Cyprus
  ethnic makeup 27
  EU bail-out 46

DALYs 102, 103
death penalty 81
debt 50–51, 73
democracy 12, 74, 75, 76, 77
Denmark, disease burden 102
dictatorships 74, 76, 77
dietary deficiencies 90, 91
  excess of calories 92, 93
  lack of Vitamin A 90
disasters 106, 107
discrimination 25, 26, 78, 79, 84, 85, 86, 87
disease
  cancer 96–97
  caused by excess weight 92
  caused by smoking 94
  living with 89, 102–03
displaced persons 68
diversity 19, 26–27
  of cities 34–35
drones, use of 64, 65
Dubai, sex trafficking to 80

economic
  crisis 10, 35, 36, 38, 39, 40, 46, 50, 51
  growth 9, 18, 19, 104
  impact of war 66
  significance of tourism 52–53
education 30–31, 43, 54
Egypt 35, 77
energy 114–15
environmental issues 13, 14, 104–19
Estonia, cyber attack 64
ethnicity 26–27
European Union 11, 14, 38
execution 80, 81

food 90, 91, 92–93, 101
forests 55, 109
France
  GNI compared to bank wealth 47
  military spending 63
  overseas aid 54
  Paris 33, 34
  sex trafficking in 80

gay rights 86–87
gender inequality 31, 55, 84–85
Georgia, cyber attack on 65
Germany
  billionaires in 40
  GNI compared to bank wealth 47
  military spending 63
  overseas aid 54
Gini index 40–41
global warming *see* climate change
Greece, EU bail-outs 46
gross national income 38–39
  as component of HDI 43
  compared to bank wealth 46
  compared to corporation wealth 44
  cost of terror as percentage of 64
  cost of tourism as percentage of 52–53

happiness 42
health care 13, 88, 89, 99, 100
Hinduism 28–29
HIV/AIDS 55, 89, 98–99
Honduras, sex trafficking in 80
Hong Kong, billionaires in 41
Human Development Index 43–44
human rights 57, 74, 75
  abuses of 80–81

Iceland
  banking crisis 46
  disease burden 102
IDPs 68
illiteracy 30–31
India
  billionaires in 41
  change in GNI 10, 38, 91
  Delhi 33
  Kolkata 33
  Mumbai 33, 35, 65, 112
  overseas aid 54
  undernourished 91
  vulture deaths 107
  water resources 110, 111
indigenous religions 28–29
Indonesia
  attitude to gay people 87
  Bali bombing 65
  Jakarta 33, 35
  official languages 27
inequality 10, 40–41
  of city wealth 34–35
internet availability 55
invasive species 107
Iran
  cyber attacks on 65
  Global Happiness Index 42
  Tehran 34, 35
Iraq
  abuse of gay people 87
  refugees from 68
  war 58

Ireland
bank bail-out 46
plastic bag tax 113
Islam 28–29, 78

Japan
billionaires in 40
change in GNI 38
military spending 63
Osaka–Kobe 33
overseas aid 54
Tokyo 33, 34, 35
Judaism 28–29

languages
official 26–27
number spoken in various cities 34, 35
Lebanon, legal system in 79
Libya, special forces in 64
life expectancy 24–25, 43, 96

literacy 30–31

Madagascar, lemurs 106
malaria 55
malnutrition 14, 54, 88, 90–91
map projections 16
maternal mortality 55
Mauritania, abuse of gay people 86
mental health 89, 100–01
Mexico
drugs money 60
Mexico City 32, 34, 35
migrants 26
military spending 11, 62–63
militias *see* warlords
Millennium Development Goals 10, 35, 54–55, 57, 72
monarchy 76, 77
monsoons 117

Nepal, armed groups 61
Nestlé 44, 45
Nigeria
drugs money 61
Lagos 34
non-believers 28
North Korea 42, 65
nuclear weapons 62, 63

obesity 14, 88, 92–93
ocean
acidification 107, 118, 119
dead zones 106
overseas aid 54
ozone depletion 118, 119

Pakistan
death of Osama bin-Laden in 65
floods 107
Karachi 33, 35
refugees from 68
terrorist attacks in 65
Palestine 68, 83
Papua New Guinea, official languages 27
peacefulness 26, 28, 56, 57, 72–73
peacekeeping 70–71

Peru
glacial melt 106
sex trafficking in 80
piracy 64, 65
planetary boundaries 118–19
plastics 112, 113
political systems 14, 76–77
pollution 35, 118, 119
population growth 18, 22–23, 96
in cities 18, 32–33, 34, 35
Portugal, EU bail-out 46
poverty 10, 35, 41, 54
protected areas 108

refugees 68–69, 80, 81
religious beliefs 28–29
religious rights 78–79
renewable energy 115
Russia
billionaires in 41
disease burden 102
fires 107
military spending 63
Moscow 33
overseas aid 54
special forces 65
terrorism in 65

sanitation 112
Saudi Arabia, sex trafficking 80
sea-level rise 107, 117
sex trafficking 80
shadow economy 48
Sierra Leone, disease burden 102
Sikhism 29
slavery 80, 81
smoking 89, 94–95
Somalia
non-ratification of UN Convention 83
piracy 65
refugees from 68
South Africa, official languages 27
South Korea, Global Happiness Index 42
South Sudan 21
sovereignty 20–21
Soviet Union, former, 9, 21, 25
Spain
billionaires in 40
economic crisis 46
GNI compared to bank wealth 47
Madrid bombing 64
special forces, use of 64, 65
stateless persons 69
Sudan, refugees from 68
suicide 101

Taiwan, billionaires in 40
tax 48, 49
terrorism 64, 65, 66
theocracy 76, 77
threatened species 108, 109
tourism 34, 52–53
trade 50, 55
transnational corporations 44–45
tuberculosis 55
Turkey
billionaires in 40
Istanbul 34, 35
legal system of 79

Uganda, terrorist attack in 65
UK
banking crisis 46
billionaires in 40
cyber attack 64
GNI compared to bank wealth 47
life expectancy of homeless 24
London 33, 34, 64
military spending 63
overseas aid 54
sex trafficking to 80
undernourished 90, 91
United Nations 11, 20
peacekeeping 70–71
urbanization 18, 32–33
USA
9/11 terrorist attack 9, 62, 64
Alaska, permafrost melt 106
banking crisis 46
billionaires in 40
California, plastic bag ban 113
change in GNI 38
Chicago 32
cyber attack on 65
cyber war games 65
debt 50
disease burden 102
Global Happiness Index 42
GNI compared to bank wealth 47
Hawaii, plastic bag ban 113
military spending 62, 63
New York 32, 34
non-ratification of UN Convention 83
obesity 92
overseas aid 54
poverty 38
sex trafficking in 80

Venezuela, Global Happiness Index 42

warlords 60–61
wars *see* armed conflicts
waste 104, 112–13
water 104, 110–11, 118, 119
improved access to 111
women
illiteracy 31
in government 84, 85
rights of 83–85

Yemen, attacks on schools 83